# Microsimulation Modelling of Taxation and the Labour Market

# Microsimulation Modelling of Taxation and the Labour Market

The Melbourne Institute Tax and Transfer Simulator

John Creedy
*The Truby Williams Professor of Economics, Department of Economics and MIESR, University of Melbourne, Australia*

Alan S. Duncan
*Professor of Microeconomics, University of Nottingham, Institute for Fiscal Studies, London, UK and MIESR, University of Melbourne, Australia*

Mark Harris
*Senior Research Fellow, University of Melbourne, Australia*

*and*

Rosanna Scutella
*Research Fellow, MIESR, University of Melbourne, Australia*

**Edward Elgar**
Cheltenham, UK • Northampton, MA, USA

Published by
Edward Elgar Publishing Limited
The Lypiatts
15 Lansdown Road
Cheltenham
Glos GL50 2JA
UK

Edward Elgar Publishing, Inc.
William Pratt House
9 Dewey Court
Northampton
Massachusetts 01060
USA

Reprinted 2010, 2016


A catalogue record for this book
is available from the British Library

**Library of Congress Cataloguing in Publication Data**
Microsimulation modelling of taxation and the labour market : the Melbourne
Institute tax and transfer simulator / John Creedy ... [et al.].
    p. cm.
    Includes index.
    1. Melbourne Institute tax and transfer simulator. 2. Taxation—Australia—
Mathematical models. 3. Labor market—Australia—Mathematical models.
I. Creedy, John, 1949–

    HJ3019 M53 2002
    331.1'01'13—dc21

                                           2002024375


ISBN 978 1 84376 063 4

Printed on FSC approved paper
Printed and bound in Great Britain by Marston Book Services Ltd, Oxfordshire

# Contents

# Preface

The production of a large-scale behavioural microsimulation model such as the Melbourne Institute Tax and Transfer Simulator (MITTS) inevitably involves teamwork and is reliant on substantial research grants. The extensive work on MITTS over several years has been supported by a number of grants. A special University of Melbourne Faculty of Economics and Commerce grant enabled John Creedy to work part time in the Melbourne Institute for three years. Two visits of Alan Duncan to the Melbourne Institute were supported by Visiting Research Scholar grants from the Faculty of Economics and Commerce. Visits to the University of York were made by John Creedy in 1998, and by Rosanna Scutella and Mark Harris in 1999. Rosanna Scutella visited the University of Nottingham in 2000. The hospitality shown by the respective economics departments is warmly appreciated.

The building of the model also received substantial funding from the Department of Family and Community Services. Indeed the MITTS model is jointly owned intellectual property of the Melbourne Institute and the Department of Family and Community Services. The Department's continued support is making possible the further development of MITTS.

The continued encouragement and enthusiasm of Peter Dawkins, the Director of the Melbourne Institute, is also acknowledged. In the early development stages of the work, valuable discussions were held with Andrew Dilnot, the Director of the Institute for Fiscal Studies in London. Indeed the work on MITTS has benefited substantially from the accumulated knowledge built up by the microsimulation modellers at the Institute for Fiscal Studies.

Some of the following chapters are based on work that has appeared separately. Chapter 2 uses material from Creedy (2001a); chapter 3 is based on Creedy, Duncan, Harris and Scutella (2001); chapters 4 and 5 are based on Creedy and Duncan (2000, 2002); chapter 6 uses material from Creedy and Duncan (2002) and Creedy (2001b); chapters 7 and 8 are based on draft material produced by Duncan and Harris; chapter 9 is based on Creedy (2001c); chapters 10, 11 and 12 use material from Creedy and Duncan (2001a); a first draft of chapter 13 was produced by Scutella.

As with all large scale models of this kind, work never really stops. The wage equations and the preference functions are in the process of being re-estimated. Feedback effects on wages of labour supply changes have been considered by Creedy and Duncan (2001b), and an extensive policy simulation using MITTS is reported in Creedy, Kalb and Kew (2001). The measurement of welfare changes is examined in Creedy and Kalb (2001). The present form of MITTS owes much to the work of Guyonne Kalb and Hsien Kew, who joined the Melbourne Institute early in 2001.

# Part I

# Introduction

# Chapter 1

# Introduction and Outline

Microsimulation models can help to provide a valuable contribution to tax policy debates. When reporting simulation results for particular hypothetical or actual policy changes, it is not possible, given the scale and complexity of models, to give details regarding the modelling approach and assumptions used. It is therefore important to provide this kind of information in easily accessible form. This book is concerned with the Melbourne Institute Tax and Transfer Simulator, referred to as MITTS. This microsimulation model was designed to examine the effects on individuals and households in Australia of policy changes to any component of the income tax and transfer payments system.

The aims of this book are twofold. First, it provides information about, and discusses the rationale for, the basic modelling approach adopted, along with details of econometric methods used to estimate behavioural relationships. Second, it describes the MITTS model in detail, giving information about its main features, installation and use. The emphasis throughout is on modelling. Hence this book does not report particular policy simulations.

Microsimulation models must inevitably undergo a continuous process of development. Extensions are made to the types of analysis that can be carried out and the form of the output from the model and new data need to be incorporated into the model. Furthermore, it is necessary to revise

1

econometric estimates as often as possible, making use of new methods and data as they arise. While some of the details described in this book are therefore likely to become out of date relatively quickly, the basic structure and modelling approach remain relatively stable.

MITTS actually consists of two closely integrated simulation models. First, an arithmetic model, MITTS-A, examines the effects of a specified change in the direct tax and transfer system, assuming that the labour supply, and hence pre-tax and transfer income, of each individual remains fixed. Second, a behavioural model, MITTS-B, allows for the effects of labour supply variations in response to changes in the tax and transfer system.

Like all existing microsimulation models, MITTS is a supply-side partial equilibrium model. In particular, the behavioural component, MITTS-B, concentrates on examining the effects of changes in the tax structure on variations in the hours of work that individuals wish to supply. Hence, in interpreting the output from MITTS, it should be recognised that, depending on what happens to the demand for labour, individuals may not in reality be able to work their desired number of hours; they may be constrained as a result of demand-side considerations. Large changes in the tax structure, designed for example to increase the labour force participation of benefit recipients, may also have effects on the demand for labour. In addition, changes in the tax and transfer system are assumed to have no effect on individuals' wage rates. Future modelling developments are likely to be concerned with such feedback effects.

With the above aims in mind this book naturally divides into three parts. Part I concentrates on introductory material, and chapter 2 provides a general introduction to tax modelling and discusses the need for, and limitations of, alternative types of model. Stress is placed on the need to allow for potential labour supply responses to changes in direct taxes and transfers.

Part II examines alternative modelling methods in detail and presents estimates on which MITTS is based. Any model must have the ability to simulate individuals' net incomes at hours points other than those observed in the database. For this to be possible, information about the individual's hourly wage rate must be provided, along with other characteristics. The wage rate is typically evaluated by dividing total earned income by the reported number of hours worked. For non-working individuals, an appropriate wage rate must be imputed, usually based on an estimated wage function. Such a function is normally estimated using the same data set that forms the basis of the simulation model, allowing for many individual characteristics. It must also deal with the sample selection involved in observing only the wage rates of individuals who work in the sample period. Chapter 3 presents estimates of wage functions for Australians in several demographic groups. These groups include married (or partnered) males and females, single males and females, and sole parents (the majority of whom are female). The problem of obtaining imputed wages for non-workers, using these estimated wage functions, is also considered.

Chapter 4 presents an efficient method of producing exact budget constraints for individuals. A common approach is simply to compute net incomes for a large number of levels of hours worked, but this is inefficient and does is not guaranteed to identify kinks and discontinuities exactly. The method presented in chapter 4, and implemented in MITTS, is computationally efficient and produces exact constraints.

Chapter 5 presents a general overview of the treatment of labour supply in microsimulation modelling. This includes models involving continuous hours, based on specified labour supply functions or utility functions, and discrete hours models in which workers are considered to face a limited choice of hours.

Chapter 6 provides an efficient algorithm for determining each individual's labour supply, given a labour supply function or direct utility function, in the context of continuous microsimulation. Methods of obtaining welfare changes are also presented.

Chapters 7 and 8 present econometric estimates, for Australian demographic groups, of preference functions. The approaches are based on discrete hours models. These estimates make use of the imputed wage rates for non-workers, obtained using the results of chapter 3. The preference functions are based on quadratic direct utility functions. Chapter 9 provides further details of the properties of such functions, including the implied expenditure functions.

Part III is concerned with the details of the MITTS model. Chapter 10 provides a general description of the structure of the model and its main features. Chapter 11 describes the installation of MITTS and outlines the structure of data and program files. Chapter 12 provides extensive instructions for the use of MITTS and gives examples of the tables and figures displayed when the model is run. A major consideration when designing and building MITTS was the need for flexibility and ease of use. For example, it is possible to make substantial changes to an existing tax and transfer system during the running of MITTS, without the need for further programming. There are nevertheless several Australian tax systems programmed and directly available for use. To give some indication of the complexity of the tax structure in Australia, chapter 13 describes the system in operation at March 1998.

# Chapter 2

# Tax Modelling

Tax models come in all shapes and sizes, depending on the nature of the policy issues examined. The policy questions may relate to specific problems, concerning perhaps the revenue implications of a particular tax, or they may involve an extensive analysis of the cost and redistributive effects of a large number of taxes and transfer payments. Small tax models can help to provide useful general lessons and guiding principles for tax reform. However, specific analyses that can be directly related to practical policy questions, and can provide direct inputs into rational policy debate, require the construction of larger tax simulation models. Rapid developments in computing hardware and software have removed an earlier major obstacle to their construction. Examples include SWITCH from the ESRI in Dublin, TAXBEN from the IFS in London, POLIMOD from the Microsimulation Unit in Cambridge, and STINMOD from NATSEM in Canberra.

The chapter provides an informal introduction to microsimulation modelling. The distinguishing feature of such models is the use of a large cross-sectional data set giving information about the characteristics of individuals and households, including their labour supply, earnings and (possibly) expenditure. Emphasis is placed on the precise design of tax and transfer systems. Microsimulation models are therefore able to replicate more closely the considerable degree of heterogeneity observed in the population.

5

First, the general need for tax models is discussed in section 2.1. Section 2.2 discusses the main features and the role played by microsimulation models. Sections 2.3 and 2.4 discuss non-behavioural and behavioural models in turn. Brief conclusions are in section 2.5.

## 2.1   The Need for Tax Models

There is no escape from the need to use some kind of tax model. As soon as tax issues begin to be examined, their many complexities force economists to produce a simplified framework in which the various inter-relationships become more manageable and transparent. Thinking in terms of models forces analysts, as far as possible, to be explicit about their simplifications and what is being ignored. Hence the inevitable limitations of models can be clearly recognised.

Taxation affects everyone at virtually all stages of the life cycle, so everyone has a personal interest in tax policy. Every tax policy change involves losers and gainers. Hence, distributional value judgements are unavoidable. It is argued here that the most useful role of models is in supporting rational policy analysis. By this is meant the examination and reporting of the implications of alternative policies, so that policy-makers can form their own judgements. It also involves the determination of the appropriate policies that are implied by the adoption of a range of clearly specified value judgements.

This suggests that, although government departments will probably wish to develop some limited internal modelling capacity, there is a major role for independent tax modellers, or researchers who are independent of government or special-interest groups. However, in view of the high costs of model building, it is likely that they need financial support from research grants or government departments. A strong advantage is that independent modellers are obliged to publish full details of models. This public knowledge can help to stimulate a wider assessment of approaches as well as imposing a constraint on the inappropriate use of models. Indeed a strong case can be made for the support of several models so that the benefits of alternative strategies are obtained and the abuse of a single model can be controlled.

A common vice is the tendency to treat even simple models as if they were real, and to make strong policy recommendations on the basis of highly simplified tractable models. Similarly, there is a tendency to treat comparative static results as if they automatically provide realistic information about the dynamics of adjustments. Reminders must regularly be issued regarding the need to treat models as providing, at best, tentative guidance about the possible implications of tax changes in well-specified circumstances. Some people will nevertheless be tempted to use models inappropriately, or for purposes for which they were never constructed. For example, models designed to examine only small tax changes are sometimes used to consider policies that involve more than marginal adjustments.

If the need for models is accepted, what kind of model should be built? What makes a good model? All models are unrealistic, so the difficult challenge in any kind of economic modelling is to simplify the problem in such a way that attention can be concentrated on the essential questions, without assuming away the crucial elements.

The inevitable lack of reality of models means, among other things, that the idea of producing an ideal or complete tax model that is capable of providing answers to all tax policy questions is a chimera. A complete model would need to be a life-cycle, overlapping generations, dynamic general equilibrium open economy model. It would also allow endogenous choices regarding the education, occupational choice, labour supply, household formation, consumption and saving behaviour of all individuals. It should reflect a vast range of demographic heterogeneity.

As soon as the crudest description along these lines is given, it is clear that model construction and solution algorithm limitations alone make such a model infeasible. Also, the data requirements far exceed available sources, or even data that could in principle be obtained. Any model involves a certain amount of calibration, or the imposition of parameter values that are not based on direct econometric estimates. However, it is best to keep this to manageable proportions so that imposed values do not dominate results and appropriate sensitivity analyses can be performed. A comprehensive model would have little transparency; it would, for the vast majority of users, be simply a 'black box'. Furthermore, developments in modelling strategies and computer technology are likely to limit the longevity of any particular approach. An implication of this argument is that there is a need for a range of models, using different approaches and reflecting different strengths.

## 2.2   Microsimulation Models

Practical policy analysis typically requires information about the effects of tax reform on a range of narrowly defined demographic groups. One of the most important defining characteristics of large-scale simulation models is that, based as they usually are on individual records from a cross-sectional household survey, it is possible to deal explicitly with considerable heterogeneity.

There are three components which combine to form a behavioural microsimulation model. The first is an accounting or arithmetic microsimulation model (sometimes called a static model) with which to impute net household incomes for a representative sample of households, and for both incumbent and counterfactual tax-benefit regimes. The second component is a quantifiable behavioural model of individual tastes for net income and labour supply (or equivalently, non-work time), with which individuals' preferred labour supply for a given set of economic circumstances may be simulated. For the purposes of behavioural microsimulation this essentially relates to the budget constraint faced by the individual under a given tax and benefit regime. The third component is a mechanism to allocate to each individual a preferred supply of hours in the face of any tax-benefit system. Analysing simulated changes in this allocation, between some base tax system and a counterfactual regime, forms the essence of behavioural microsimulation.

An immediate characteristic of larger-scale tax models is that their construction and maintenance require teamwork. The data handling and computer programming requirements are greater, and the range of skills required is also considerable. For example, a detailed knowledge of tax and social security systems is required. These sometimes involve several government departments and their full details are rarely codified in accessible forms. In the case of behavioural models, economic modelling and econometric skills are obviously important. The need for teams inevitably raises the cost of such models. For examples and broad discussions of microsimulation modelling, see Orcutt *et al.* (1986), Harding (ed.) (1996), Atkinson and Sutherland (1988, 1998), Redmond *et al.* (1998), Immervoll *et al.* (1999), Gallagher (1990), Hellwig (1990), Sutherland (ed.) (1997), Heimler and Meulders (eds.) (1993).

## 2.2.1 The Tax and Transfer System

Actual tax and transfer systems are typically extremely complex and contain a large number of taxes and benefits which, having been designed and administered by different government departments, are usually poorly integrated. The complexity increases where several means-tested benefits are available, because of the existence of numerous eligibility requirements and special conditions. It is only when a great deal of detailed information about individuals is available that it becomes possible to include the complexities of actual tax and transfer systems in a simulation model.

However, it is unlikely that household surveys contain sufficient information to replicate realistic tax systems fully. There are several reasons for this. In some cases, for example where asset values are required in the administration of means tests, it may be necessary to impute values. Imputations may not always be possible. Furthermore, regulations regarding the administration of taxes and transfers often leave room for some flexibility in interpretation. In particular, the administration of means tests or other benefits may allow a degree of discretion to be exercised by benefit officers who deal directly with claimants; changes in the interpretation of (possibly ambiguous) rules, or the degree to which some rules are fully enforced, can take place over time; there may be changes in people's awareness of the benefits available, and the eligibility rules, thereby affecting the degree of take-up.

In view of these limitations, even large-scale models may not be able to replicate actual systems entirely. Thus they may not accurately reproduce aggregate expenditure and tax levels. Similarly, the same problems may give rise to distortions in measuring the extent to which redistribution occurs. Another difficulty is that household surveys may contain non-representative numbers of some types of household and benefit recipient. It is usually necessary to apply a set of grossing up factors, depending on the properties of the sampling framework and survey responses.

## 2.2.2   Partial Equilibrium Modelling

The emphasis on population heterogeneity has meant that the large-scale tax microsimulation models are partial equilibrium in nature. They focus on the commodity demands, labour supplies and incomes of individuals and households, along with the associated taxes and transfer payments. Insofar as they deal with consumption, they only deal with the demand side, and insofar as they deal with labour supplies, they only handle the supply side of the labour market. In practice, particularly for large tax changes, the resulting reallocation of resources may be expected to give rise to changes in factor prices. As mentioned earlier, it has not so far been possible to construct general equilibrium models having extensive household components, though experiments have been made involving linkages between two different models.

This aspect of partial equilibrium models should always be kept in mind when considering simulation results. They describe what, under specified situations, may happen to only one side of the relevant market; they cannot produce a new equilibrium resulting from economy-wide adjustments. The models are also static in the sense that there is usually no attempt to model a time sequence of changes.

In the case of models which include endogenous consumption demands, the analysis of changes in indirect taxes may often require the construction of an auxiliary tax incidence model, in which the effects on consumer prices can first be traced under specific assumptions about the degree of tax shifting. This is particularly important where, as for example in Australia, there are many indirect taxes imposed at different stages in the production process. Such a tax incidence model is likely to be partial-equilibrium in nature and rely on the use of input-output data. For a tax incidence model covering indirect taxes in Australia, see Scutella (1999). Other indirect tax incidence models concern, for example, the effects on prices of a carbon tax; see Proops *et al.* (1993), Symons *et al.* (1994), and an application to Australia in Cornwell and Creedy (1997).

## 2.2.3 Data Limitations

Reference has already been made to the data requirements of tax models. This raises special problems for modellers in Australia. The two large-scale household surveys that are potentially useful are the Household Expenditure Survey and the Income Distribution Survey. The former does not contain sufficient information about hours worked by individuals while the latter does not contain information about expenditure patterns. It is well known that the measurement of income in the Household Expenditure Survey is unreliable, so that in developing models for the analysis of direct taxes and transfer payments, it is not surprising that reliance has been placed on the Income Distribution Survey. The extension of models to cover consumption taxes will require some elaborate data merging.

## 2.3   Non-Behavioural Tax Models

The majority of large-scale tax simulation models are non-behavioural. That is, no allowance is made for the possible effects of tax changes on individuals' consumption plans or labour supplies. These models are described as being arithmetic. It is sometimes said that they provide information about the effects of tax changes on the 'morning after' the change.

Advantages of the non-behavioural models include the fact that they are much more straightforward to build and maintain. For example, they do not involve the need for estimation of econometric relationships, such as labour supply or commodity demand functions. They are relatively easy to use and quick to run. They can therefore be accessed by a wide range of users. Furthermore, in view of the fact that no econometric estimation is required, they retain the full extent of the heterogeneity contained in the basic survey data used.

When examining the effects of policy changes, these models generally rely on tabulations and associated graphs, for various demographic groups, of the amounts of tax paid (and changes in tax) at various percentile income levels. It would be useful to extend the range of distributional analyses, using these models, to examine a number of inequality and tax progressivity measures, along with social welfare function evaluations. There is an extensive literature on measuring the impact of taxes and transfers; see the comprehensive study by Lambert (1993). It would be possible to apply some of the lessons from that literature.

The models are typically used to generate profiles, again for various household types, of net income at a range of gross income levels. These profiles are useful for highlighting certain discontinuities, and are helpful when trying to redesign tax and transfer systems in order to overcome discontinuities and excessively high marginal tax rates over some income ranges.

It is perhaps surprising that few of the non-behavioural models provide the facility for users to produce policy changes that are, say, revenue-neutral. This would require iterative search methods in which certain tax parameters (chosen by the user) are automatically adjusted in response to some specified policy change. Such search methods are much easier to carry out when there are no adjustments to individuals' behaviour to accommodate.

## 2.4  Behavioural Microsimulation Models

The production of behavioural microsimulation tax models represents a substantial challenge. It is a relatively new departure, particularly where labour supply variations are modelled. On labour supply modelling in the context of tax simulation models, see, for example, Apps and Savage (1989), Banks *et al.* (1996), Blundell *et al.* (1986), Duncan (1993), Duncan and Giles (1996) and Moffit (1992). On behavioural responses in EUROMOD, see Klevmarken (1997).

Behavioural models are needed because many tax policy changes are designed with the aim of altering the consumption of certain goods. These involve environmental taxes such as carbon taxes, or sumptuary taxes to reduce the consumption of harmful goods. Also, some policies are designed to induce more individuals to participate in paid employment or, for those already working, to increase their hours of work.

Measures of the welfare losses, for example resulting from increases in indirect taxes, are also overstated by non-behavioural models that rely on 'morning after' changes in tax paid, rather than allowing for substitution away from goods whose relative prices increase. In addition, estimates of the distributional implications of tax changes may be misleading unless behavioural adjustments are modelled. Estimates of tax rates required to achieve specified revenue levels are likely to be understated.

The existing behavioural microsimulation models are nevertheless restricted in the types of behaviour that are endogenous. At most, individuals' labour supplies and household demands are modelled. Variables such as household formation, marriage and births, along with retirement, labour training and higher education decisions, are considered to be exogenous and independent of the tax changes examined. Independence between commodities and leisure is also assumed. There is essentially a two-stage procedure in which a decision is made regarding labour supply (and hence income), and then the allocation of the resulting net income over commodities is made. Typically, labour supply in just one job is examined, so that the possibility of working additional hours at a different wage rate is ignored. Indeed, the wage rate is typically calculated by dividing total earnings by the total number of reported hours worked.

A component that evaluates the net income corresponding to any given number of hours worked by each individual is required at an early stage in the construction of a behavioural model. It contains all the details of the tax and transfer system, and is used to produce, for each individual, the precise budget constraint relating net income to hours worked. The behavioural part of the model can then evaluate which part of each individual's constraint is optimal.

It might be said that the evaluation of the net incomes, using the tax and transfer system, is in effect an associated non-behavioural model. However, it does not mean that any existing non-behavioural model can be augmented by a behavioural component. The complex architecture of microsimulation models requires the kind of integration that can only be achieved by simultaneously planning and producing all the components. For example, non-behavioural models are not usually concerned with the production of net incomes corresponding to various hours worked by each individual, but with the relationship between net and gross income for well-defined demographic types.

## 2.4.1 Population Heterogeneity

Behavioural microsimulation models have, to some extent, a lower degree of population heterogeneity than non-behavioural models. This is because econometric estimation of the important relationships must involve the use of a limited range of categories. For example, in estimating labour supply behaviour, individuals may be divided into groups such as couples, single males and single females, and single-parent households. The number of groups may be limited by the sample size. Nevertheless, many variables, such as age, location, occupation and education level, are used to estimate the relevant functions. However, individual-specific variability may be re-introduced to ensure that the optimum labour supply in the face of current taxes actually corresponds, for each individual, to the level that is observed in the current period.

In addition, some households may have to be eliminated from the base sample if, following econometric estimation, individuals in the household do not conform to the assumptions of the underlying economic model. For example, implied indifference curves must display decreasing marginal rates of substitution. If the number of hours worked is the dependent variable in a labour supply equation, the integrability condition needs to be satisfied in order for hours to be regarded as the outcome of utility maximisation. In other words it must be possible to recover the indirect utility function by integration; see, for example, Stern (1986).

### 2.4.2   Labour Force Participation

An important policy issue relates to the nature of tax and transfer changes designed to encourage more people to participate in the labour market. Hence, this is likely to provide a focus for behavioural microsimulation studies. However, it should be recognised that this is precisely the area which raises the greatest difficulty for modellers. There are several reasons for this. First, there is less information about non-participants in survey data. For example, it is necessary to impute a wage rate for non-workers, using estimated wage equations and allowing for selectivity issues. Also, variables such as industry or occupation are not available for non-workers, but these are often important in wage equations. A second problem is that there are fixed costs associated with working, irrespective of the number of hours worked. These are usually difficult to estimate in view of data limitations.

A third problem is that there may be constraints on the hours worked, so that individuals may not be able to vary hours continuously as is often, though not always, assumed in labour supply models. Methods involving discrete numbers of hours have been developed both for estimation and simulation purposes. Finally, labour supply models typically treat non-participation as a voluntary decision giving rise to a corner solution. However, demand-side factors may be important and there may be a discouraged worker effect of unemployment, which is difficult to model.

An important issue concerns the choice between continuous and discrete simulation; this is discussed in detail in Part II. Continuous simulation contrasts with discrete microsimulation, where net incomes before and after a policy reform are required only for a finite set of hours points. Each method has its costs and benefits. Discrete simulation is computationally simpler, but it is likely that simulated hours do not cover the full range of feasible hours choices open to the individual. Secondly, the precise detail of the budget constraint is lost in simulation. Thirdly, it is computationally non-trivial to calibrate the econometric model to replicate observed behaviour. There are, however, many advantages concerning the use of discrete hours in estimation.

## 2.5 Conclusions

It has been argued that tax models provide a necessary input into rational policy analysis. Valuable lessons can be learned from the use of relatively small, though often surprisingly complicated, models. However, direct policy advice requires the use of microsimulation models that can reflect the kind of population heterogeneity found in practice. Nevertheless, all models have their limitations and these must be recognised when producing policy simulations. Indeed, the use of formal models helps to make the assumptions explicit.

Despite difficulties, the development of behavioural simulation models presents exciting challenges for tax modellers. Improvements in data and in labour supply models and estimation methods will help to overcome some of the problems. As always, given that no model is without its limitations, it is necessary to treat the output from microsimulation models with caution. But given the importance of the issues examined, such models can provide a valuable element of policy analysis and can thereby help to provide a counterweight against the rhetoric and special pleading that otherwise play a major role in tax policy debates.

# Part II

# Estimation and Modelling

# Chapter 3

# Wage Functions

Wage functions provide much useful descriptive information about those characteristics of individuals which are associated with relatively high or low wage rates. Earnings functions have often been estimated, but these combine hours and wage rate variations. In any cross-sectional survey there are many individuals who are not working at the time the survey is carried out. Such people may be sick or temporarily unemployed, in which case a current wage rate is not available, or they may not be participating in the labour market, in which case there may not even be a previous wage to record. The estimation procedure obviously needs to allow for this sample selection aspect.

An additional value of wage functions is that they can be used to assign a wage rate to non-working individuals on the basis of their observed characteristics. A context in which this is required is the analysis of labour supply and, in particular, examination of the effects of taxes and transfers. For example, many tax policies are specially designed in an attempt to encourage more people to participate in paid employment. There would therefore be little value in restricting analyses of the effects of tax changes on labour supply to those currently working. Labour supply analyses require an individual-specific budget constraint relating net income to the number of hours worked by each person. Therefore it is not sufficient to obtain the relationship between gross and net income, which depends on a range of characteristics. A wage rate must be assigned to non-workers.

This chapter reports estimates of wage functions for Australians, using information from the 1995 and 1996 Income Distribution Surveys. The estimation procedure allows for the sample selection bias that would otherwise arise from the fact that only the wage rates of those currently working are observed. A second aim of the chapter is to consider the question of how such wage functions can be used to impute wage rates to non-workers. This issue is complicated by the fact that the wage equations may contain variables, such as industry and occupation, that are not recorded for non-workers for the same reason that wage rates are not available. It is nevertheless deemed to be desirable to include as many relevant individual characteristics as possible in the wage functions.

The selection model is described in section 3.1. Estimates are reported in section 3.2. The problem of assigning wage rates to non-workers is examined in section 3.3.

## 3.1   The Model

This section briefly describes the estimation approach used, which follows the standard procedure involving two equations. The first equation determines selection (employment) using a probit equation, and the second is the regression model which determines wage rates, conditional on employment.

### 3.1.1   The Selection Model

As in the standard selection model, each individual's observed employment outcome is regarded as being the result of an unobservable index of employability, $E_i^*$, which varies with personal characteristics, $z_i$. The variables included in $z$ may include both supply and demand side variables. Hence:

$$E_i^* = z_i'\gamma + u_i \tag{3.1}$$

Where $u_i$ is assumed to be independently distributed as $N(0, 1)$. As there is no information about the scale of $E^*$, the variance of $u$ cannot be identified and is therefore set equal to unity. Although the $E_i^*$ are unobservable, the realisation of this latent variable is that the individual is either employed, whereby $E_i = 1$, or unemployed, whereby $E_i = 0$. The selection model is such that:

$$E_i = \begin{cases} 1 \text{ if } E_i^* > 0 & \text{with prob } \Phi(z_i'\gamma) \\ 0 \text{ if } E_i^* \leq 0 & \text{with prob } 1 - \Phi(z_i'\gamma) \end{cases} \tag{3.2}$$

where $\Phi(z_i'\gamma)$ is the standard normal cumulative distribution function evaluated at $z_i'\gamma$, and $\phi(z_i'\gamma)$ denotes the associated density function. The parameters of (3.2) can be consistently estimated by a standard probit model; see Maddala (1983).

## 3.1.2 The Regression Model

Let $w_i$ denote the logarithm of the wage rate of the $i$th individual, and $x_i$ a vector of characteristics determining wage rates. The regression model is written as:

$$w_i|_{E_i=1} = x_i'\beta + \varepsilon_i \tag{3.3}$$

The $u_i$, from equation (3.1) and $\varepsilon_i$ are assumed to be jointly normally distributed as $N(0, 0, 1, \sigma_\varepsilon^2, \rho)$. The covariance between $u_i$ and $\varepsilon_i$ is thus $\rho\sigma_\varepsilon$. In order to avoid selectivity bias, this is estimated using:

$$w_i|_{E_i=1} = x_i'\beta + \rho\sigma_\varepsilon^2\widehat{\lambda}_i + v_i \tag{3.4}$$

The term $\widehat{\lambda}_i$ is an estimate of the inverse Mills ratio for each individual. Having estimated (3.2), it is possible to calculate the $\widehat{\lambda}_i$s using:

$$\widehat{\lambda}_i = \frac{\phi(z_i'\overline{\gamma})}{\Phi(z_i'\overline{\gamma})} \tag{3.5}$$

Equation (3.3) takes into account the correlation between $u_i$ and $\varepsilon_i$. Allowance also needs to be made for the fact that the variance of $v_i$, $\sigma_i^2$, is heteroscedastic, since:

$$\sigma_i^2 = \sigma_\varepsilon^2 \left(1 - \rho^2 \delta_i\right) \tag{3.6}$$

where:

$$\delta_i = \lambda_i \left(\lambda_i + z_i' \gamma\right) \tag{3.7}$$

For further details of efficient estimation of this model see, for example, Greene (1981, pp.980-981).

## 3.2   Empirical Results

This section presents the main empirical results. The first two subsections describe the data and report basic summary statistics. The final two subsections report the estimated selection and wage equations.

### 3.2.1   The Data

The data used in this analysis are taken from the 1995 and 1996 Income Distribution Surveys, available from the Australian Bureau of Statistics in the form of confidential unit record files (CURFs). The survey collects information on the sources and amounts of income received by persons resident in private dwellings throughout Australia. It provides information on a range of characteristics of income units and persons surveyed. The survey is continuous with around 650 households interviewed every month during the financial year. In the 1995 and 1996 surveys information is available respectively for 14,017 and 14,595 individuals over the age of 15.

Earlier Income Distribution Surveys were carried out, but the 1995 survey is the first to provide published data on the precise hours worked (up to 50 hours per week) by each worker in the sample; earlier surveys contain only grouped information, with very broad groups. The details of hours worked are required for the calculation of a wage rate, which is obtained for each individual as the ratio of total earnings to hours worked. Hence the following

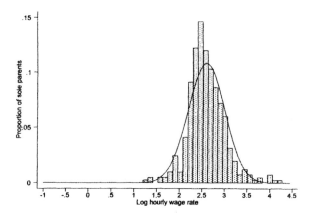

Figure 3.1: Sole Parents

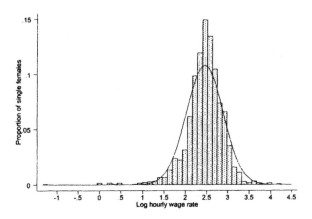

Figure 3.2: Single Females

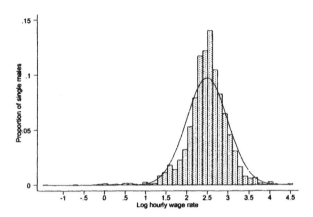

Figure 3.3: Single Males

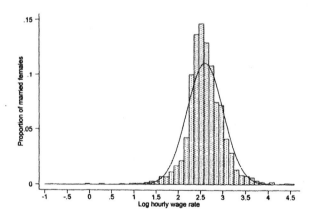

Figure 3.4: Married Females

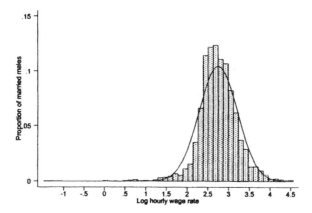

Figure 3.5: Married Males

analysis ignores the possibility that individuals may obtain overtime premia, or may work in more than one job. Where individuals worked more than 50 hours, the number was set at 50; this obviously produces an upward bias in the wage rate for those people.

The majority of the data comprising the explanatory variables were re-coded as zero-one dummy variables. To keep the variables to scale all of the non-wage income variables were divided by 1,000. Any inconsistencies between wages and hours, that is positive wages for zero hours or zero wages for positive hours, were treated as a zero hourly wage. To avoid the problem of taking the logarithm of zero in the wage equation and to ensure consistency between the employment and wage equations, employment status was determined with reference to the wage rate. Thus, any person with a zero wage rate per hour was treated as being unemployed, regardless of the actual employment status defined in the original data set. Those individuals not in the labour force were omitted from the sample so that only persons employed or unemployed remained. In the two surveys used, there were 1,208 people either at school or studying full-time. There were 69 unpaid voluntary work-

ers and 188 individuals permanently unavailable for work. There were 1,825
self employed people. In addition 425 females and 27 males were deemed not
to be in the labour force.

The two surveys were pooled and the sample was divided into five broad
demographic groups: sole parents, single females without dependents, single
males without dependents, married females and married males. It was not
possible to divide the sole parent group into males and females, in view of
the small number of male sole parents in the sample. There were 104 male
sole parents, compared with 857 females.

Examples of distributions of the logarithms of hourly wage rates for the
five demographic groups are shown in Figures 3.1 to 3.5. These are based
on February 1995 wages. These histographs suggest that the distributions of
wage rates are approximately lognormal.

### 3.2.2   Summary Statistics

Summary statistics for the various demographic groups are shown in Tables
3.1 and 3.2. These tables show the sample averages. Since many variables
are dummy variables taking (0,1) values, the values in the tables show the
proportions in each category. Two tables are required because the samples
used in the selection equation and the wage equations are different.

### 3.2.3   Selection Equations

The results of estimating the selection equations for each demographic group
are shown in Tables 3.4, 3.5 and 3.6. These are based on sample sizes, for
married men, married women, single men, single women and sole parents respectively, of $5,689$, $4,333$, $2,857$, $2,264$ and $509$. The column headed $df/dx$
shows the marginal effects on the probability of being employed, evaluated
at sample means of variables (in most cases these are the effects of a discrete
change from 0 to 1 in the dummy variable). The majority of coefficients are

Table 3.1: Sample Averages: Selection Equations

| variable | Single Prnts | Single Men | Sngl Women | Mrd Men | Mrd Women |
|---|---|---|---|---|---|
| aged 15 to 19 | 0.0059 | 0.1400 | 0.1643 | 0.0012 | 0.0060 |
| aged 20 to 24 | 0.0452 | 0.2891 | 0.2765 | 0.0311 | 0.0542 |
| aged 25 to 29 (ref group) | 0.1198 | 0.1883 | 0.1661 | 0.0976 | 0.1219 |
| aged 30 to 34 | 0.1709 | 0.1173 | 0.0830 | 0.1448 | 0.1507 |
| aged 35 to 39 | 0.2220 | 0.0739 | 0.0658 | 0.1596 | 0.1629 |
| aged 40 to 44 | 0.2338 | 0.0655 | 0.0490 | 0.1580 | 0.1703 |
| aged 45 to 49 | 0.1316 | 0.0459 | 0.0742 | 0.1571 | 0.1650 |
| aged 50 to 54 | 0.0452 | 0.0340 | 0.0561 | 0.1185 | 0.1018 |
| aged 55 to 59 | 0.0196 | 0.0287 | 0.0415 | 0.0796 | 0.0487 |
| aged 60 to 64 | 0.0059 | 0.0137 | 0.0150 | 0.0380 | 0.0132 |
| separated/widowed | 0 | 0.0021 | 0.0044 | | |
| Australia (reference group) | 0.7760 | 0.1579 | 0.2164 | 0.7311 | 0.7579 |
| Europe/Middle East | 0.7780 | 0.8523 | 0.8631 | 0.1992 | 0.1636 |
| Asia | 0.1552 | 0.1001 | 0.0848 | 0.0496 | 0.0542 |
| America/Africa | 0.0413 | 0.0036 | 0.0362 | 0.0202 | 0.0242 |
| postgraduate qualification | 0.0255 | 0.0112 | 0.0159 | 0.0670 | 0.0544 |
| undergraduate qualification | 0.0628 | 0.0308 | 0.0490 | 0.1114 | 0.1165 |
| diploma | 0.0943 | 0.0970 | 0.1378 | 0.1197 | 0.0997 |
| vocational qualification | 0.0845 | 0.0809 | 0.0906 | 0.2918 | 0.1941 |
| no formal qualifications (ref) | 0.2240 | 0.2324 | 0.1811 | 0.4101 | 0.5350 |
| non-labour income unit income | 0.5324 | 0.5586 | 0.5380 | 0.3020 | 0.5605 |
| child support income | 0.0190 | 0.0089 | 0.0734 | 0.0000 | 0.0098 |
| NSW (reference group) | 0.0242 | 0.0000 | 0.0535 | 0.2238 | 0.2315 |
| Victoria | 0.1847 | 0.2359 | 0.2266 | 0.2144 | 0.2075 |
| Queensland | 0.2043 | 0.2048 | 0.2403 | 0.1733 | 0.1710 |
| South Australia | 0.1513 | 0.1733 | 0.1731 | 0.1085 | 0.1140 |
| Western Australia | 0.1198 | 0.1085 | 0.1056 | 0.1378 | 0.1290 |
| Tasmania | 0.1375 | 0.1435 | 0.1334 | 0.0673 | 0.0653 |
| ACT/Northern Territory | 0.0963 | 0.0571 | 0.0658 | 0.0749 | 0.0817 |
| capital city | 0.1061 | 0.0770 | 0.0552 | 0.6027 | 0.5982 |
| number of children | 0.5737 | 0.6220 | 0.6789 | 1.2153 | 1.0425 |
| youngest child aged 0 to 2 | 1.5992 | 0 | 0. | 0.1833 | 0.1163 |
| youngest child aged 3 to 4 | 0.0982 | 0 | 0 | 0.0745 | 0.0639 |
| youngest child aged 5 to 9 | 0.1139 | 0 | 0 | 0.1484 | 0.1410 |
| youngest child aged 10 to 15 | 0.2927 | 0 | 0 | 0.1188 | 0.1336 |
| owned/mortgaged (reference) | 0.2868 | 0 | 0 | 0.7715 | 0.7891 |
| rented | 0.4460 | 0.1827 | 0.6718 | 0.2048 | 0.1874 |
| other tenure | 0.5265 | 0.5870 | 0.5455 | 0.0237 | 0.0235 |
| partner employed | 0.0275 | 0.2303 | 0.2275 | 0.5753 | 0.7334 |
| partner has postgraduate qual | | | | 0.0410 | 0.0621 |
| partner has undergraduate qual | | | | 0.1007 | 0.1108 |
| older than partner | | | | 0.1100 | 0.0097 |
| younger than partner | | | | 0.0123 | 0.1216 |
| university qual x (aged 20 to 24) | | 0.0000 | 0.0000 | 0.0229 | 0.0057 |
| university qual x (aged 25 to 29) | 0 | 0.0301 | 0.0508 | 0.0118 | 0.0226 |
| university qual x (aged 30 to 34) | 0 | 0.0357 | 0.0473 | 0.0239 | 0.0254 |
| university qual x (aged 35 to 39) | 0.0196 | 0.0228 | 0.0261 | 0.0323 | 0.0355 |
| university qual x (aged 40 to 44) | 0.0373 | 0.0109 | 0.0230 | 0.0380 | 0.0321 |
| university qual x (aged 45 to 49) | 0.0413 | 0.0116 | 0.0088 | 0.0341 | 0.0277 |
| university qual x (aged 50 to 54) | 0.0393 | 0.0077 | 0.0119 | 0.0206 | 0.0145 |
| university qual x (aged 55 to 59) | 0.0118 | 0.0042 | 0.0066 | 0.0114 | 0.0046 |
| vocational qual x (aged 20 to 24) | 0.0020 | 0.0105 | 0.0265 | 0.0116 | 0.0162 |
| vocational qual x (aged 25 to 29) | 0.0177 | 0.0914 | 0.0857 | 0.0401 | 0.0335 |
| vocational qual x (aged 30 to 34) | 0.0393 | 0.0714 | 0.0517 | 0.0559 | 0.0501 |
| vocational qual x (aged 35 to 39) | 0.0550 | 0.0410 | 0.0190 | 0.0679 | 0.0508 |
| vocational qual x (aged 40 to 44) | 0.0550 | 0.0294 | 0.0186 | 0.0631 | 0.0478 |
| vocational qual x (aged 45 to 49) | 0.0805 | 0.0231 | 0.0146 | 0.0682 | 0.0455 |
| vocational qual x (aged 50 to 54) | 0.0393 | 0.0161 | 0.0208 | 0.0503 | 0.0319 |
| vocational qual x (aged 55 to 59) | 0.0138 | 0.0137 | 0.0168 | 0.0308 | 0.0129 |
| vocational qual x (aged 60 to 64) | 0.0059 | 0.0112 | 0.0115 | 0.0178 | 0.0025 |

Table 3.2: Sample Averages: Wage Equations

| Variable | Sngle Prnts | Sngle Men | Sngl Women | Mrd Men | Mrd Women |
|---|---|---|---|---|---|
| aged 15 to 19 | 0.0048 | 0.1264 | 0.1455 | 0.0008 | 0.0045 |
| aged 20 to 24 | 0.0361 | 0.2945 | 0.2792 | 0.0307 | 0.0549 |
| aged 25 to 29 (ref group) | 0.1082 | 0.1956 | 0.1740 | 0.1034 | 0.1249 |
| aged 30 to 34 | 0.1659 | 0.1199 | 0.0885 | 0.1499 | 0.1484 |
| aged 35 to 39 | 0.2356 | 0.0778 | 0.0677 | 0.1568 | 0.1621 |
| aged 40 to 44 | 0.2356 | 0.0672 | 0.0488 | 0.1617 | 0.1740 |
| aged 45 to 49 | 0.1370 | 0.0460 | 0.0748 | 0.1572 | 0.1682 |
| aged 50 to 54 | 0.05048 | 0.0318 | 0.0570 | 0.1180 | 0.1038 |
| aged 55 to 59 | 0.0192 | 0.0254 | 0.0407 | 0.0770 | 0.0435 |
| aged 60 to 64 | 0.0072 | 0.0142 | 0.0163 | 0.0339 | 0.0188 |
| aged 65 to 69 | 0 | 0.0004 | 0.0458 | | |
| professional | 0.2332 | 0.1819 | 0.2096 | 0.3120˙ | 0.2200 |
| para-professional | 0.1034 | 0.0744 | 0.1200 | 0.1075 | 0.1397 |
| clerical/sales | 0.4159 | 0.1986 | 0.5158 | 0.1495 | 0.4658 |
| traditional labour (ref group) | 0.2476 | 0.5451 | 0.1546 | 0.4310 | 0.1745 |
| agriculture/forestry (ref group) | 0.0216 | 0.0357 | 0.0076 | 0.0282 | 0.0151 |
| mining | 0.0048 | 0.0129 | 0.0031 | 0.0223 | 0.0045 |
| manufacturing | 0.1106 | 0.1986 | 0.0814 | 0.2115 | 0.0979 |
| construction | 0.0144 | 0.0881 | 0.0076 | 0.0804 | 0.0187 |
| sales | 0.1418 | 0.2158 | 0.2106 | 0.1607 | 0.1666 |
| transport | 0.0216 | 0.0563 | 0.0204 | 0.0705 | 0.0214 |
| communications | 0.0240 | 0.0305 | 0.0132 | 0.0291 | 0.0137 |
| financial/business sector | 0.0937 | 0.1135 | 0.1679 | 0.1320 | 0.1524 |
| service industries | 0.5577 | 0.2395 | 0.4837 | 0.2456 | 0.5049 |
| Australia (reference group) | 0.7885 | 0.8573 | 0.8657 | 0.7339 | 0.7668 |
| Europe/Middle East | 0.1442 | 0.0980 | 0.0829 | 0.1974 | 0.1590 |
| Asia | 0.0384 | 0.0327 | 0.0356 | 0.0481 | 0.0475 |
| America/Africa | 0.0288 | 0.0120 | 0.0158 | 0.0205 | 0.0267 |
| postgraduate qualification | 0.0769 | 0.0357 | 0.0534 | 0.0703 | 0.0578 |
| undergraduate qualification | 0.0961 | 0.1066 | 0.1490 | 0.1131 | 0.1236 |
| diploma | 0.0889 | 0.0825 | 0.0941 | 0.1251 | 0.1030 |
| vocational qualification | 0.2043 | 0.2382 | 0.1750 | 0.2927 | 0.1933 |
| no formal qual (reference) | 0.5337 | 0.5365 | 0.5254 | 0.3987 | 0.5223 |
| New South Wales (ref) | 0.1827 | 0.2498 | 0.2335 | 0.2247 | 0.2337 |
| Victoria | 0.2019 | 0.1991 | 0.2462 | 0.2155 | 0.2094 |
| Queensland | 0.149 | 0.1694 | 0.1679 | 0.1714 | 0.1685 |
| South Australia | 0.1082 | 0.1045 | 0.1007 | 0.1070 | 0.1122 |
| Western Australia | 0.1394 | 0.1423 | 0.1328 | 0.1395 | 0.1275 |
| Tasmania | 0.1034 | 0.0533 | 0.0641 | 0.0646 | 0.0639 |
| ACT/Northern Territory | 0.1154 | 0.0817 | 0.0549 | 0.0772 | 0.0847 |
| capital city | 0.5793 | 0.6363 | 0.6948 | 0.6185 | 0.6121 |
| university qual x (age 20 to 24) | 0 | 0.0339 | 0.0544 | 0.0223 | 0.0061 |
| university qual x (age 25 to 29) | 0 | 0.0387 | 0.0504 | 0.0134 | 0.0236 |
| university qual x (age 30 to 34) | 0.0168 | 0.0258 | 0.0285 | 0.0254 | 0.0267 |
| university quax (age 35 to 39) | 0.0457 | 0.0125 | 0.0259 | 0.0323 | 0.0375 |
| university qual x (age 40 to 44) | 0.0433 | | | 0.0400 | 0.0335 |
| university qual x (age ≥ 35) | 0.0457 | 0.0133 | 0.0092 | | |
| university qua x (age 45 to 49) | 0.0144 | 0.0082 | 0.0132 | 0.0313 | 0.0301 |
| university qual x (age 50 to 54) | 0.0072 | 0.0043 | 0.0071 | 0.0211 | 0.0158 |
| university qual x (age 55 to 59) | 0 | 0.0021 | 0.0081 | 0.0116 | 0.0053 |
| university qual x (age 60 to 64) | 0 | 0.0258 | 0.0041 | 0.0047 | 0.0026 |
| vocational qual x (age ≤ 24) | 0.0120 | | | | |
| vocational qual x (age 20 to 24) | | 0.0941 | 0.0860 | 0.0114 | 0.0174 |
| vocational qual x (age 25 to 29) | 0.0264 | 0.0744 | 0.0524 | 0.0427 | 0.0341 |
| vocational qual x (age 30 to 34) | 0.0649 | 0.0434 | 0.0285 | 0.0589 | 0.0499 |
| vocational qual x (age 35 to 39) | 0.0577 | 0.0309 | 0.0259 | 0.0681 | 0.0494 |
| vocational qual x (age 40 to 44) | 0.0697 | 0.0249 | 0.0092 | 0.0648 | 0.0502 |
| vocational qual x (age 45 to 49) | 0.0408 | 0.0159 | 0.0132 | 0.7049 | 0.0467 |
| vocational qual x (age 50 to 54) | 0.0144 | 0.0146 | 0.0071 | 0.0508 | 0.0335 |
| vocational qual x (age 55 to 59) | 0.0072 | 0.0086 | 0.0081 | 0.0303 | 0.0106 |
| vocational qual x (age 60 to 64) | | 0.0047 | 0.0041 | 0.0158 | 0.0021 |

significantly different from zero and the coefficient signs appear to accord with expectations.[1]

A 'hit and miss' table can be constructed to evaluate how well the selection model predicts. However, if standard techniques are used to do this (based on the maximum probability rule), the models generally tend to overpredict the empirically most frequently chosen outcome. Indeed, this is true of the present models, with the employed being somewhat overpredicted for each demographic group. Such a result stems from the fact that the random elements of the model are explicitly ignored in its evaluation.

An alternative method is to utilise the underlying economic model and to simulate it by repeated draws of the unobserved random variates (that is, from the standard normal distribution). For each random draw, the probabilistic expressions are evaluated and the outcome which yields the maximum probability is the one predicted for that repetition. A predicted probabilities of $\geq 0.5$, give rise to a predicted value of unity (employed) and zero (unemployed) otherwise. Each separate hit and miss table is collected, and the simulated hit and miss table is the average of all of these independent ones. The results are reported in Table 3.3, which summarises actual versus predicted values, using 1000 random draws. It can be seen that in each case the probit model provides close predictions of the numbers employed.

Considering the results, state of residence seems to be of more importance to employment patterns of women than for men, whereas living in a capital city is associated with a higher probability of employment for all demographic groups. In the case of married women the probability of employment is higher for those with a tertiary qualification than for those without any qualification, whereas this is not true of married men. The probability of employment is higher for sole parents with a diploma or vocational qualification than for

---

[1]Direct comparisons with results in Miller and Rummery (1991) are not possible because the latter have just two demographic groups (males and females) and include a much smaller set of variables than are used here.

Table 3.3: Simulated Hit/Miss Results

| Actual | Predicted 0 | Predicted 1 | Total |
|--------|------|------|-------|
|        | **Sole Parents** | | |
| 0      | 26.5 | 66.5 | 93 |
| 1      | 66.3 | 349.67800 | 416 |
| Total  | 92.9 | 416.1400 | 509 |
|        | **Single Females** | | |
| 0      | 57.2 | 240.8 | 298 |
| 1      | 241.3 | 1724.7 | 1966 |
| Total  | 298.5 | 1965.5 | 2264 |
|        | **Single Males** | | |
| 0      | 122.0 | 409.0 | 531 |
| 1      | 409.3 | 1917.0 | 2326 |
| Total  | 531.3 | 2326.0 | 2857 |
|        | **Married Females** | | |
| 0      | 128.6 | 417.4 | 546 |
| 1      | 418.1 | 3369.0 | 3787 |
| Total  | 546.7 | 3786.0 | 4333 |
|        | **Married Males** | | |
| 0      | 146.6 | 619.4 | 766 |
| 1      | 620.4 | 4303.0 | 4923 |
| Total  | 767.0 | 4922.0 | 5689 |

those without any qualification. Couples where the partner is employed are significantly more likely to be in employment than couples where the partner is out of work. Also women whose partner has a postgraduate qualification have a lower probability of employment.

As the number of dependent children increases, the probability of employment falls for either member of a couple. For single parents, employment status is unaffected by the number of children. The age of the youngest child has opposite effects for married men and women. Coefficients on the age of the youngest child indicator variables are all positive and significant (at least at the ten per cent level) for men. This counteracts the negative coefficient on the number of children. In the case of married women, negative coefficients on the age of youngest child variables reinforce the negative effect of the number of dependent children on the probability of employment. Thus, employment is relatively less likely for women with children under the age of 9. However, for men with children under the age of 15, the probability of employment is higher than for those without children or with older children. All groups, apart from sole parents, are more likely to be employed if their homes are either owned outright or if they have a mortgage.

In addition to variables relating to age, location, qualifications and number and ages of children (in the case of married and sole parent groups), interaction terms for qualification and age were also found to be significant. These suggest, as expected, that age-earnings profiles differ between education groups.

Maximum likelihood estimation of discrete choice models, such as the selection model used here, is based upon a specified distribution of the unobserved elements of the underlying economic model. However, unlike the traditional linear regression model, if the distributional assumptions in such non-linear models are invalid, parameter estimates are both biased and inconsistent. For this reason, diagnostic testing procedures in a discrete choice framework have been suggested; see Olsen (1982), Blundell and Meghir

Table 3.4: Selection Terms: Married Men and Women

| variable | Men coeff | SE | df/dx | Women coeff | SE | df/dx |
|---|---|---|---|---|---|---|
| constant | 0.8037 | 0.1175 | | 0.8628 | 0.1302 | |
| aged 15 to 19 | -0.8862 | 0.5082 | -.2623 | | | |
| aged 20 to 24 | 0.0596 | 0.1891 | .0112 | -0.1008 | 0.1721 | -.0180 |
| aged 25 to 29 (ref) | | | | | | |
| aged 30 to 34 | 0.0490 | 0.1279 | .0094 | 0.0692 | 0.1328 | .0113 |
| aged 35 to 39 | -0.1290 | 0.1273 | -.0265 | 0.2088 | 0.1414 | .0321 |
| aged 40 to 44 | -0.0154 | 0.1338 | -.0030 | 0.0380 | 0.1381 | .0063 |
| aged 45 to 49 | -0.1611 | 0.1250 | -.0335 | -0.0681 | 0.1351 | -.0118 |
| aged 50 to 54 | -0.1515 | 0.1368 | -.0317 | -0.1686 | 0.1520 | -.0311 |
| aged 55 to 59 | -0.1754 | 0.1441 | -.0373 | -0.2893 | 0.1660 | -.0576 |
| aged 60 to 64 | -0.2780 | 0.1835 | -.0628 | -0.3709 | 0.2480 | -.0783 |
| separated/widowed | | | | | | |
| Australia (ref group) | | | | | | |
| Europe/Middle East | -0.0630 | 0.0571 | -.0126 | -0.2125 | 0.0712 | -.0394 |
| Asia | -0.1630 | 0.1012 | -.0346 | -0.5582 | 0.1059 | -.1267 |
| America/Africa | -0.0888 | 0.1602 | -.0182 | 0.4843 | 0.2508 | .0597 |
| postgraduate | 0.0712 | 0.1587 | .0133 | 0.7528 | 0.2302 | .0806 |
| undergraduate | -0.1544 | 0.1474 | -.0323 | 0.7657 | 0.2193 | .0875 |
| diploma | -0.3613 | 0.2572 | -.0824 | -0.2897 | 0.4337 | -.0567 |
| vocational | -0.5214 | 0.2501 | -.1153 | -0.4443 | 0.4260 | -.0892 |
| no formal qual (ref group) | | | | | | |
| non-labour income unit inc | 0.0565 | 0.1056 | .0110 | 0.0570 | 0.1055 | .0096 |
| child support income | | | | 0.0245 | 2.5755 | .0041 |
| NSW (reference) | | | | | | |
| Victoria | -0.0462 | 0.0672 | -.0092 | -0.0747 | 0.0827 | -.0130 |
| Queensland | -0.0030 | 0.0706 | -.0006 | -0.1183 | 0.0854 | -.0210 |
| South Australia | -0.1304 | 0.0810 | -.0270 | -0.1891 | 0.0966 | -.0350 |
| Western Australia | 0.0072 | 0.0765 | .0014 | -0.1952 | 0.0921 | -.0362 |
| Tasmania | -0.1133 | 0.0933 | -.0234 | -0.1436 | 0.1158 | -.0263 |
| ACT/Northern Territory | 0.2156 | 0.1019 | .0376 | 0.2021 | 0.1205 | .0305 |
| capital city | 0.2759 | 0.0496 | .0557 | 0.2458 | 0.0597 | .0429 |
| number of children | -0.0569 | 0.0291 | -.0110 | -0.0939 | 0.0394 | -.0159 |
| youngest child 0 to 2 | 0.1857 | 0.0943 | .0337 | -0.3061 | 0.1173 | -.0600 |
| youngest child 3 to 4 | 0.2306 | 0.1133 | .0399 | -0.3287 | 0.1371 | -.0665 |
| youngest child 5 to 9 | 0.1540 | 0.0937 | .0281 | -0.3163 | 0.1166 | -.0618 |
| youngest child 10 to 15 | 0.1662 | 0.0904 | .0300 | -0.1124 | 0.1096 | -.0200 |
| owned/mortgaged (ref) | | | | | | |
| rented | -0.2794 | 0.0557 | -.0600 | -0.2376 | 0.0696 | -.0442 |
| other tenure | -0.2781 | 0.1341 | -.0630 | -0.3127 | 0.1566 | -.0636 |
| partner employed | 0.5288 | 0.0629 | .1085 | 0.8078 | 0.0879 | .1728 |
| partner has postgrad qual | -0.0540 | 0.1279 | -.0108 | -0.2443 | 0.1232 | -.0473 |
| partner has undergrad qual | 0.1253 | 0.0883 | .0230 | -0.0600 | 0.0962 | -.0105 |
| older partner | -0.1177 | 0.0680 | -.0242 | -0.3789 | 0.2420 | -.0804 |
| younger partner | -0.0137 | 0.1923 | -.0027 | -0.0679 | 0.0786 | -.0119 |
| university qual x ( 20 to 24) | -0.0182 | 0.4884 | -.0036 | -0.6433 | 0.4625 | -.1567 |
| university qual x ( 25 to 29) | 1.0848 | 0.4418 | .1067 | -0.5428 | 0.2971 | -.1247 |
| university qual x ( 30 to 34) | 0.2481 | 0.2321 | .0418 | -0.4859 | 0.2920 | -.1084 |
| university qual x ( 35 to 39) | 0.0673 | 0.2000 | .0126 | -0.4229 | 0.2787 | -.0909 |
| university qual x ( 40 to 44) | 0.1639 | 0.2074 | .0291 | -0.4806 | 0.2735 | -.1065 |
| university qual x ( 45 to 49) | 0.1399 | 0.2295 | | | | |
| university qual x ( 50 to 54) | 0.1322 | 0.2670 | .0251 | -0.1817 | 0.3688 | -.0344 |
| university qual x ( 55 to 59) | -0.0411 | 0.3392 | .0238 | | | |
| vocational qual x ( 20 to 24) | 0.3396 | 0.3559 | .0538 | 0.8797 | 0.5179 | .0827 |
| vocational qual x ( 25 to 29) | 0.7096 | 0.2648 | .0912 | 0.4560 | 0.4404 | .0577 |
| vocational qual x ( 30 to 34) | 0.6532 | 0.2828 | .0882 | 0.4499 | 0.4490 | .0578 |
| vocational qual x ( 35 to 39) | 0.5559 | 0.2762 | .0801 | 0.3149 | 0.4489 | .0440 |
| vocational qual x ( 40 to 44) | 0.4912 | 0.2805 | .0732 | 0.6943 | 0.4552 | .0764 |
| vocational qual x ( 45 to 49) | 0.6938 | 0.2759 | .0926 | 0.5903 | 0.4531 | .0692 |
| vocational qual x ( 50 to 54) | 0.6425 | 0.2840 | .0868 | 0.7229 | 0.4698 | .0768 |
| vocational qual x ( 55 to 59) | 0.5978 | 0.2956 | .0816 | 0.1379 | 0.4811 | .0213 |
| vocational qual x ( 60 to 64) | 0.4493 | 0.3246 | .0666 | 0.0371 | 0.6330 | .0061 |

Table 3.5: Selection Terms: Single Men and Women

| variable | Men coeff | SE | df/dx | Women coeff | SE | df/dx |
|---|---|---|---|---|---|---|
| constant | 1.2671 | 0.1424 | | 2.1158 | 0.2072 | |
| aged 15 to 19 | -0.1691 | 0.1174 | -.0456 | -0.5443 | 0.1579 | -.1238 |
| aged 20 to 24 | 0.0300 | 0.1133 | .0076 | -0.2223 | 0.1615 | -.0435 |
| aged 25 to 29 (ref group) | | | | | | |
| aged 30 to 34 | -0.1042 | 0.1328 | -.0276 | 0.0246 | 0.2060 | .0045 |
| aged 35 to 39 | 0.0222 | 0.1808 | .0056 | -0.5705 | 0.2498 | -.1385 |
| aged 40 to 44 | -0.1903 | 0.1782 | -.0523 | -0.4315 | 0.2548 | -.0994 |
| aged 45 to 49 | -0.0771 | 0.2090 | -.0203 | -0.3867 | 0.2382 | -.0863 |
| aged 50 to 54 | -0.5788 | 0.2267 | -.1823 | -0.2631 | 0.2642 | -.0557 |
| aged 55 to 59 | -0.2219 | 0.2316 | -.0621 | -0.3237 | 0.2687 | -.0709 |
| aged 60 to 64 | 0.0832 | 0.3340 | .0204 | 1.0595 | 0.6457 | .0987 |
| aged 65 to 69 | -1.8938 | 0.6660 | -.6563 | 0.7190 | 0.9215 | .0823 |
| separated/widowed | -0.0200 | 0.0983 | -.0051 | -0.2742 | 0.1361 | -.0555 |
| Australia (ref group) | | | | | | |
| Europe/Middle East | -0.1631 | 0.0979 | -.0441 | -0.2881 | 0.1284 | -.0611 |
| Asia | -0.4797 | 0.1438 | -.1466 | -0.3677 | 0.1890 | -.0825 |
| postgraduate | 0.7401 | 0.2634 | .1298 | 0.1443 | 0.2483 | .0245 |
| undergraduate | 0.4046 | 0.1561 | .0874 | 0.1575 | 0.2043 | .0270 |
| diploma | -0.2220 | 0.4762 | -.0615 | -1.5634 | 0.6089 | -.4877 |
| vocational | -0.1596 | 0.4687 | -.0423 | -1.8176 | 0.6031 | -.5388 |
| no formal qual (ref group) | | | | | | |
| non-labour income unit inc | -0.4504 | 0.5276 | -.1149 | -1.8168 | 0.7151 | -.3344 |
| NSW (reference group) | | | | | | |
| Victoria | -0.2895 | 0.0871 | -.0797 | -0.1521 | 0.1120 | -.0294 |
| Queensland | -0.2396 | 0.0922 | -.0656 | -0.2690 | 0.1147 | -.0551 |
| South Australia | -0.3588 | 0.1033 | -.1033 | -0.4293 | 0.1300 | -.0962 |
| Western Australia | -0.2432 | 0.0968 | -.0670 | -0.2084 | 0.1241 | -.0421 |
| Tasmania | -0.3607 | 0.1285 | -.1054 | -0.1944 | 0.1572 | -.0396 |
| ACT/Northern Territory | 0.1088 | 0.1337 | .0265 | -0.0305 | 0.1765 | -.0057 |
| capital city | 0.2606 | 0.0639 | .0684 | 0.2841 | 0.0820 | .0557 |
| owned/mortgaged (ref) | | | | | | |
| rented | -0.3070 | 0.0911 | -.0763 | -0.7058 | 0.1257 | -.1263 |
| other tenure | -0.4989 | 0.1038 | -.1427 | -0.9068 | 0.1411 | -.2200 |
| university qual x ( 20 to 24) | 0.0600 | 0.2599 | .0149 | 0.2287 | 0.2835 | .0369 |
| university qual x ( 35 to 39) | 0.0343 | 0.4247 | .0086 | 0.8703 | 0.5081 | .0924 |
| university qual x ( 40 to 44) | 0.2458 | 0.4303 | .0556 | 0.1754 | 0.4924 | .0289 |
| university qual x ( 45 to 49) | -0.4403 | 0.4265 | -.1341 | 0.6003 | 0.5446 | .0750 |
| university qual x ( 50 to 54) | -0.0413 | 0.4932 | -.0107 | 0.0272 | 0.6506 | .0049 |
| vocational qual x ( 15 to 19) | -0.0157 | 0.5294 | -.0040 | 1.7386 | 0.6331 | .1138 |
| vocational qual x ( 20 to 24) | 0.2899 | 0.4821 | .0657 | 1.7282 | 0.6192 | .1342 |
| vocational qual x ( 25 to 29) | 0.3280 | 0.4874 | .0726 | 1.5641 | 0.6161 | .1192 |
| vocational qual x ( 30 to 34) | 0.4430 | 0.5005 | .0915 | 1.4555 | 0.6808 | .1082 |
| vocational qual x ( 35 to 39) | 0.2882 | 0.5208 | .0641 | 2.0729 | 0.6870 | .1135 |
| vocational qual x ( 40 to 44) | 0.5819 | 0.5314 | .1106 | 1.9094 | 0.6975 | .1111 |
| vocational qual x ( 45 to 49) | 0.1799 | 0.5462 | .0421 | 1.7544 | 0.6740 | .1121 |
| vocational qual x ( 50 to 54) | 0.9002 | 0.5690 | .1419 | 1.9444 | 0.7006 | .1121 |
| vocational qual x ( 55 & over) | -0.2718 | 0.5580 | -.0779 | 1.4334 | 0.6977 | .1059 |

Table 3.6: Selection Terms: Sole Parents

| variable | coefficient | SE | df/dx |
|---|---|---|---|
| constant | 1.4189 | 0.4327 | |
| aged 15 to 19 | -0.8461 | 0.8229 | -.2744 |
| aged 20 to 24 | -0.9708 | 0.3994 | -.3171 |
| aged 25 to 29 (ref) | | | |
| aged 30 to 34 | -0.4026 | 0.3058 | -.1070 |
| aged 35 to 39 | -0.0056 | 0.3206 | -.0013 |
| aged 40 to 44 | -0.0082 | 0.3518 | -.0019 |
| aged 45 to 49 | -0.2783 | 0.4121 | -.0720 |
| aged 50 to 54 | 0.3342 | 0.6466 | .6623 |
| aged 55 to 59 | -0.6849 | 0.6073 | -.2113 |
| separated/widowed | -0.1917 | 0.2033 | -.0424 |
| Australia (ref group) | | | |
| Europe/Middle East | -0.4270 | 0.1906 | -.1150 |
| Asia | -0.3466 | 0.3509 | -.0943 |
| undergraduate qual | -0.1359 | 0.2599 | -.0336 |
| diploma | 1.0094 | 0.4156 | .1466 |
| vocational qual | 0.6592 | 0.3215 | .1269 |
| no formal qual (ref group) | | | |
| non-labour income unit inc | 3.7022 | 1.7325 | .8670 |
| child support income | -0.8672 | 1.3786 | -.2031 |
| NSW (reference group) | | | |
| Victoria | -0.0777 | 0.2263 | -.0186 |
| Queensland | 0.0876 | 0.2452 | .0199 |
| South Australia | -0.3420 | 0.2574 | -.0907 |
| Western Australia | 0.1172 | 0.2578 | .0262 |
| Tasmania | 0.4141 | 0.2969 | .0807 |
| ACT/Northern Territory | 0.4408 | 0.3049 | .0853 |
| capital city | 0.2952 | 0.1642 | .0707 |
| number of children | -0.0626 | 0.1032 | -.0147 |
| youngest child 0 to 2 | -0.2858 | 0.3696 | -.0748 |
| youngest child 3 to 4 | -0.4499 | 0.3300 | -.1239 |
| youngest child 5 to 9 | -0.2156 | 0.2715 | -.0528 |
| youngest child 10 to 15 | 0.1991 | 0.2431 | .0446 |
| owned/mortgaged (ref) | | | |
| rented | -0.1086 | 0.1664 | -.0253 |
| other tenure | 0.5529 | 0.5800 | .0963 |
| vocational qual x ( 25 to 29) | -1.6139 | 0.5058 | -.5612 |
| vocational qual x ( 35 to 39) | -0.7766 | 0.4800 | -.2415 |
| vocational qual x ( 40 to 44) | -1.4658 | 0.4403 | -.4988 |
| vocational qual x ( 45 to 49) | -0.7649 | 0.5431 | -.2390 |
| vocational qual x ( 50 to 54) | -1.3088 | 0.8753 | -.4552 |

Table 3.7: Specification Tests for Selection Equations (P-Values)

| Demographic Group | Normality | Heteroscedasticity |
|---|---|---|
| Sole parents | 0.026 | 0.428* |
| Single females | 0.940* | 0.324* |
| Single males | 0.705* | 0.492* |
| Married females | 0.157* | 0.550* |
| Married males | 0.549* | 0.272* |

*Cannot reject at 5% level.

(1987), Chesher and Irish (1987a,b), Gourieroux *et al.* (1987) and Pagan and Vella (1989).

Thus the first stage in checking model specification is to test the specification of these selection equations. Following Pagan and Vella (1989), tests for both normality and heteroscedasticity were undertaken. The results are reported in Table 3.7. These results show that the assumption of homoscedasticity appears valid for all of the demographic groups. Also, the assumption of normality cannot be rejected (at the 5% level) for all demographic groups except for sole parents.

## 3.2.4 Wage Equations

The estimated wage equations conditional on being in employment are reported for each demographic group in Tables 3.8, 3.9 and 3.10. These are based on sample sizes, for married men, married women, single men, single women and sole parents respectively, of 4923, 3787, 2326, 1966 and 416. The inverse Mills ratio was retained in each case although the estimated $t$ statistics are low (except for single women). For prediction purposes it is useful to include this variable, along with other non-significant variables. With the exception of the sole parents, the coefficient on the Mills ratio is positive. The interpretation of negative inverse Mills ratios in this context was discussed by Ermisch and Wright (1994). Miller and Rummery (1991) found a positive value for women and a negative value for men. They also review results found in previous Australian studies. In each table the 'estimated standard error' and 'estimated correlation coefficient' refer to $\sigma_\epsilon$ and $\rho$ respectively.

The coefficients display the expected variation with age, industry and educational qualifications. Wage rates of professionals, para-professionals, and clerical/salespersons are significantly higher than for trades persons or labourers across all groups. Wage rates also tend to increase with the level of educational qualification across all groups.

Couples living in New South Wales experience higher wage rates than those living in the other States, while those residing in the Territories receive even higher wages; residents of the Australian Capital Territory dominate this category. Married men and women in capital cities are paid higher wage rates than their counterparts living in other areas of the country. Wage rates of married men and women are generally higher in all industries compared with the agriculture and forestry industry (the reference industry). Single males in the mining industry earn higher wages whereas there is no significant difference in the wage rates across industries for single females without dependents and sole parents.

The specification of the present model is also based on the joint normality of both the selection and regression equations. If the selection equation is misspecified, the same is true of the correction term in the regression equation, resulting in biased and inconsistent estimates of the determinants of wages; see Olsen (1982). Following Pagan and Vella (1989) it is possible to test the assumption of joint normality by including the product of the linear prediction terms of the selection equation (to powers 1, 2 and 3) and the inverse Mills ratio for each individual. The null hypothesis of joint normality is rejected if these three additional variables are jointly significant. The likelihood ratio tests for these restrictions are reported in Table 3.11.

Table 3.11 shows that the null hypothesis of joint normality cannot be rejected for three out of the five regressions, and for one of the others the test could not be computed. This was caused by the multicolinearity arising

Table 3.8: Wage Equations: Married Men and Women

| variable | Men coeff | SE | Women coeff | SE |
|---|---|---|---|---|
| constant | 2.3829 | 0.0551 | 2.3170 | 0.0973 |
| aged 15 to 19 | -0.4420 | 0.2722 | | |
| aged 20 to 24 | -0.1231 | 0.0555 | -0.0724 | 0.0427 |
| aged 25 to 29 (ref group) | | | | |
| aged 30 to 34 | 0.0441 | 0.0367 | 0.0585 | 0.0334 |
| aged 35 to 39 | 0.1092 | 0.0385 | 0.0464 | 0.0327 |
| aged 40 to 44 | 0.1070 | 0.0381 | -0.0190 | 0.0312 |
| aged 45 to 49 | 0.1023 | 0.0388 | 0.0247 | 0.0313 |
| aged 50 to 54 | 0.0662 | 0.0406 | -0.0323 | 0.0358 |
| aged 55 to 59 | -0.0345 | 0.0442 | -0.0388 | 0.0464 |
| aged 60 & over | 0.0434 | 0.0644 | 0.1426 | 0.0775 |
| professional | 0.1886 | 0.0189 | 0.2947 | 0.0251 |
| para-professional | 0.1472 | 0.0222 | 0.2390 | 0.0268 |
| clerical/sales | 0.0626 | 0.0202 | 0.1064 | 0.0174 |
| tradesperson/labourer (ref) | | | | |
| agriculture/forestry (ref) | | | | |
| mining | 0.6171 | 0.0599 | 0.2953 | 0.1278 |
| manufacturing | 0.1824 | 0.0481 | 0.1190 | 0.0970 |
| construction | 0.1538 | 0.0516 | 0.1433 | 0.1072 |
| sales | 0.0452 | 0.0483 | 0.0786 | 0.0949 |
| transport | 0.2003 | 0.0514 | 0.2018 | 0.1028 |
| communications | 0.2499 | 0.0576 | 0.2889 | 0.1067 |
| financial/business sector | 0.1699 | 0.0491 | 0.1541 | 0.0947 |
| service industries | 0.1015 | 0.0472 | 0.0969 | 0.0940 |
| Australia (ref group) | | | | |
| Europe/Middle East | -0.0245 | 0.0167 | -0.0270 | 0.0184 |
| Asia | -0.1776 | 0.0312 | -0.0762 | 0.0331 |
| America/Africa | -0.1148 | 0.0447 | -0.0423 | 0.0378 |
| postgraduate | 0.3163 | 0.0503 | 0.2840 | 0.0478 |
| undergraduate | 0.1885 | 0.0467 | 0.2283 | 0.0425 |
| diploma | -0.0511 | 0.1100 | 0.1132 | 0.1095 |
| vocational | -0.1034 | 0.1089 | 0.0357 | 0.1083 |
| no formal qual (ref group) | | | | |
| New South Wales (ref group) | | | | |
| Victoria | -0.0641 | 0.0192 | -0.0379 | 0.0189 |
| Queensland | -0.0466 | 0.0205 | -0.0470 | 0.0204 |
| South Australia | -0.0714 | 0.0238 | 0.0092 | 0.0231 |
| Western Australia | -0.0158 | 0.0216 | -0.0726 | 0.0222 |
| Tasmania | -0.0218 | 0.0291 | -0.0170 | 0.0287 |
| ACT/Northern Territory | 0.0830 | 0.0290 | 0.0784 | 0.0272 |
| capital city | 0.0860 | 0.0170 | 0.0524 | 0.0157 |
| university qual x ( 20 to 24) | -0.0716 | 0.1494 | -0.1765 | 0.0944 |
| university qual x ( 25 to 29) | -0.0532 | 0.0736 | -0.0986 | 0.0604 |
| university qual x ( 30 to 34) | 0.0326 | 0.0633 | -0.0550 | 0.0589 |
| university qual x ( 35 to 39) | 0.0116 | 0.0597 | | |
| university qual x ( 40 to 44) | 0.0314 | 0.0625 | 0.0177 | 0.0553 |
| university qual x ( 45 to 49) | 0.1959 | 0.0683 | -0.0055 | 0.0560 |
| university qual x ( 50 to 54) | 0.2006 | 0.0805 | -0.0352 | 0.0671 |
| university qual x ( 55 to 59) | 0.2420 | 0.1202 | -0.0124 | 0.0977 |
| university qual x ( 60 to 64) | 0.2387 | 0.1330 | -0.0572 | 0.1411 |
| vocational qual x ( 20 to 24) | 0.2146 | 0.1101 | -0.0391 | 0.1230 |
| vocational qual x ( 25 to 29) | 0.2015 | 0.1146 | -0.0246 | 0.1126 |
| vocational qual x ( 30 to 34) | 0.1296 | 0.1152 | -0.0370 | 0.1138 |
| vocational qual x ( 35 to 39) | 0.1791 | 0.1147 | -0.0114 | 0.1139 |
| vocational qual x ( 40 to 44) | 0.1582 | 0.1152 | -0.0382 | 0.1135 |
| vocational qual x ( 45 to 49) | 0.1967 | 0.1164 | -0.0358 | 0.1136 |
| vocational qual x ( 50 to 54) | 0.3070 | 0.1200 | 0.0018 | 0.1164 |
| vocational qual x ( 55 to 59) | 0.1271 | 0.1338 | 0.0291 | 0.1331 |
| Inverse Mills ratio | 0.0069 | 0.0645 | -0.0190 | 0.0514 |
| estimated SE | 0.4083 | | 0.3578 | |
| estimated correlation coeff | 0.0169 | | -0.0532 | |

Table 3.9: Wage Equations: Single Men and Women

| variable | Men coeff | SE | Women coeff | SE |
|---|---|---|---|---|
| constant | 2.5723 | 0.1370 | 2.5191 | 0.2543 |
| aged 15 to 19 | -0.4444 | 0.0638 | -0.3319 | 0.0478 |
| aged 20 to 24 | -0.1741 | 0.0492 | -0.0268 | 0.0410 |
| aged 30 to 34 | 0.1289 | 0.0647 | 0.0301 | 0.0533 |
| aged 35 to 39 | 0.0895 | 0.0737 | 0.1668 | 0.0697 |
| aged 40 to 44 | 0.0865 | 0.0831 | -0.0036 | 0.0669 |
| aged 45 to 49 | 0.1585 | 0.0883 | 0.0909 | 0.0559 |
| aged 50 to 54 | 0.2831 | 0.1371 | 0.0629 | 0.0597 |
| aged 55 to 59 | 0.0370 | 0.1075 | -0.0295 | 0.0704 |
| aged 60 to 64 | 0.1831 | 0.1390 | -0.0621 | 0.1009 |
| aged 65 to 69 |  |  | -0.1479 | 0.1380 |
| professional | 0.2518 | 0.0333 | 0.2724 | 0.0335 |
| para-professional | 0.1945 | 0.0376 | 0.2537 | 0.0373 |
| clerical/sales | 0.1504 | 0.0259 | 0.1225 | 0.0229 |
| mining | 0.5072 | 0.1220 | 0.3802 | 0.2854 |
| manufacturing | 0.0371 | 0.1016 | -0.1490 | 0.2524 |
| construction | 0.0752 | 0.1043 | -0.1460 | 0.2646 |
| sales | -0.0481 | 0.1011 | -0.1439 | 0.2512 |
| transport | 0.1664 | 0.1067 | -0.0024 | 0.2551 |
| communications | 0.1351 | 0.1132 | -0.0207 | 0.2604 |
| financial/business sector | 0.0179 | 0.1037 | -0.1177 | 0.2492 |
| service industries | -0.0756 | 0.1016 | -0.1523 | 0.2495 |
| Europe/Middle East | 0.0500 | 0.0443 | 0.0186 | 0.0355 |
| Asia | 0.0657 | 0.0863 | 0.0516 | 0.0519 |
| America/Africa | 0.0450 | 0.0856 | -0.0691 | 0.0711 |
| postgraduate | 0.0955 | 0.1177 | 0.3163 | 0.0752 |
| undergraduate | 0.0237 | 0.0925 | 0.2654 | 0.0694 |
| diploma | 0.2077 | 0.1539 | 0.0835 | 0.0730 |
| vocational | 0.1824 | 0.1425 | 0.0903 | 0.0672 |
| Victoria | 0.0542 | 0.0455 | -0.0173 | 0.0264 |
| Queensland | 0.0573 | 0.0447 | -0.0202 | 0.0308 |
| South Australia | 0.0113 | 0.0563 | 0.0360 | 0.0370 |
| Western Australia | 0.0875 | 0.0455 | -0.0353 | 0.0321 |
| Tasmania | 0.1252 | 0.0685 | -0.0518 | 0.0421 |
| ACT/Northern Territory | 0.0615 | 0.0548 | 0.0949 | 0.0471 |
| capital city | -0.0300 | 0.0418 | -0.0083 | 0.0247 |
| university qual x ( 20 to 24) | 0.0168 | 0.1029 | -0.2261 | 0.0794 |
| university qual x ( 25 to 29) | -0.0163 | 0.0940 | -0.1644 | 0.0808 |
| university qual x ( 35 to 39) | -0.0549 | 0.1395 | -0.0427 | 0.1047 |
| university qual x ( 40 to 44) | 0.1163 | 0.1442 | -0.0034 | 0.1267 |
| university qual x ( 45 to 49) | 0.2528 | 0.1711 | -0.0732 | 0.1101 |
| university qual x ( 50 to 54) | 0.0442 | 0.2224 | 0.0297 | 0.1325 |
| university qual x ( 55 to 59) | 0.1447 | 0.2239 | -0.0199 | 0.1252 |
| university qual x ( 60 to 64) | -0.9790 | 0.2283 | -0.3011 | 0.1737 |
| vocational qual x ( 20 to 24) | -0.0529 | 0.1557 | -0.0499 | 0.0773 |
| vocational qual x ( 25 to 29) | -0.0814 | 0.1578 | -0.0242 | 0.0833 |
| vocational qual x ( 30 to 34) | -0.2267 | 0.1716 | 0.0106 | 0.1018 |
| vocational qual x ( 35 to 39) | -0.0776 | 0.1734 | -0.0671 | 0.1124 |
| vocational qual x ( 40 to 44) | -0.0860 | 0.1900 | -0.0074 | 0.1159 |
| vocational qual x ( 45 to 49) | -0.1857 | 0.1884 | -0.0621 | 0.1032 |
| vocational qual x ( 50 to 54) | -0.6505 | 0.2397 | 0.0500 | 0.1082 |
| vocational qual x ( 55 to 59) | 0.0775 | 0.2257 | 0.0344 | 0.1300 |
| vocational qual x ( 60 to 64) | -0.1567 | 0.2477 | 0.1035 | 0.1845 |
| Inverse Mills ratio | -0.5242 | 0.2985 | -0.2284 | 0.1150 |
| estimated SE | 0.5165 |  | 0.3725 |  |
| estimated correlation coeff | -1.0151 |  | -0.6131 |  |

Table 3.10: Wage Equation: Sole Parents

| variable | coeff | SE |
|---|---|---|
| constant | 2.7077 | 0.2416 |
| aged 15 to 19 | -0.4127 | 0.3590 |
| aged 20 to 24 | -0.0409 | 0.1630 |
| aged 25 to 29 (ref group) | | |
| aged 30 to 34 | -0.0992 | 0.0962 |
| aged 35 to 39 | -0.0935 | 0.0790 |
| aged 40 to 44 | -0.1726 | 0.0816 |
| aged 45 to 49 | -0.0737 | 0.0943 |
| aged 50 to 54 | -0.1396 | 0.1218 |
| aged 55 to 59 | -0.1343 | 0.1731 |
| professional | 0.2654 | 0.0694 |
| para-professional | 0.1614 | 0.0806 |
| clerical/sales | 0.0819 | 0.0480 |
| traditional labour (ref group) | | |
| agriculture/forestry (ref group) | | |
| mining | | |
| manufacturing | -0.1950 | 0.2345 |
| construction | -0.2390 | 0.2637 |
| sales | -0.2876 | 0.2326 |
| transport | -0.1453 | 0.2553 |
| communications | -0.1280 | 0.2473 |
| financial/business sector | -0.1588 | 0.2294 |
| service industries | -0.2020 | 0.2256 |
| Australia (ref) | | |
| Europe/Middle East | -0.0190 | 0.0693 |
| Asia | -0.1326 | 0.1113 |
| America/Africa | 0.1371 | 0.1126 |
| postgraduate | 0.3932 | 0.1804 |
| undergraduate | 0.2682 | 0.1919 |
| diploma | 0.0110 | 0.1652 |
| vocational | -0.0458 | 0.1535 |
| no formal qual (ref group) | | |
| New South Wales (ref group) | | |
| Victoria | -0.1065 | 0.0661 |
| Queensland | -0.0948 | 0.0701 |
| South Australia | -0.1255 | 0.0821 |
| Western Australia | -0.0186 | 0.0714 |
| Tasmania | -0.0117 | 0.0784 |
| ACT/Northern Territory | 0.1230 | 0.0856 |
| capital city | 0.0411 | 0.0532 |
| university qual x ( 35 and over) | 0.0067 | 0.1823 |
| vocational qualx ( 24 or less) | 0.0652 | 0.3066 |
| vocational qual x ( 25 to 29) | -0.2620 | 0.2245 |
| vocational qual x ( 30 to 34) | 0.1056 | 0.1890 |
| vocational qual x ( 35 to 39) | 0.0031 | 0.1758 |
| vocational qual x ( 40 to 44) | 0.2766 | 0.1790 |
| vocational qual x ( 45 to 49) | 0.1431 | 0.1878 |
| Inverse Mills ratio | 0.1738 | 0.2300 |
| estimated SE | 0.3457 | |
| estimated correlation coeff | 0.5028 | |

Table 3.11:  Joint Normality Tests for the Heckman-Selection Model (P-Values)

| Demographic Group | Joint Normality |
|---|---|
| Sole parents | 0.593* |
| Single females | 0.002 |
| Single males# | - |
| Married females | 0.295* |
| Married males | 0.873* |

#Unable to be computed.
*Cannot reject joint normality at 5% level.

from the additional terms in this case. Although the sole parent group fails the normality assumption in the selection equation, the assumption of joint normality cannot be rejected, suggesting confidence in the validity of these results. On the other hand, one might be wary of placing too much emphasis on the results of the determinants of the wages of single females.

## 3.3   Wage Predictions

This section considers the question of how a wage rate may be assigned to unemployed individuals. In the simple case where the selection and wage equations contain a common set of variables, consider first the conditional mean log-wage rate for an individual with given characteristics. For those who are employed, this is given by:

$$E\left(w_i|_{E_i=1}\right) = x_i'\widehat{\beta} + \widehat{\rho}\widehat{\sigma}_\varepsilon\widehat{\lambda}_i \tag{3.8}$$

Imputed wage rates for those who are unemployed can be obtained using the expression:

$$E\left(w_i|_{E_i=0}\right) = x_i'\widehat{\beta} + \widehat{\rho}\widehat{\sigma}_\varepsilon\left\{\frac{-\phi\left(z_i'\widehat{\gamma}\right)}{1-\Phi\left(z_i'\widehat{\gamma}\right)}\right\} \tag{3.9}$$

The use of the conditional mean log-wage is perhaps the most obvious choice for the predicted wage. It is also possible, for example, to take a random draw, for each individual, from the relevant conditional distribution. Indeed, in labour supply analyses there is no necessity to be restricted to using observed wage rates for those employed in the sample period: it would also be possible to take random draws from the relevant conditional distributions.

### 3.3.1 Missing Variables for Non-workers

In the present context, the expression in (3.9) cannot be used without modification because some variables used in the estimation of the wage functions are not available for non-workers. In addition to the wage rate, neither the occupation nor the industry of non-workers is known. Although these variables could not be included in the selection equations, they were included in the wage equations because of their demonstrated importance in wage determination.

The treatment of this issue can be illustrated using a simplified example of two occupations. Suppose there are two occupations, denoted 0 and 1. Individual wages, $w_i$, in each occupation are given by:

$$w_i \; = \; a_0 + u_i \qquad \text{if in occupation 0} \qquad (3.10)$$

$$= \; a_1 + u_i \qquad \text{if in occupation 1} \qquad (3.11)$$

where $u_i$ is distributed as $N\left(0, \sigma_u^2\right)$. Suppose that $n_0$ and $n_1$ are the numbers of individuals in each occupation, and $n = n_0 + n_1$. The average wage, $\overline{w}$, is therefore:

$$\overline{w} = a_0 \frac{n_0}{n} + a_1 \frac{n_1}{n} \qquad (3.12)$$

One approach is to give the non-working individuals the sample average, as in equation (3.12). This can be achieved as follows. Carry out a dummy variable regression of the form:

$$w_i = a_0 + a_1' d_i + u_i \qquad (3.13)$$

where $a_1' = (a_1 - a_0)$ measures the differential effect of being in occupation 1 compared with occupation 0. Consider the following predicted wage, $\widehat{w}$, for those individuals whose occupation is not known:

$$\widehat{w} = a_0 + a_1' \frac{n_1}{n} \tag{3.14}$$

A little rearrangement shows that $\widehat{w} = \overline{w}$.

However, it is possible, indeed likely, that the distribution across occupations differs between the employed and the unemployed workers. Therefore the above method would impart a bias to the predictions. However, extraneous information may be used to obtain the proportion of non-workers in occupation 1, say $n_1^*$. An alternative predictor is therefore simply:

$$\widehat{w}^* = a_0 + a_1' \frac{n_1^*}{n} \tag{3.15}$$

Instead of the above approach, a regression may be carried out of the form:

$$w_i = a + a_0 d_{0i} + a_1 d_{1i} + u_i \tag{3.16}$$

where $d_{0i} = 1$ if the individual is in occupation 0, and $d_{0i} = 0$ otherwise; and $d_{1i} = 1$ if the individual is in occupation 1, and $d_{1i} = 0$ otherwise. Hence $d_{0i} + d_{1i} = 1$. The regression equation (3.16) can be estimated subject to the constraint that $a_0 + a_1 = 0$. Thus, using $a_1 = -a_0$, (3.16) can be rearranged to give:

$$w_i = a + a_0 (d_{0i} - d_{1i}) + u_i \tag{3.17}$$

The predicted wage can easily be obtained from (3.17) for those whose occupation is known. For the non-workers, whose occupation is not known, consider setting both dummies in (3.17) equal to zero. This gives the predictor, $\widetilde{w}$, where:

$$\widetilde{w} = a \tag{3.18}$$

However, from (3.17) the average wage, $\overline{w}$, is given by:

$$\overline{w} = a + a_0 \left( \frac{n_0}{n} - \frac{n_1}{n} \right) \tag{3.19}$$

A comparison with (3.18) shows immediately that $\widetilde{w} = a \neq \overline{w}$. Hence the preferred prediction method is to use (3.15).

Table 3.12: Occupation and Industry Proportions: Unemployed June 1995

| Category | Males | Females |
|---|---|---|
| Industry Division | | |
| Agriculture, Forestry and Fishing | 0.06568 | 0.03792 |
| Manufacturing | 0.24968 | 0.17465 |
| Construction | 0.17768 | 0.01896 |
| Wholesale Trade | 0.03958 | 0.02595 |
| Retail Trade | 0.13684 | 0.19661 |
| Accommodation, Cafes and Restaurants | 0.04968 | 0.09980 |
| Transport and Storage | 0.02894 | 0.04797 |
| Property and Business Services | 0.05684 | 0.08483 |
| Gov Admin and Defence | 0.04547 | 0.04291 |
| Education | 0.01979 | 0.05389 |
| Health and Community Services | 0.01389 | 0.11177 |
| Cultural and Recreational Services | 0.01853 | 0.02894 |
| Personal and Other Services | 0.02021 | 0.03992 |
| Other industries | 0.05010 | 0.05489 |
| Occupational Group | | |
| Managers and admin | 0.04755 | 0.02095 |
| Professionals | 0.05597 | 0.06686 |
| Para-professionals | 0.03072 | 0.04690 |
| Tradespersons | 0.22601 | 0.04291 |
| Clerks | 0.04545 | 0.25149 |
| Sales and personal service | 0.09932 | 0.29441 |
| Plant and machine ops and drivers | 0.14351 | 0.04391 |
| Labourers and related | 0.35143 | 0.23253 |

## 3.3.2 Selected Examples

This subsection provides selected examples of predicted wages obtained when unemployed individuals are assigned the sample occupation and industry characterisics. These are compared with the above procedure involving the use of extraneous information on unemployment rates by industry and occupation. Information about the last full time job of those unemployed in June 1995, taken from the *Labour Force Survey* (ABS Catalogue, number 6203, Table 28), were used to construct the proportions given in Table 3.12.

Consider first a female unemployed lone parent with the following characteristics: aged 30 to 34 years; separated/widowed from a previous relationship; European born; residing in ACT/NT in a non-capital city; with no other income unit income; with two dependent children aged 5-9 years and 10-15 years; in 'other tenure'. The predicted or imputed wage obtained using (employed) sample averages for industry and occupation groups is found to be $16.91 per hour. Proportions relating to the unemployed, based on extraneous information from the ABS *Labour Force Survey,* are listed in the appendix. These give an imputed wage of $14.98 per hour.

Second, consider a single female with: no children; never married; aged 20 to 24 years; Australian born; residing outside the Sydney metropolitan region in NSW; with a vocational qualification; living in 'other tenure' with no other income. The initial imputed hourly wage is found to be $14.18, whereas it is reduced to $13.98 when extraneous information is used.

Third, consider an unemployed single male with: no children; never married; aged 20 to 24 years; Australian born residing outside the Brisbane metropolitan region in Queensland; in rented accommodation. The imputed wage based on sample averages is $15.32, which in this case is increased to $16.54 per hour when the extraneous information is used.

Fourth, consider an unemployed married female: aged 40 to 44 years; with one dependent child aged over 15 years; European born; residing in Perth; with no formal educational qualifications; partner has vocational qualification but is currently not employed; other income is $25 per week; owns home outright. The basic imputed wage is $13.49 per hour, and this is only slightly reduced to $13.11 an hour.

Finally, consider an unemployed married male: aged 45 to 49 years with five dependent children (three of which are aged 5 to 9 years, two are aged 10 to 15 years); European born; residing in Melbourne; with a diploma; partner has no formal qualifications and is currently not employed; no other income; own home outright. The basic hourly rate is $20.54 per hour, and this is reduced to $18.24 by the use of extraneous information.

## 3.4 Conclusion

This chapter has reported estimates of wage equations for Australian workers, using pooled data from the Income Distribution Surveys for 1995 and 1996, the first two years for which continuous hours information is available for each individual. The problem of assigning a wage rate to non-workers, for example in the context of labour supply analysis, was also examined. The use of extraneous information regarding the occupation and industry characteristics of the unemployed was recommended.

# Chapter 4

# Budget Constraints

This chapter presents a method of obtaining exact budget constraints relating net incomes to hours worked for each individual. The existence of a large number of overlapping taxes and benefits, and the heterogeneity of households and income units, means that it is not practical to attempt to construct analytical formulae for each constraint, based on the basic regulations.

A common approach to calculating budget constraints involves the evaluation of net income for a large number of labour supply intervals. Small time intervals are needed, in order to identify the corners and discontinuities reasonably accurately. However, with a large number of different individuals, this would be computationally cumbersome and inefficient. It requires the same number of evaluations of net income irrespective of the complexity of an individual's budget constraint. In addition, it may not precisely identify the position of each kink. Budget constraints can be obtained more efficiently and accurately using the procedure described here.

Knowledge of the precise form of budget constraints is useful in tax planning, where it may be desired to avoid discontinuities or ranges with very high marginal tax rates. Furthermore, for the application of behavioural microsimulation methods using continuous hours, full details are required. In the case of discrete hours microsimulation, such detail is not necessary and only net incomes at a discrete collection of hours points are required.

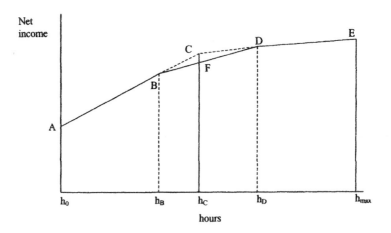

Figure 4.1: A Budget Constraint with Three Linear Segments

Sections 4.1 and 4.2 discuss convex and non-convex budget sets respectively. An example is given in section 4.3, while 4.4 concludes.

## 4.1  Convex Budget Sets

Consider the constraint shown in Figure 4.1 consisting of three linear sections. This represents a convex budget set associated with an increasing marginal rate structure. The algorithm begins by taking the minimum and maximum number of hours, $h_0$ and $h_{max}$ respectively, adding a small increment, $\Delta h$, to the first and subtracting it from the second, and evaluating the net incomes corresponding to the resulting four values of $h$. These values can be used to construct the straight lines shown as AC and CE, which are found to intersect at point C. The net income corresponding to the labour supply at C is evaluated and compared with actual net income at C. The comparison reveals that C is not on the budget constraint.

The algorithm continues by considering the two separate ranges, one between $h_0$ and $h_C$ and another between $h_C$ and $h_{max}$. This involves finding the equations of the budget lines either side of point F and the intersection with lines from A and E (the slopes at $h_0$ and $h_{\max}$ having already been computed). The intersection points, B and D, are found to be on the budget constraint. Also, the slopes of these lines are the same. Hence BF and FD are found to be on the same segment of the budget constraint, so they form the line segment BD.

However, it cannot be assumed without further checking that the constraint between points A and B, and between D and E, are in fact straight lines; there may be other kinks or discontinuities. It is necessary to consider the lines obtained by moving to the left and right hand sides of each of the points B and D respectively. Comparisons reveal that the line on the left side of $h_B$ coincides with the line from $h_0$, and the intersection of the two relevant lines, a common line, defines the range AB of the true budget constraint. Similarly, the line on the right of $h_D$ is found to coincide with that on the left of $h_{\max}$, which generates the linear section DE of the budget constraint. The algorithm therefore rapidly identifies the budget constraint as the piecewise linear constraint ABDE. The procedure assumes that, where lines from two points are found to coincide, there are no intermediate kinks involved. This is because is it improbable that any actual budget constraint would take such a form.

In this example, 13 evaluations of net income are required to find the exact budget constraint. In the case of a budget constraint consisting of two linear sections, and hence one kink, only seven evaluations of net income corresponding to seven different values of hours worked are required. This algorithm is obviously much more efficient than the use of small increments over the complete range of hours, with the evaluation of net income for each hours level.

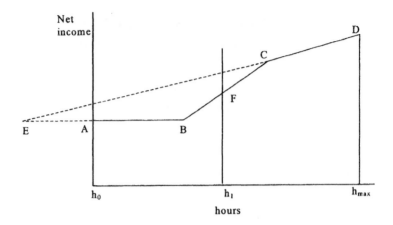

Figure 4.2: A Non-convex Budget Set

## 4.2  Non-convex Budget Sets

Further complications arise in the case of non-convex budget sets. Consider
Figure 4.2, showing the budget constraint ABCD. In this case, starting from
$h_0$ and $h_{max}$ produces an intersection point at E, which is associated with
negative hours. The next stage is to divide the hours range, $h_0$ to $h_{max}$, in
half, giving $h_1$. Consideration of the two separate sections to the right and
left of F reveals the intersection points B and C. Examination of the lines
from B and C, moving to the left and right of each, as before, establishes
the ranges AB, BF, FC and CD. Furthermore, the slopes of the sections BF
and FC are equal, so they are indeed part of the same line. Hence discovery
of the constraint of Figure 4.2 involves the evaluation of net income for 14
different hours levels. The principle involved in this case is that when an
intersection point occurs outside the relevant range of hours, it is necessary
to divide the range in half.

Figure 4.3 shows an example of a non-convex budget constraint involving
a discontinuity between B and C. Starting from the limits, $h_0$ and $h_{max}$,

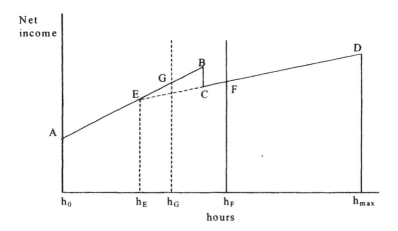

Figure 4.3: A Budget Constraint with a Discontinuity

generates the intersection point E, corresponding to $h_E$, which is found to
be on the budget constraint. Examination of the line to the left of point E
generates the section AE as part of the constraint; the line from A coincides
with that from E. But taking the right hand side of E in combination with the
left hand side of D again gives E as the point of intersection. In cases where
such a fixed point occurs, it is again necessary to divide the relevant range,
this time between $h_E$ and $h_{max}$, into half, giving hours of $h_F$ and associated
net income of F. Moving in a rightward direction from F identifies the length
FD as being on the budget constraint, since the line from F coincides with
that from D. However, moving to the left of F, combined with a move to the
right of E, produces the fixed point at E.

The next step is therefore to divide the range between $h_E$ and $h_F$ in half,
giving hours of $h_G$. Moving to the left of G gives the additional range EG,
while moving to the right of G and the left of F continues to generate the fixed
point of intersection, E. Up to this stage, 13 evaluations of net income are
required, remembering that there is no need to repeat the calculations once

net income for a particular value of hours has been found. The procedure continues by dividing the range between $h_G$ and $h_F$, in half and continuing as before. The algorithm iterates towards convergence at the discontinuity, where the number of iterations depends on the level of accuracy specified.

The general rules therefore apply of dividing the relevant range of hours in half whenever a fixed point is observed or whenever an intersection outside the relevant range is observed. Whenever an intersection point is found in the feasible range, the lines either side of that point are investigated. Sections of the budget constraint are identified when lines from two separate points are found to coincide.

In applying the algorithm, the exact number of hours of all kinks and slopes of all linear sections of the budget constraint are automatically computed. Hence it is also a simple matter to compute, for each linear segment, the intersection of that linear section when extended to the horizontal axis (at zero hours of labour supply). For each linear section, the slope is identified as the net wage rate and the intercept is the virtual income. The procedure therefore generates a set of net wages, virtual incomes and hours at which the net wage changes. In continuous hours microsimulation, these are retained for use in the solution algorithm for determining each individual's labour supply.

## 4.3   An Example

This section provides an example of the budget constraints for a sole parent before and after a hypothetical change to the January 2000 Australian system of taxes and transfer payments. This example gives an indication of the complexity of budget constraints under the Australian system. The reform consists of an alteration to the income test relating to the receipt of the Parenting Payment by sole parents, whereby the taper is reduced from 50 per cent to 40 per cent. Recipients of the Parenting payment must have

a qualifying child under 16 or a Child Disability Allowance child over 16
(for sole parents only). The basic rates of payment is \$366.50, and there
is a pharmaceutical allowance of \$5.40 per fortnight. An education entry
payment of \$200 may be payable and an employment entry payment of \$100
may be payable.

The income test applied is the same as for a single age pensioner. This
is described as follows. Let $Y$ denote the person's income and $RA$ Rent
Assistance. The reduction in the benefit per fortnight is given, where $AP_B$
is the basic pension, as follows. Let

$$AP_1 = AP_B + RA + 5.40 - max[0, 0.5(Y - 102)] \qquad (4.1)$$

Then $AP = max[0, AP_1)$. The \$5.40 refers to the Pharmaceutical Allowance.
For each additional child, add \$24 per child to the threshold. The reform
of interest involves changing the above component, $max[0, 0.5(Y - 102)]$, to
$max[0, 0.4(Y - 102)]$.

Consider the situation facing a particular sole parent facing a wage rate
of \$14.73 per hour, who does not pay rent and has 1 child in the age range
5-12 years, with two children in the range 13+ years. This individual was
observed to be working for 22 hours per week. The piecewise-linear budget
constraint is shown in Figure 4.4. The solid line is for the January 2000
system, while the broken line is for the hypothetical policy change.

The reduction in the taper rate involves a small increase in net income for
a wide range of hours worked (between about 5 hours and 38 hours). It also
eliminates a non-convex range of the budget set (where the marginal tax rate
falls over a range of hours) at around 30 hours of work. A discontinuity is
introduced in the reform system where the more generous Parenting Payment
(single) cuts out. As the maximum level of Family Payment is automatic, for
anyone entitled to any other form of income support, the cut out point for
the basic benefit leads to a substantial reduction in net income as the income
test for Family Payment is now introduced at a higher level of income.

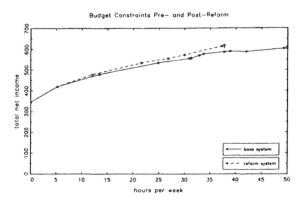

Figure 4.4: Total Net Income

Further details of the budget constraint are shown in Figure 4.5, which gives the effective marginal tax rate corresponding to each level of hours worked. The solid line again refers to the January 2000 system, with the broken line showing the hypothetical reform. While net income under the reformed system is either the same as or greater than the base system at all hours, there are nevertheless hours ranges where the marginal rate is relatively higher under the reform system. The main hours range where the the effective marginal tax rate is higher under the reform system is between the 31 and 34 hour range where Parenting Payment plus the Pharmaceutical Allowance cuts out under the base system. However, it continues to be payable under the reform. There are other hours ranges where effective rates are higher under the reform due to the introduction of higher marginal tax rates at lower hours levels as a result of the increase in taxable income. The base and reform systems display a small range of hours over which the marginal tax rate slightly exceeds 100 per cent. This is due to a combination

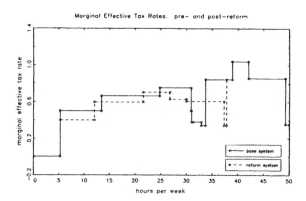

Figure 4.5: Marginal Effective Tax Rate

of marginal tax rates on income, the withdrawal of family payments and the introduction of the medicare levy.

Tables 4.1 and 4.2 give further details, for the base system of January 2000 and the hypothetical reform respectively. Each table gives the hours level at which each new marginal effective rate applies, the corresponding gross and net earnings levels, the effective rate and the probable reason for the change in the rate.

## 4.4  Conclusions

This chapter has presented an efficient algorith for the accurate construction of an individual's budget constraint, given an arithmetic tax model that is able to compute net income for any given number of hours worked. The algorith is used in MITTS, as described in Part III.

Table 4.1: Reasons for Kinks: January 2000 Tax System

| Hours | Gross Inc | Net Inc | EMTR | Probable reason for kink |
|---|---|---|---|---|
| 0 | 0 | 344.74 | 0 | Constraint starts |
| 5.25 | 75.01 | 419.75 | 0.5 | MR changes for Taxable Allowance |
| - | - | - | - | and for Sole Parent Pension Rebate |
| 13.42 | 191.87 | 478.17 | 0.662 | (Kink not recognised) |
| 24.81 | 354.65 | 533.11 | 0.752 | MR changes for Low Income Rebate |
| 30.89 | 441.50 | 554.60 | 0.505 | Taxable Allowance stops |
| - | - | - | - | MR changes for Low Income Rebate |
| - | - | - | - | and for Sole Parent Pension Rebate |
| 30.99 | 442.91 | 555.30 | 0.38 | Sole Parent Pension Rebate stops |
| 31.27 | 446.9 | 557.78 | - | Discontinuity |
| 31.27 | 446.92 | 555.09 | 0.38 | Pharm Allowance stops |
| 32.90 | 470.21 | 569.53 | 0.34 | Low Income Rebate stops |
| 33.70 | 481.69 | 577.11 | 0.84 | MR changes for Family Payment |
| 38.88 | 555.65 | 588.94 | 1.04 | Medicare Levy starts |
| 42.03 | 600.71 | 587.14 | 0.855 | MR changes for Medicare Levy |
| 49.27 | 704.21 | 602.16 | 0.355 | MR changes for Family Payment |

Table 4.2: Reasons for Kinks: Second Tax System

| Hours | Gross Inc | Net Inc | EMTR | Probably reason for change |
|---|---|---|---|---|
| 0 | 0 | 344.74 | 0 | Constraint starts |
| 5.25 | 75.01 | 419.75 | 0.4 | MR changes for Taxable Allowance |
| - | - | - | - | and for Sole Parent Pension Rebate |
| 12.06 | 172.39 | 478.17 | 0.595 | (Kink not recognised) |
| 21.55 | 308.04 | 533.11 | 0.703 | MR changes for Low Income Rebate |
| 26.78 | 382.76 | 555.30 | 0.628 | Sole Parent Pension Rebate stops |
| 29.96 | 428.25 | 572.22 | 0.604 | Low Income Rebate stops |
| 30.38 | 447.4 | 579.81 | 0.904 | MR changes for Family Payment |
| 37.30 | 533.13 | 613.75 | 0.34 | Taxable Allowance stops |
| 37.77 | 539.87 | 618.21 | - | discontinuity |
| 37.78 | 539.89 | 586.42 | 0.84 | MR changes for Family Payment |
| | | | | Pharm Allowance stops |
| 37.73 | 555.65 | 588.94 | 1.04 | Medicare Levy starts |
| 40.79 | 600.71 | 587.14 | 0.855 | MR changes for Medicare Levy |
| 50.00 | 714.61 | 608.86 | | Constraint ends |

# Chapter 5

# Labour Supply

This chapter reviews alternative approaches to labour supply in the context of behavioural microsimulation modelling. Some basic theory of labour supply is first described in section 5.1. Section 5.2 discusses alternative methods by which such models may be estimated. The major issue in this regard is the choice of a continuous or discrete hours mode of estimation; the merits of both are discussed and the appropriateness of each of continuous and discrete hours models for behavioural microsimulation is examined. The treatment of preference heterogeneity is discussed in section 5.3, and brief conclusions are in section 5.4.

## 5.1 Some Basic Theory

The simplest approach to the analysis of labour supply involves maximisation of a direct utility function, $U(h, c)$, where $h$ and $c$ represent hours worked and consumption (or net income, where the price index is normalised to unity), subject to a budget constraint. Unlike the standard commodity demand model in which prices are constant irrespective of the amount of each good consumed, the individual faces a variety of net wage rates. The actual wage depends on the chosen position on the budget constraint and is therefore, like the number of hours worked, endogenous. However, an interior (tangency) solution can be regarded as if it were generated by a simple linear constraint of the form:

$$wh + \mu = c \qquad\qquad (5.1)$$

where $w$ and $\mu$ represent the appropriate net wage rate and virtual income respectively. Virtual income is distinct from actual non-wage income, since it is an intercept corresponding to the particular associated net wage. The concept of the virtual wage is the same as that of the virtual price used in the theory of rationing.

Care must be taken in the choice of the direct utility function to be used when deriving labour supply functions, and the more tractable direct utility functions often lead to labour supply functions which are insufficiently flexible for practical labour supply modelling. See Stern (1986, pp.181-184) for a discussion of the properties of a wide range of candidate labour supply functions, either specified directly (for example, the semi-log supply function) or derived from direct utility (the linear expenditure system, the CES, quadratic direct utility and direct translog) and indirect utility functions (the indirect quadratic, or indirect translog).

Solving the first-order conditions for utility maximisation, starting from a direct utility function, may not be possible. Further progress often involves making use of duality results, starting with either the indirect utility function, $V(w, \mu)$, and associated expenditure function, $\mu(w, U)$, or the labour demand function itself. This section discusses the latter approach.

A choice can be made concerning the way in which the expenditure function is expressed. One approach involves writing it in terms of the individual's full income defined as $M = \mu + wT$, where $T$ is the total number of hours available. Alternatively, it can be written, as here, in terms of virtual income, $\mu$. The two approaches give equivalent results, but the use of $\mu$ avoids the need to specify $T$. However, the use of virtual income can create problems if

$\mu$ is zero or negative. See also Stern (1986, p.148).

## 5.1.1 Labour Supply and Indirect Utility

In specifying a form of labour supply function to be used in behavioural microsimulation, care must be taken to choose a model which is sufficiently flexible to account for a wide range of behavioural responses in estimation. The model must, when used in simulation, be consistent with utility maximising behaviour for a high proportion of the sample over a wide range of hours choices. If the empirical model used in simulation is not broadly consistent with the normal axioms of utility theory, then it is unclear how to rationalise simulated behavioural responses to a policy reform.

Two alternatives are available. One option is to specify directly the form of the labour supply function. This option tends to be favoured in continuous studies which place emphasis on the flexibility of the relationship between hours and wage rates. However, to compute an individual's utility at any point on the budget constraint, it is necessary to derive the indirect utility function from the particular labour supply function used. The second approach is to specify the model directly in terms of the direct utility function. This is typically the most appropriate option when estimating discrete models of labour market status, although it is again necessary to derive the desired hours function if the estimated model is to be applied to continuous hours behavioural microsimulation.

If a labour supply function is specified directly, it is important to use a labour supply function that allows for a backward bending range at higher wage rates, while having a positive slope at lower wages. This is particularly important when modelling female labour supply. The need for flexibility rules out the use of a linear function.

An alternative approach is to specify a direct utility function. For example, suppose the direct utility function takes the quadratic form:

$$U(h, c) = \alpha c^2 + \beta h^2 + \gamma ch + \delta c + \varepsilon h \qquad (5.2)$$

where parameters $\delta$ and $\varepsilon$ are allowed to depend on the characteristics of the individual. This specification corresponds to a labour supply function of the form:

$$h = \frac{2\alpha\mu w + \gamma\mu + \delta w + \varepsilon}{-2(\alpha w^2 + \gamma w + \beta)} \qquad (5.3)$$

This can admit backward-bending labour supply at higher hours for certain combinations of parameters. Substituting (5.3) and $c = wh + \mu$ in (5.2) yields the indirect utility function.

## 5.2 Estimating Models of Labour Supply

There exist many practical difficulties in estimating empirical models of labour supply. These include the incorporation of taxes; dealing with endogeneity and random preference heterogeneity; eliminating the reservation wage condition in a manner consistent both with estimation and behavioural microsimulation; accommodating stochastic elements in microsimulation; dealing with incomplete welfare programme participation.

There are essentially two routes available when seeking to resolve some of these difficulties. One involves a continuous mode of estimation, while the other uses a discrete estimation procedure. There are advantages and disadvantages with both, and the arguments are rehearsed below.

### 5.2.1 Discrete versus Continuous Labour Supply

The traditional approach to the modelling of labour supply maintains that the decision variable, hours of work, is continuous and unconstrained. Individuals are assumed to derive utility from net household income $c$ and leisure $L = T - h$. Let these preferences be represented by:

$$U = U(h, c; X) \qquad (5.4)$$

where $X$ represents individual characteristics. Behavioural decisions are constrained to lie within a budget set defined in terms of gross wage rates $w$, non-wage income, $\mu$, and the tax system $T(h, w, \mu; X)$, where $h = T - L$ for some time endowment $T$. The budget set takes the following general form:

$$c = wh + \mu - T(h, w, \mu; X) - F(Z_c) \qquad (5.5)$$

where $T(h, w, \mu; X)$ represents tax payments minus benefit receipts, assumed to depend on hours, wages, unearned income and household characteristics; $F(Z_c)$ represents the fixed cost of employment for someone with characteristics $Z_c$. In the standard continuous model, households are assumed to maximise (5.4) subject to (5.5) over a continuum of hours. That is, desired hours $h^*$ for each household member stem from the solution to the following problem:

$$\max_H U(c, T - h) \text{ s.t. } c \le wh + \mu - T(h, w, \mu; X) - F(Z_c) \qquad (5.6)$$

The maximisation problem is complicated by the non-linear character of the tax function $T(.)$. What tends instead to happen instead is that (5.6) is solved for a constant marginal tax rate to recover parametric forms for the Marshallian labour supply functions $h^* = h(w, \mu; X)$. The complexities of the tax schedule are then dealt with in estimation.

However, a number of recent studies have examined policy issues using labour supply models characterised by a discretised budget set. There are a several reasons for this. Firstly, analysts increasingly question whether a model which allows continuous substitution of hours for leisure constitutes a realistic representation of the supply choices open to the individual. For many socio-demographic groups labour market participation takes the form of fixed wage and hours contracts, with individuals choosing from among a discrete set of hours combinations (most often at part-time levels of around 20 hours, and at full-time levels of between 38 and 40 hours per week). Secondly, there are statistical and practical reasons to favour a discrete approach to the modelling of labour supply in preference to continuous models. These largely stem from the difficulties associated with the treatment of non-linear budget constraints in continuous estimation.

The strategy adopted in the discrete approach is to replace the budget set with a finite number of points, and optimise only over those discrete points. The procedure supposes that hours choices can be approximated by the discretized hours level $h_{(.)} \in \{h^1, h^2, .., h^P\}$ according to the grouping rule:

$$
\begin{aligned}
h_{(.)} &= h^1 \quad \text{if } h \le h_1^B \\
&= h^2 \quad \text{if } h_1^B < h \le h_2^B
\end{aligned}
$$

$$
\ldots\ldots\ldots\ldots
$$

$$
\begin{aligned}
&= h^{P-1} \text{ if } h_{P-2}^B < h \le h_{P-1}^B \\
&= h^P \quad \text{if } h > h_{P-1}^B
\end{aligned}
\tag{5.7}
$$

giving $P$ alternative values for $h_{(.)}$. For example, a five-state labour supply regime might be described by the choice set $h_{(.)} = \{0, 10, 20, 30, 40\}$ where $h_1^B = 5$, $h_2^B = 15$, $h_3^B = 25$, and $h_4^B = 35$. Household net incomes may be calculated for the set of discrete hours combinations $h_{(.)}$ as:

$$
c[h_{(.)}] = wh_{(.)} + \mu - T(h_{(.)}, w, \mu; X)
\tag{5.8}
$$

for $h_{(.)} \in \{h^1, h^2, .., h^P\}$. The household is assumed to maximise:

$$
U(c[h_{(.)}], T - h_{(.)})
\tag{5.9}
$$

for $h_{(.)} \in \{h^1, h^2, .., h^P\}$. This approach removes from the optimisation problem many of the complexities of a nonlinear tax schedule, but at the cost of introducing rounding errors in the hours levels used for estimation. The degree of aggregation may therefore have a potentially detrimental effect on the authenticity of the parameters estimated under a discrete regime, and ought at the very least to be subjected to sensitivity analysis.

## 5.2.2 Discrete Hours Model in Reduced Form

Estimation of the discrete choice model requires a specification both of the preference function and of the stochastic structure. One approach specifies directly a series of state-specific utilities at each discrete hours regime $h_{(.)} \in \{h^1, h^2, .., h^P\}$. Let state specific utilities be represented by:

$$U_{h(.)} = U_h(c_{h(.)}; Z, X) \tag{5.10}$$

where $c_{h(.)}$ represents the net household income at $h_{(.)}$. Utility is specified as a linear combination of state-specific incomes and household characteristics, such that $U_{h(.)} = X'\beta_{h(.)} + \gamma.c_{h(.)}$. Random disturbances are added to utilities in each state of the world, leading to a stochastic utility specification of the form:

$$U^*_{h(.)} = X'\beta_{h(.)} + \gamma.c_{h(.)} + \varepsilon_{h(.)} \tag{5.11}$$

for $h(.) = h^1, h^2, .., h^P$. By introducing stochastic structure, probabilistic expressions can be derived for the likelihood of choosing any labour market regime by application of the maximum utility criterion in (5.9). Hence, the probability that the individual works $h^j \in \{h^1, h^2, .., h^P\}$ hours is:

$$
\begin{aligned}
\Pr(h_{(.)} = h^j) &= \Pr[U^*_{h^j} > U^*_{h^p} \text{ for all } j \neq p, p \in \{1, .., P\}] \\
&= \Pr[X'\beta_{h^j} + \gamma.Y_{h^j} + \varepsilon_{h^j} > X'\beta_{h^p} + \gamma.c_{h^p} + \varepsilon_{h^p}] \\
&= \Pr[\varepsilon_{h^p} - \varepsilon_{h^j} < X'_i(\beta_{h^j} - \beta_{h^p}) - \gamma.(c_{h^p} + c_{h^j})] \quad (5.12)
\end{aligned}
$$

The probability (5.12) depends both on state-invariant individual characteristics and state-varying characteristics (specifically, net income at different hours levels). The parameters of (5.11) can be estimated via a likelihood formed from probabilities, (5.12), for a sample of data once assumptions are made about the distribution of random components $\varepsilon_{h(.)}$. In fact, only $P - 1$ sets of parameters $\beta_{H(.)}$ can be identified. Typically, a reference state of the world is chosen for which $\beta_0 = 0$. For example, if it is assumed that each $\varepsilon_{h^j}$

in (5.11) is distributed as a Type I Extreme Value error, then parameters may be estimated using standard Multinomial Logit methods.

One problem with this approach is the difficulty of testing the statistical model against economic theory. The parameters of the utilities in each state are estimated independently, so it is not easy to confirm that the preference function itself is consistent with theory. Moreover, the number of parameters multiplies in direct proportion to the number of distinct labour market states, and in practice such models can yield imprecisely determined parameters. This can make simulated responses volatile. For this reason, there is perhaps greater potential with a more structural approach.

### 5.2.3   A Structural Model of Labour Supply

A more structural approach to modelling household labour supply behaviour derives from Van Soest (1995) and Keane and Moffitt (1998), who model hours behaviour as the outcome of a discrete choice among a finite set of hours alternatives. The approach allows both for random preference heterogeneity and state-specific errors in perception, and can incorporate either directly estimated or indirectly imputed fixed costs in estimation. To see the essence of their approach, let:

$$U_{h(.)} = U(T - h_{(.)}, c_{h(.)}; X) \tag{5.13}$$

for $h_{(.)} \in \{h^1, h^2, .., h^P\}$, where the unified preference function now depends both on discrete hours $h_{(.)}$ and income $c_{h(.)}$. Compared with the discrete approach, this method is parsimonious in its parameterisation and preserves the same preference structure over the whole range of hours. Random disturbances are added to utilities in each state $h_{(.)} \in \{h^1, h^2, .., h^P\}$, as with the discrete approach, to give random utilities:

$$U^*_{h(.)} = U(T - h_{(.)}, c_{h(.)}; X) + \varepsilon_{h(.)} \tag{5.14}$$

Each $\varepsilon_{h(.)}, h_{(.)} \in \{h^1, h^2, .., h^P\}$ is assumed to be independently distributed as a Type I Extreme Value. The probability of choosing state $h_{(.)} = h^j$ is therefore:

$$\Pr[h_{(.)} = h^j)] = \Pr[U^*_{h^j} > U^*_{h^p} \text{ for all } j \neq p, p \in \{1, .., P\}]$$
$$= \frac{\exp[U(T - h^j, c_{h^j}; X)]}{\sum_{k=1}^{P} \exp[U(T - h^k, c_{h^k}; X)]} \quad (5.15)$$

### 5.2.4   Some Refinements

**Unobserved Wage Rates**

It is not usually possible to observe wage rates for non-working individuals. This poses a problem when simulating behavioural responses, since the budget constraint over which the non-working individual is supposed to optimise requires a value for the gross hourly wage rate. For practical microsimulation it is necessary to estimate the expected market wage rate commanded by individuals with a given set of observed characteristics. This conditional wage expectation is used in place of missing data for non-workers in the continuous method of microsimulation. Econometric methods also make it possible to factor unobserved characteristics into this expectation, particularly those unobserved characteristics thought specifically to influence the level of the market wage available to non-working individuals in the sample. The method of estimating wage rates also offers the possibility of repeated sampling from conditional wage distributions in simulation, given pre-estimated expressions for expected wage rates conditional on observed characteristics.

**Modelling Non-participation**

The participation decision is probably the hardest aspect of the labour supply decision to get right. Yet the impact at the point of participation is often the most important consideration when assessing the incentive and welfare effects of tax or benefit reform proposals. For example, in the UK, the Family Credit system of in-work support has seen three relatively recent structural reforms, each of which was designed with the objective of encouraging participation. Empirical evidence suggests that the participation elasticity is large relative to conditional hours elasticities, implying a low reservation wage for many groups.

Most microsimulation studies of the impact of tax reform on labour supply deal with participation simply by assuming that reservation wages exceed the market wage available. However, there is empirical evidence suggesting that this corner solution characterisation of non-participation is unsustainable. Other reasons for observing individuals out of the labour market include involuntary unemployment, and potential participants being discouraged from seeking work as a result of fixed costs or search costs of employment. These affect the likelihood that a potential worker will move into paid employment, and they can be controlled for in estimation. Hence, ideally they should also be accommodated in microsimulation applications. Blundell *et al.* (1987) discussed a likelihood-based approach which exploits sample information to differentiate those who are unemployed, but seeking work, from those who are self-reported non-participants.

Perhaps the main reason why most microsimulation studies adhered to the corner solution notion of non-participation is the expectation that the tax and benefit reform should have some impact on the likelihood of voluntary labour market participation. The implementation of selection-type models to separate the participation decision from the choice of hours, conditional on participation, is consistent with fixed costs in estimation. However, the participation decision is typically modelled in reduced form, to the extent that the choice does not explicitly depend on the full detail of the tax and benefit system. Consequently, such models make an uneasy transition into microsimulation, where tax and benefit changes ought explicitly to affect participation decisions.

Sources of microdata identify various types of individual not in paid employment. Some people report that they are looking for work, others say that they want to work but are not looking (including those who cite the need to care for children as a reason for not looking), while some report that they do not want to work. This information can be used in estimation and simulation to differentiate individuals. Keane (1995) factored exogenous child-related and fixed costs of work into his estimation procedure by netting from the household net income of working families a state-specific average fixed cost. Callan and Van Soest (1996) introduced a method by which fixed costs may directly be imputed in estimation. Specifically, by attributing to those who want to work, but who do not look for work, an unobserved (shadow) fixed cost, and parameterising this cost in terms of observable characteristics and a random element, they were able to estimate a shadow fixed cost equation. This equation was used in microsimulation to eliminate the reservation wage condition most commonly suggested as an explanation of non-participation. The advantage of the Callan-Van Soest approach is that the fixed cost imputation can be factored directly into either continuous or discrete behavioural microsimulation.

Duncan and Giles (1998) implemented the Callan-Van Soest method in an application to UK data and analysed the potential labour market impact of the Working Families Tax Credit (WFTC) as a replacement for the UK Family Credit system of in-work benefit, concentrating on the likely effect on single parent families. They found that the imputation of fixed costs reduced significantly the inertia in discrete microsimulation that is typically found at the point of non-participation.

### 5.2.5 Choice of Mode of Estimation

Whether using a continuous or a structural discrete mode of estimation for an empirical model of labour supply, the successful application of continuous behavioural microsimulation methods requires a quantifiable model both for preferences over any combination of net income and hours of work, and a model which predicts the preferred supply of hours for any combination of marginal net wage rate and virtual income. Ideally, the empirical model should also have the potential to factor fixed or child-related work costs into the behavioural model. This serves to eliminate the reservation wage condition in estimation, and also offers an opportunity to simulate the behavioural impact of policy reforms designed to compensate for expenditures on child-care.

Among the alternative estimation methods available, the Keane-Moffitt approach is perhaps best suited to address these various concerns, for a variety of reasons. The estimation strategy is consistent with the presence of taxes and observed and unobserved heterogeneity is incorporated in estimation. The behavioural model may be applied equally well to continuous or discrete microsimulation and fixed and child-related costs may be imputed in estimation and altered in simulation. Stochastic elements of the behavioural model may be factored into behavioural microsimulation. Finally, incomplete participation in welfare programmes may be controlled for in estimation and imputed in simulation.

### 5.2.6   Choice of Functional Form

For continuous estimation, a prime concern when choosing an appropriate functional form for hours of work is the flexibility of the potential behavioural responses, coupled with the availability of manageable utility functions, either direct or indirect. It is rare to find specifications which are flexible and which yield explicit forms for both versions of utility; see Stern (1986). Most of the more recent contributions to the continuous labour supply literature have chosen functional forms which are either quadratic or log-linear in the marginal wage, and are linear in non-labour income.

For the implementation of the structural discrete approach, Van Soest

(1995) and Callan and Van Soest (1996) used a direct translog utility function
for (5.14) whereby:

$$U(h,c) = \alpha_{cc} \ln c^2 + \alpha_{hh} \ln(T-h)^2 + \alpha_{ch} \ln c \ln(T-h) + \beta_c \ln c + \beta_h \ln(T-h)$$

$$(5.16)$$

for some pre-specified value for the time endowment, $T$. Equation (5.16)
requires net household incomes, $c_{h(.)}$, to be positive for all hours alternatives.
This may cause a problem when netting fixed costs from household income in
the estimation procedure, in which case the difference can become negative
for low-earning households with high fixed costs.

The quadratic direct utility function was favoured by Keane and Moffitt
(1998), where:

$$U(h,c) = \alpha_{cc}c^2 + \alpha_{hh}h^2 + \alpha_{ch}ch + \beta_c c + \beta_h h \qquad (5.17)$$

for parameters $\phi = \{\alpha_{cc}, \alpha_{hh}, \alpha_{ch}, \beta_c, \beta_h\}$. This function is tractable, yet permits a wide range of possible behavioural responses.

Whether (5.16) or (5.17) is chosen, observed heterogeneity can be introduced linearly through parameters $\beta_c$ and $\beta_h$. Specifically:

$$\beta_c = \beta_{c0} + \beta_c' X \qquad (5.18)$$
$$\beta_h = \beta_{h0} + \beta_h' X \qquad (5.19)$$

To incorporate random preference heterogeneity, a subset of the parameters
in (8.8) may be randomised. For example, the linear utility parameters, $\beta_c$
and $\beta_h$, can be randomised, giving:

$$\beta_c^* = \beta_{c0} + \beta_c' X + v_c \qquad (5.20)$$
$$\beta_h^* = \beta_{h0} + \beta_h' X + v_h \qquad (5.21)$$

where $\{v_c, v_h\}$ are assumed to be jointly normal with variances $\{\sigma_c, \sigma_h\}$.
The estimation of this model with random preference heterogeneity requires

simulation methods, either using a simple method of Simulated Maximum Likelihood or the more complex Method of Simulated Moments.

When choosing a functional specification for direct utility, it is necessary to have some regard to the application in hand. If the principal concern is with continuous behavioural microsimulation, then the main requirement is the flexibility and consistency of the behavioural model, and the availability of tractable forms for the various functions (direct and indirect utility and labour supply). Given these criteria, the direct quadratic utility specification is preferred.

## 5.2.7   A Solution Algorithm for Discrete Hours

For a discrete choice model of labour market status of the form described in (7.12) there is inevitably less accuracy both in the budget constraint information brought to bear in estimation, and in the simulated hours responses to a tax policy reform. Specifically, hours responses are limited in accuracy to the number of discrete hours bands into which the simulation sample is divided, and the nominal value for hours of work allocated to observations falling within each band. This may be appropriate for certain demographic groups, such as married male workers, and certain tax reforms, but it is by no means a universally acceptable feature. It is known, for example, that the labour market decisions of one-parent households are relatively marginal or flexible, reflecting the high value such households place on non-work time. It is therefore desirable to extend both estimation and simulation methods for such groups to embrace a wider set of hours alternatives and a variety of reasons for non-participation. However, such households tend to have complex budget constraints, so the estimation of continuous hours models is particularly problematic and prone to bias. This leaves one alternative, which is to estimate a discrete choice model based upon a large number of labour market states, of the form described in, say, Callan and Van Soest (1996).

The methods by which discrete models of labour market status are applied to discrete microsimulation are to some extent under-developed. One approach is to restrict attention to aggregated groups in the simulation sample and to summarise probabilities of occupation of each discrete state before and after some policy reform. This tends to conceal the impact of reform at the individual level, making it difficult to assess how the behaviourally-adjusted cost of the reform might be judged, and the impact of a reform targetted either at a specific demographic group or over a specific range of hours.

If simulated responses at the level of the individual are required, it is not obvious which is the more appropriate strategy to adopt. In continuous hours microsimulation, the optimal hours before and after a policy reform are solved and fed back into a static microsimulation model to generate behaviourally-adjusted costings and distributional results. This raises the question of what parallel approach might be adopted using discrete hours models.

Discrete hours simulated responses are sometimes based on a maximum probability rule as a 'one-shot' or 'all-or-nothing' mode of individual allocation, disregarding the probabilistic nature of the model specification. This approach is wasteful of information, and it can be demonstrated that the maximum-probability rule method of simulating labour market transitions is biased, particularly in discrete models where some states are either sparsely or densely represented in the sample. A second strategy is to respect the probabilistic form of the discrete model by basing the behavioural simulation directly on predicted state probabilities. For a simple two-state model this strategy is relatively straightforward. Suppose $\widehat{p}_{i0}^B$ and $\widehat{p}_{i1}^B$ represent predicted probabilities for two labour market states (of work or non-work, say) for the $i$th individual under some base system, $B$. Further, let $\widehat{p}_{i0}^R$ and $\widehat{p}_{i1}^R$ represent equivalent probabilities under a reformed tax system, $R$. The correct transitions probabilities are:

$$P_{i(0\to0)} \quad = \quad \min\{\widehat{p}_{i0}^{B} , \widehat{p}_{i0}^{R}\} \tag{5.22}$$

$$P_{i(0\to1)} \quad = \quad \mathbf{1}[\widehat{p}_{i0}^{B} > \widehat{p}_{i0}^{R}].(\widehat{p}_{i0}^{B} - \widehat{p}_{i0}^{R}) \tag{5.23}$$

$$P_{i(1\to0)} \quad = \quad \mathbf{1}[\widehat{p}_{i0}^{B} < \widehat{p}_{i0}^{R}].(\widehat{p}_{i0}^{R} - \widehat{p}_{i0}^{B}) \tag{5.24}$$

$$P_{i(1\to1)} \quad = \quad \min\{\widehat{p}_{i1}^{B} , \widehat{p}_{i1}^{R}\}. \tag{5.25}$$

In other words, it is necessary only to difference the two state probabilities to obtain a measure of the probability of transition. Only one of the off-diagonal transitions probabilities can be non-zero. However, it is difficult to extend these formulae to higher-dimensional problems. Suppose, for example, that a matrix of transitions probabilities for a five-state labour supply model is required. The conditional integrals which underpin the formulations (5.22) to (5.25) become practically insoluble in multiple dimensions. It is tempting to form a matrix of transition probabilities simply using the arithmetic product of predicted state probabilities pre-and post-reform. Hence, for example, $\widehat{p}_{i0}^{B}\widehat{p}_{i0}^{R}$ would become the joint probability that state 0 is chosen both before and after the reform. However, this formulation is incorrect because it assumes inappropriately that the probabilities are independent.

A way of extending (5.22) to (5.25) to higher dimensions is by the following computationally time-consuming method. Apply resampling methods to draw repeated realisations of the stochastic elements of the discrete choice model. In the model of Keane and Moffitt (1998), this would involve draws from Type I Extreme Value and Multivariate Normal Distributions for, respectively, state specific errors and random taste parameters. Apply the maximum-probability rule to allocate each individual to the most probable state following each random draw. Average these resampled transitions frequencies to arrive at a simulated version of (5.22) to (5.25) in higher dimensions.

## 5.3 Preference Heterogeneity in Simulation

When examining the labour supply effects of a change in the tax and transfer system, it may sometimes be convenient to ensure that the pre-change optimal choice of each individual, given the estimated labour supply function, corresponds to the actual choice made. This is relevant when the analysis of a policy reform involves a comparison of static and behavioural costings and distributional results. However, the parameters of the labour supply function are expressed as functions of a wide range of individual and demographic characteristics. The values assigned to a particular type of person are based on the conditional expected values, so there is no guarantee that the optimal choice of any individual of that type corresponds to the actual choice.

The required correspondence can be obtained by interpreting any difference between observed and predicted hours under an incumbent tax system as individual random preference heterogeneity. Then this term can be factored back into the underlying preference structure as an individual-specific parameter. These are strong assumptions, given the range of reasons for a difference between observed and predicted behaviour. However, it provides a useful benchmark against which more sophisticated stochastic structures might be compared. Moreover, the manner by which such correspondence can be brought about depends on whether the method of behavioural simulation is continuous or discrete.

Consider first the continuous case, using:

$$h = \alpha + \beta \log w + \gamma \mu / w \tag{5.26}$$

as an example of a continuous hours function. Individual-specific heterogeneity can be introduced in the constant term, $\alpha$, based on the observed error. If the individual is observed to be at a point on one of the linear segments, which must therefore correspond to a tangency solution, then using the appropriate values of the net wage $w$ and virtual income $\mu$ for that section, the observed error $\varepsilon$ is:

$$\varepsilon = h_0 - (\alpha + \beta \log w + \gamma \mu / w) \tag{5.27}$$

where $h_0$ is the individual's observed labour supply. By interpreting this error as an individual-specific random preference component, the value of $\alpha$ in (5.26) can be adjusted by adding $\varepsilon$. This has a consequent effect on the indirect utility function. Each individual is thereby associated with a unique utility function.

If the individual is observed to be on a flat linear section, corresponding to a zero net wage, this cannot be made to correspond to a tangency position, given the property of diminishing marginal rates of substitution between net income and leisure; that person is consequently said to be supply-constrained. A similar conclusion is made if the individual is observed on a segment where the corresponding tangency cannot be made to correspond to a globally optimum position by a simple change in $\alpha$.

A complication arises in cases where the individual is observed to be on a kink in the budget constraint. Simply adjusting the constant term, $\alpha$, to push the optimum position to the required kink would introduce excessive sensitivity to a change in the tax system (although all retired individuals would obviously be treated as being permanently retired). This can be overcome in several ways. One option is to assign to the individual not the actual error but the conditional mean for the given type of person. However, the use of such a conditional mean generates considerable inertia as a small change in the tax and transfer system is unlikely to move any individuals away from their corner solutions. An alternative procedure would involve assigning to each individual a random value taken from the conditional distribution. A further option, particularly in the case of a non-worker, may be to adjust the imputed wage obtained from the estimated earnings function.

For the labour supply to be consistent with utility maximising behaviour, the Slutsky condition must also be satisfied at the optimum hours. Substituting $\partial h/\partial w$ and $\partial h/\partial \mu = \gamma/w$ into the Slutsky condition gives the requirement that:

$$\beta - \gamma \{\alpha + \beta \log w + \mu (1 + \gamma)/w\} \geq 0 \qquad (5.28)$$

The need for the specified labour supply function to satisfy the Slutsky condition in as many cases as possible places a further constraint on the form that can be used. It is not always possible to ensure the global satisfaction of the Slutsky condition. If (5.28) is not satisfied, then the interpretation of the simulated response is difficult. One can simply exclude from the sample those individuals who fail (5.28), although this would cause problems if some demographic groups systematically failed the Slutsky condition more frequently than others. An alternative is to force such cases to remain at their pre-reform supply of hours under an alternative assumption that their failure to satisfy Slutsky is due not to pure preferences, but to some other factor (for example, institutional constraints on hours). However, both approaches are clearly second-best.

When the method of behavioural microsimulation is discrete, calibration is less straightforward, particularly when random preference heterogeneity combines with state-specific preference errors in estimation. In one approach recently considered by Duncan and Weeks (1998) in the context of standard Multinomial Probit models of labour market status, the observed distribution of (discretised) hours was replicated by drawing conditionally from the multivariate stochastic error structure. The simulated transitions frequencies based on calibrated models of discrete choice were shown in Monte Carlo experiments to be unbiased.

## 5.4 Conclusions

This chapter has discussed alternative methods of simulating labour supply responses to changes in direct taxes and benefits, concentrating on those factors which influence the choice of a continuous or a discrete mode of es-

timation or simulation. The ease with which fixed costs, child-related costs
and incomplete programme participation may be factored into the microsimulation process formed a major criterion.

It was suggested that for estimation the structural discrete choice approach offers much potential for behavioural microsimulation. In particular, the Keane-Moffitt method allows for the direct estimation of preference
functions in a manner consistent with the presence of taxes and incomplete
welfare programme participation. The model extends to household preference structures, as for example in Van Soest (1995). Their model may also
be augmented to impute a fixed costs component in estimation. This is a
desirable extension to the basic method, since it avoids the corner-solution
or reservation wage characterisation of non-participation which represented
a major problem with previous microsimulation methods. A second reason for favouring this style of model specification is that, despite estimating
the model as a discrete choice, either discrete or continuous microsimulation
techniques can be applied using the same underlying preference structure.

Stochastic elements in the econometric specification may be factored into
the behavioural microsimulation in a number of ways. For continuous microsimulation methods the model may be calibrated to replicate observed
behaviour under the assumption that errors may be interpreted as random
preference heterogeneity. For discrete methods of microsimulation a similar
calibration may be achieved with suitable draws from the conditional distribution of stochastic elements in the model specification.

# Chapter 6

# Labour Supply with Continuous Hours

This chapter discusses labour supply in the presence of piecewise linear tax structures, where hours worked are allowed to vary continuously. Emphasis is given to the efficient computation of local optima for a tax structure having any number of effective marginal tax rates. The approach to the determination of labour supply presented here is particularly well-suited to behavioural microsimulation modelling. The calculation of welfare changes, in terms of compensating and equivalent variations, arising from tax changes is also examined.

The basic approach to labour supply modelling is described in section 6.1. The form of the piecewise linear budget constraint is set out in section 6.2. This is usually specified in terms of income thresholds and marginal effective tax rates. However, for labour supply analysis it is necessary to convert this information into a unique budget constraint for each individual, depending on the gross wage rate. The budget constraint is defined in terms of a set of marginal wage rates and virtual incomes which define the slope and the intercept of each linear segment.

An algorithm for the efficient identification of local optima, either tangency or corner solutions, is presented in section 6.3. The evaluation of welfare changes in the context of labour supply variations is examined in section 9.3. In this context a change in the tax structure may affect the (endogenous) net wage rate, and therefore the effective price of leisure, as well as having an income effect.

The procedures for obtaining labour supply and welfare changes can be applied given either direct or indirect forms of the utility function. In order to provide more detail concerning the procedures, section 6.5 discusses the special case of the Cobb-Douglas direct utility function and reports some numerical examples.

## 6.1 Labour Supply

The following analysis applies to a single individual who is able continuously to vary labour supply, defined as the number of hours worked, rather than effort, in one job. The individual faces a fixed gross hourly wage rate. No allowance is given for overtime rates.

Let $c$ and $h$ represent consumption (or net income, where the price index is normalised to unity) and hours worked. The simplest approach to the analysis of labour supply involves maximisation of a direct utility function, $U(c, h)$, subject to a budget constraint. Unlike the standard commodity demand model in which prices are constant irrespective of the amount of each good consumed, the individual faces a variety of net wage rates. Although the gross wage is assumed to remain constant (independent of the number of hours worked), varying effective marginal tax rates associated with the piecewise linear nature of the budget constraint means that the net wage varies with $h$. The actual net wage depends on the chosen position on the budget constraint and is therefore, like the number of hours worked, endogenous.

With a piecewise linear budget constraint any interior or tangency solution and corner solution can be regarded as being generated by a simple linear constraint of the form:

$$c = wh + \mu \tag{6.1}$$

In the case of such tangency solutions, $w$ and $\mu$ represent the appropriate net wage rate and virtual income respectively. Virtual income is the intercept (where $h = 0$) corresponding to the relevant segment of the budget constraint and associated net wage; it is therefore distinct from actual non-wage income. In the case of a corner solution, the appropriate virtual income is defined as the value generated by a linear constraint having a net wage, the virtual wage, equal to the slope of the indifference curve at the kink. The concept of the virtual wage is the same as that of the virtual price used in the theory of rationing.

Suppose the direct utility function is specified and the associated labour supply corresponding to any combination of $w$ and $\mu$ can be expressed explicitly. It is possible to evaluate the range of gross wage rates (giving a set of wage limits) for which any corner solution is relevant. For non-convex ranges of the budget constraint (arising from a decrease in the marginal tax rate), further complications arise. There is a switching gross wage rate at which the individual jumps from one segment to another as the wage rate increases. This arises because an indifference curve can be simultaneously tangential to two adjacent sections. Alternatively it is possible to jump from a corner to a segment, or a segment to a corner. One approach to the determination of the optimal position is to compare an individual's wage with the various wage limits, to determine which local optima are relevant, and then compare the associated utility levels to find the global optimum.

However, explicit expressions for the switching wage cannot always be obtained, so that numerical solutions may be required; for a detailed treatment of several examples involving budget constraints with just two linear segments, see Lambert (1993) and Creedy (1996). Evaluation of the local optima in this way is therefore very cumbersome, particularly if the budget constraint consists of many segments. The method would also be wasteful as it is likely that a number of irrelevant wage thresholds would be computed. Instead, this chapter describes an efficient search procedure that can be applied to any piecewise linear budget constraint. Furthermore, the approach can be used where the labour supply function is specified and the associated indirect utility function is obtained by integration. First the budget constraint is needed, and this is the subject of the next section.

## 6.2   The Budget Constraint

Descriptions of direct tax and transfer systems typically involve a number of effective marginal tax rates and gross earnings values at which the marginal rates change. This information is often depicted diagrammatically with gross and net incomes on horizontal and vertical axes respectively. However, each individual's budget constraint is unique. It is necessary to convert the information about the tax structure into a budget constraint for an individual facing a given gross wage rate. This section describes how the transformation is achieved.

Consider a tax and transfer system with a series of $n$ gross income thresholds, $y_i$, and effective marginal tax rates, $t_i$, for $i = 1, ..., n$. The initial threshold, $y_1$, is set equal to zero. The following discussion makes the simplifying assumption that there are no discontinuities. Given a fixed gross wage rate, $w_g$, the thresholds and rates must be transformed into a set of virtual incomes, $\mu_i$, and net wages, $w_i$, which describe respectively the intercept and the slope of each of the $n$ linear segments of the budget constraint.

The virtual income at the start of the first segment of the budget constraint must be known. With this value, it is possible, given the gross wage rate, to determine the precise hours levels at which the marginal rates change, along with the remaining set of virtual income levels. First, the net wages are:

$$w_i = w_g \left(1 - t_i\right) \tag{6.2}$$

Along the $i$th linear segment, net income, $z$, corresponding to $h$ hours of work is:

$$z = \mu_i + w_i h \tag{6.3}$$

Let $h_i^*$ denote the hours of work for which the specified gross earnings thresholds are equal to gross earnings. Clearly, $h_1^* = 0$. Given that two adjacent segments, $i$ and $i - 1$, must intersect at point $h_i^*$, it must be true that:

$$\mu_i + w_g \left(1 - t_i\right) h_i^* = \mu_{i-1} + w_g \left(1 - t_{i-1}\right) h_i^* \tag{6.4}$$

Hence, for $i = 2, ..., n$:

$$h_i^* = \frac{\mu_i - \mu_{i-1}}{w_g \left(t_i - t_{i-1}\right)} \tag{6.5}$$

Next, consider the net incomes at the earnings thresholds. For $i = 1$, $y_1 = 0$, and $z = \mu_1$. At $y_2$ net income is $\mu_1 + y_2(1 - t_1)$ and for $i = 3, ..., n$:

$$z = \mu_1 + \sum_{j=2}^{i-1} y_j \left(t_j - t_{j-1}\right) + y_i \left(1 - t_{i-1}\right) \tag{6.6}$$

Equating these with the corresponding values of $\mu_{i-1} + w_g \left(1 - t_{i-1}\right) h_i^*$, and substituting for $h_i^*$ from (6.5), it can be seen that, for $i = 2, ..., n$:

$$\mu_i = \mu_{i-1} + y_i \left(t_i - t_{i-1}\right) \tag{6.7}$$

The piecewise linear budget constraint for any value of $w_g$, corresponding to a given set of $y_i$ and $t_i$ (along with $\mu_1$) is thus fully defined by these values of $w_i$ and $\mu_i$. These are used directly in the search for local optima, as explained in the next section.

## 6.3 Utility Maximisation

This section describes an algorithm for determining the individual's labour supply by systematically investigating the local optima on linear sections and corners of a piecewise linear budget constraint. Once a local optimum has been found, only those further ranges where another corner or tangency

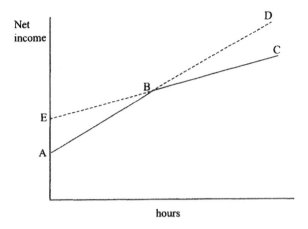

Figure 6.1: Two Segments of a Nonlinear Constraint

position could exist are examined. The utility associated with each local optimum is evaluated and the position giving the global optimum is identified as labour supply.

The procedure requires the following information. Either the direct utility function is specified and the interior solution for labour supply is derived (in terms of $w$ and $\mu$), or the labour supply function, $h(w, \mu)$, is specified directly and the associated indirect utility function is derived by integration. In the case where the direct utility function is specified in terms of leisure, labour supply is a function also of the maximum number of hours, $T$, available for work. This way of writing direct utility is not necessary, but $T$ must be specified to restrict the range of the budget constraint.

Consider Figure 6.1, which shows the first two linear sections, AB and BC, of a budget constraint. The first section, AB, is associated with a net wage of $w_1$ and virtual income of $\mu_1$ while the second section, BC, is associated with $w_2$ and $\mu_2$ respectively. The first step involves substituting the values $w_1$ and $\mu_1$ into the labour supply function. If the resulting value of $h$ is less than zero, the corner solution at point A, involving no work, is identified as a local optimum.

If only the indirect utility function is available, the evaluation of the utility associated with this point must be obtained by first calculating the virtual wage and virtual income associated with the corner solution. The virtual income in this case is $\mu_1$. The virtual wage is that which would generate the optimal position as a tangency position. The approach at this non-working corner involves solving for the virtual wage as the value of $w$ for which $h(w, \mu)$ is zero. This may require an iterative numerical method. If measures of welfare change are subsequently required, these virtual values must be calculated, even if the direct utility function is known explicitly. The virtual wage is given by the slope of the indifference curve. The remaining sections of the budget set then need to be examined for non-convexities, as there can be no other local optima if the marginal tax rates increase (given decreasing marginal rates of substitution).

If the resulting value of $h$ lies between points A and B, it is identified as a local maximum, associated with a tangency position, for which the utility is readily evaluated. Again, if it is known that the budget set is everywhere convex, there is no need to look for other positions.

A third possibility is that the value of $h$ obtained from the use of $w_1$ and $\mu_1$ lies to the right of B along the extension BD, in which case no clear identification can be made until the next linear section is investigated. The next stage therefore involves substituting $w_2$ and $\mu_2$ into $h(w, \mu)$. If the value of $h$ lies along the extension EB, the corner, B, is a local optimum. The associated virtual wage and income are then obtained. If only the indirect utility function is available, then the virtual wage and income must, as before, be calculated by solving the two simultaneous equations given by $\mu = c - wh$ and $h = h(w, \mu)$, where $c$ is the relevant net income.

Alternatively, the value of $h$ obtained from the use of $w_1$ and $\mu_1$ may be between B and C, in which case it provides a local optimum as a tangency solution. If the budget set is known to be convex, there is no need to look

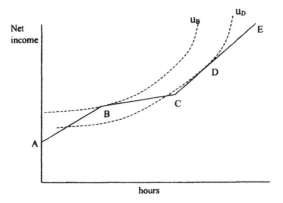

Figure 6.2: Corner and Tangency Solutions

for other positions. But if the budget set has non-convexities, the procedure moves to the appropriate section and continues as before. In this way each local optimum and its net wage, or if necessary the virtual wage, and virtual income are obtained. The global optimum is chosen as the local optimum giving the greatest utility. Cases where two positions give the same utility can arise in principle with non-convex budget sets, but the probability is negligible. Further examples showing more than one local optimum are given in Figures 6.2, and 6.3. These figures show the associated indifference curves, but the indifference curves are in practice not used.

## 6.4  Welfare Changes

Welfare changes are defined in terms of the individual's expenditure function, which is usually written as $E(w, U)$; for further discussion of welfare measurement, see Creedy (1998). In the present context of labour supply variations, this can be expressed in terms of the virtual income, $\mu$, as $\mu(w, U)$. This is most convenient where the labour supply function is specified and the indirect utility function is obtained by integration. Alternatively, it may be

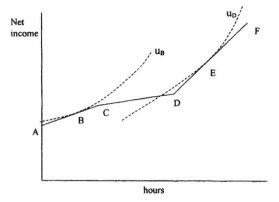

Figure 6.3: Two Tangency Solutions

written in terms of the full income, $M = wT + \mu$, where $T$ is the maximum number of hours available for work, whereby the expenditure function is written as $M(w, U)$. The latter approach is most useful where the direct utility function is specified and the indirect utility function is obtained by substitution. In either case, the expenditure function, representing the minimum level needed to achieve a specified utility level at a net wage, is obtained by inverting the indirect utility function (though this inversion may not always be possible analytically).

A change to the tax and transfer system may arise from changes in the effective marginal rates, the number of thresholds (and therefore nonlinear segments of the budget constraint), or the gross income thresholds. This may (but need not necessarily) change the individual's optimal labour supply and may produce a change in the endogenous net or virtual wage rate and virtual income. The welfare effect of such a tax change is complicated by the fact that a change in either the net or virtual wage affects both the price of leisure and the value of full (or virtual) income. It is therefore useful to decompose the welfare effect into its price and income effects.

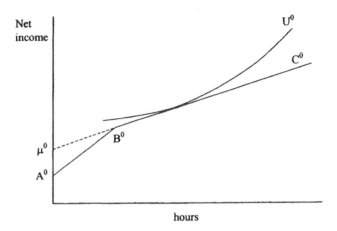

Figure 6.4: Pre-change Optimal Position: A Tangency Solution

For convenience, write the expenditure function in terms of full income, $M = \mu + wT$, and consider a change in the tax system such that the net wage and full income for an individual change from $w^0$ and $M^0$ to $w^1$ and $M^1$. The compensating and equivalent variations can be decomposed using:

$$CV = \left\{ M\left(w^1, U^0\right) - M^0 \right\} + \left\{ M^0 - M^1 \right\} \qquad (6.8)$$

$$EV = \left\{ M^1 - M\left(w^0, U^1\right) \right\} + \left\{ M^0 - M^1 \right\} \qquad (6.9)$$

These terms are defined so that a positive value indicates a reduction in welfare, while a negative value implies a welfare gain. The absolute value of the first term in curly brackets in the above expressions corresponds to an area to the left of a Hicksian (compensated) leisure demand curve between appropriate 'prices'.

In computing these welfare changes, it is necessary to use virtual wage rates when dealing with corner solutions. Suppose that the pre-change optimal position for an individual is at a tangency position on a section of the budget constraint having a net wage and virtual income of $w^0$ and $\mu^0$ respectively, giving pre-change utility, $U^0$. This tangency position is illustrated

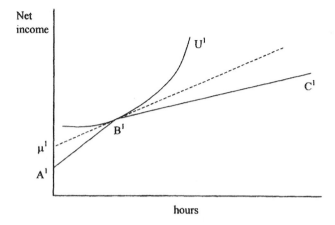

Figure 6.5: Post-change Optimal Position: A Corner Solution

in Figure 6.4. Suppose a change in the tax and transfer system causes the individual to move to another tangency position, associated with a net wage and virtual income of $w^1$ and $\mu^1$ respectively, giving $U^1$. The welfare changes can then be obtained by substituting in (6.8) and (6.9).

Alternatively, suppose that the change in the tax and transfer system causes the individual to move to a corner solution, for example the point $B^1$ in Figure 6.5. This could occur from an increase in the marginal tax rate over the range $B^0C^0$. The virtual wage and income $w^1$ and $\mu^1$, which define a linear budget constraint that would place the individual at $B^1$ as a tangency solution, are needed. It is then possible to proceed as before.

An implication of this example is that any tax change that places the individual at point $B^1$ has the same effect on the equivalent variation. For example, further changes in the effective marginal tax rate of section $B^1C^1$ do not alter the equivalent variation, so long as the corner remains fixed; this is because neither the virtual wage nor income change. This would not be true of compensating variations, which require the expenditure function to be evaluated for $w^1$ and $U^0$. However, a change to a marginal tax rate that applies to lower income ranges affects the position of the kink, $B^1$, which in turn causes the virtual income and virtual wage to change. Such a change may in some cases cause the point $B^1$ to shift up or down, and so may leave labour supply unchanged.

## 6.5   A Special Case

In this section the main results required to apply the algorithm for finding the utility maximising position on the budget constraint are presented for the special case of Cobb-Douglas utility. The expenditure functions used for the computation of welfare changes are also examined. These results are used in section 6.5.2 to produce numerical examples. The analysis of such special cases can help to elucidate the nature of the more general approach.

### 6.5.1   Cobb-Douglas Utility

Consider first the expression for labour supply arising from the Cobb-Douglas utility function. As defined above, the maximum available number of working hours is $T$. The price index of consumption goods is normalised to 1, so consumption, $c$, is equal to net income, and the direct utility function is:

$$U(c, h) = c^\alpha (T - h)^{1-\alpha} \tag{6.10}$$

Maximisation subject to the linear budget constraint, $c = \mu + wh$, gives the standard interior solutions:

$$
\begin{aligned}
c &= \alpha M \\
h &= T - (1 - \alpha)\tfrac{M}{w}
\end{aligned}
\tag{6.11}
$$

where, as above, $M$ denotes the full income, $M = wT + \mu$. The values of $w$ and $\mu$ are the endogenous net wage and virtual income corresponding to the appropriate linear section.

In the case of corner solutions, it is necessary to find the values of the virtual wage and income, $w_i^K$ and $\mu_i^K$ respectively, which would generate the same position as a tangency solution. Suppose that the corner is at the start of the $i$th linear segment, where the hours of work, $h_i^*$, are given from equation (6.5). The net income (consumption) at that point is thus given by $c_i = \mu_i + w_i h_i^*$. The virtual wage is equal to the slope of the indifference curve at the point $(c_i, h_i^*)$, so that:

$$w_i^K = \left(\frac{1-\alpha}{\alpha}\right)\frac{c_i}{T - h_i^*}$$                     (6.12)

and:

$$\mu_i^K = c_i - w_i^K h_i^*$$                                 (6.13)

Hence corner solutions can be treated in precisely the same way as tangency solutions, so long as the appropriate virtual values are used.

The indirect utility function, $V(w, U)$, is obtained by substituting (6.11) into the direct utility function, giving:

$$V(w, U) = \alpha^\alpha \left(\frac{1-\alpha}{w}\right)^{1-\alpha} M$$                     (6.14)

The expenditure function, expressed in terms of full income, is therefore given by inverting (6.14) to give:

$$E(w, U) = U\left(\frac{1}{\alpha}\right)^\alpha \left(\frac{w}{1-\alpha}\right)^{1-\alpha}$$                     (6.15)

The expenditure function could be expressed in terms of the virtual income, since $\mu = M - wT$, though the choice is purely one of convenience.

Suppose that the initial tax and transfer system gives rise to a global optimum associated with utility, $U^0$, and the values, $M^0$ and $w^0$, with $M^0 = w^0 T + \mu^0$. A change in the tax system, which may consist of changes in any of the thresholds, $y_i$, and the marginal rates, $t_i$, along with the initial virtual income, $\mu_1$. Some thresholds may be abolished or additional thresholds may be introduced. The new tax system gives rise to utility, $U^1$, and the values, $M^1$ and $w^1$, with $M^1 = w^1 T + \mu^1$. If corner solutions (either before or after the change) are relevant, the values of $w$ and $\mu$ are the associated virtual values as expressed in (6.12) and (6.13); for tangency solutions they are the net wage and virtual income corresponding to the relevant linear section of the budget constraint.

In the Cobb-Douglas case, appropriate substitution into (6.8) and (6.9) gives:

$$CV = M^0 \left\{ \left( \frac{w^1}{w^0} \right)^{1-\alpha} - 1 \right\} + \left\{ M^0 - M^1 \right\} \qquad (6.16)$$

and:

$$EV = M^1 \left\{ 1 - \left( \frac{w^0}{w^1} \right)^{1-\alpha} \right\} + \left\{ M^0 - M^1 \right\} \qquad (6.17)$$

### 6.5.2   Numerical Examples

Suppose first that an individual with a gross hourly wage rate of $w_g = 8$ has Cobb-Douglas preferences with $\alpha = 0.5$. Assume that the total number of hours available for work per week is $T = 80$. The individual faces a piecewise linear budget constraint with five segments, as shown in the top half of Table 6.1. The effective marginal tax rate increases up to the third segment, whereafter it falls from 0.60 to 0.40. The marginal rate increases again in section 5 to 0.50. The initial increase is associated with means-testing, as the benefit withdrawal or taper rate applying to benefits is first introduced and then raised from 0.5 to 0.6 at an earnings threshold of 70. From segment 4 the individual does not receive means-tested benefits, so the effective marginal tax rate falls; the budget set is non-convex over the relevant range. The income tax has a progressive rate structure, whereby the marginal rate increases to 0.50 at the earnings threshold of 350.

The upper section of the table also shows the corresponding values of virtual income and the hours levels at which each marginal tax rate begins to apply. The lower half of Table 6.1 reports the details of applying the algorithm to find local optima. A blank entry in this part of the table indicates that there is no local optimum. It can be seen that there are two tangency

Table 6.1: Tax Structure A

| Segment | | $t_i$ | $y_i$ | $\mu_i$ | $h_i^*$ |
|---|---|---|---|---|---|
| 1 | | 0.00 | 0.00 | 150.00 | 0.00 |
| 2 | | 0.50 | 30.00 | 165.00 | 3.75 |
| 3 | | 0.60 | 70.00 | 172.00 | 8.75 |
| 4 | | 0.40 | 200.00 | 132.00 | 25.00 |
| 5 | | 0.50 | 350.00 | 167.00 | 43.75 |
| Segment | Interior Solutions | | Corner Solutions | | |
| | $U$ | $h$ | $U$ | $w^K$ | $\mu^K$ |
| 1 | – | – | – | – | – |
| 2 | – | – | – | – | – |
| 3 | 119.630 | 13.125 | – | – | – |
| 4 | 117.760 | 26.250 | – | – | – |
| 5 | – | – | – | – | – |

solutions, on the third and fourth segments. There are no corner solutions, so the global optimum is seen to be on segment 3, involving labour supply of 13.125 hours, with gross and net earnings respectively of 105 and 214. The latter exceeds the former because of the fact that the individual is in receipt of the means-tested benefit.

Suppose that the tax structure changes, as shown in Table 6.2, where the higher taper rate applying to the means-tested benefit is increased to 0.70. The lower section of Table 6.2 shows that there continue to be two local optima under the new regime, but the global optimum is now a corner solution at the beginning of the third section. This section has become flatter as a result of the higher effective tax rate. There is therefore a reduction in labour supply from 13.125 to 8.75 hours, involving falls in gross and net incomes to 70 and 200 respectively. The reduction in full income resulting from the tax structure change is found to be 28. The effect of the reduction in the price of leisure alone (arising from the higher tax rate) is to produce a compensating variation of $-27.141$ and an equivalent variation of $-27.083$. Hence, the overall effect is a welfare reduction of $CV = 0.859$ or $EV = 0.917$.

Using the same approach, it can be shown that an individual with an

Table 6.2: Tax Structure B

| Segment | $t_i$ | $y_i$ | $\mu_i$ | $h_i^*$ |
|---------|-------|-------|---------|---------|
| 1 | 0.00 | 0.00 | 150.00 | 0.00 |
| 2 | 0.50 | 30.00 | 165.00 | 3.75 |
| 3 | 0.70 | 70.00 | 179.00 | 8.75 |
| 4 | 0.40 | 200.00 | 119.00 | 25.00 |
| 5 | 0.50 | 350.00 | 154.00 | 43.75 |

| Segment | Interior Solutions | | Corner Solutions | | |
|---------|--------------------|------|------------------|-------|---------|
|         | $U$ | $h$ | $U$ | $w^K$ | $\mu^K$ |
| 1 | – | – | – | – | – |
| 2 | – | – | – | – | – |
| 3 | – | – | 119.373 | 2.807 | 175.439 |
| 4 | 114.794 | 27.604 | – | – | – |
| 5 | – | – | – | – | – |

hourly wage rate of $w_g = 5$, with the same preferences of $\alpha = 0.5$, is not affected by the tax change, since that individual remains on the second segment of the budget constraint (supplying 7 hours of work). Each tax system is also associated with another local optimum at the corner where labour supply is 70 hours but, not surprisingly, this has a much lower utility level. For an individual with a higher wage of $w_g = 10$, and a higher preference for consumption of $\alpha = 0.6$, labour supply under the first tax system is at the corner at the start of segment 5, associated with labour supply of 35 hours. The effect of the tax change is actually to move the individual to a tangency solution on segment 5, where labour supply is 35.68 hours. Unlike the previous two cases, this individual is a net taxpayer, so that net income is less than gross earnings. The effect of the higher tax rate is therefore to increase the labour supply of an individual who is not actually facing the higher rate, but whose virtual income falls.

## 6.6  Conclusions

This chapter has discussed the determination of labour supply in the face of piecewise linear tax structures. The methods examined are particularly useful in behavioural microsimulation modelling where the complexity of realistic nonlinear tax and transfer systems must be modelled. They contrast with optimal tax models which use very simple tax functions, such as a linear tax or a two-rate structure allowing means testing.

The measurement of welfare changes resulting from tax structure changes was also described. This involves the use of expenditure functions and, in the case of corner solutions, the computation of virtual wage rates and income levels. Numerical examples based on Cobb-Douglas utility functions were given in order to provide further insights into the way labour supplies and welfare changes can be obtained for practical cases. Examples of labour supply functions demonstrated their complexity, something that is concealed by econometric studies which report only a few elasticities based on sample averages.

# Chapter 7

# Labour Supply of Single Persons

This chapter considers the estimation of a labour supply model for single persons, including sole parents. The modelling approach must be sufficiently flexible to incorporate a number of considerations. First, it must deal appropriately with taxes in estimation. Second, the specification must differentiate effectively among those who choose not to participate in work (often discouraged from seeking employment through fixed or search costs) and those who are involuntarily unemployed. The model must also be capable of being integrated into a microsimulation model.

The approach used here follows the discrete hours approach described in chapter 5. This has a number of advantages over continuous hours methods. First, nonlinear tax schedules are dealt with straightforwardly in estimation in a manner which does not force Slustky satisfaction on the parameters of the model. Second, the preference model is fully structural and testable against economic theory. Third, the model is extended to incorporate more recently developed methods of imputating the level of fixed costs of employment. Finally, random preference heterogeneity can be incorporated by applying Simulated Maximum Likelihood methods in estimation.

The budget constraints facing individuals, particularly sole parents, are highly nonlinear. Net incomes were generated using the Melbourne Institute

Tax and Transfer Simulator (MITTS). In Section 7.1 the basic structural discrete choice model is described. The section also describes how that model may be extended to differentiate among non-working households. Section 7.2 describes the empirical labour supply estimates.

## 7.1   The Framework

### 7.1.1   Discrete versus Continuous Labour Supply

The traditional approach to the modelling of labour supply maintains that the decision variable, hours of work, is continuous and unconstrained. Individuals are assumed to derive utility from net household income $Y$ and leisure $L$. Let these preferences be represented by:

$$U = U(Y, L; X) \tag{7.1}$$

where $X$ represents individual characteristics. Behavioural decisions are constrained to lie within a budget set defined in terms of: gross wage rates $W$; total household income $V$ from assets and other unearned sources and; the tax system $T(H, W, V; X)$, where $H = T - L$ for some time endowment $T$ yielding the budget set:

$$Y = WH + V - T(H, W, V; X) - FC(Z_c) \tag{7.2}$$

where $T(H, W, V; X)$ represents tax payments minus benefit receipts (assumed to depend on hours, wages, unearned income and household characteristics) and $FC(Z_c)$ is the fixed cost of employment for someone with characteristics $Z_c$. Households are assumed to maximise (7.1) subject to (7.2) over a continuum of hours to give desired hours $H^*$:

$$\max_H U(Y, T - H) \text{ s.t. } Y \leq WH + V - T(H, W, V; X) - FC(Z_c) \tag{7.3}$$

The fundamental nonlinearity of the tax function $T(.)$ makes this non-trivial.

Irrespective of the complexities of using a continuous approach, attention has recently turned towards labour supply models which use a discrete budget set. The reason for this is that labour market participation typically takes the form of fixed wage and hours contracts, with individuals choosing from among a discrete set of hours combinations (most often at part-time levels of around 20 hours, and at full-time levels of between 38 and 40 hours per week).

The strategy adopted in the discrete approach is to replace the entire budget set with a finite number of points thereon, and optimise only over those discrete points. The procedure supposes that hours choices can be approximated by the discretised hours level $H_{(.)} \in \{H^1, H^2, .., H^P\}$ according to the grouping rule:

$$
\begin{aligned}
H_{(.)} &= H^1 \quad \text{if } H \leq H_1^B \\
&= H^2 \quad \text{if } H_1^B < H \leq H_2^B
\end{aligned}
$$

$$\ldots\ldots\ldots\ldots$$

$$
\begin{aligned}
&= H^{P-1} \text{ if } H_{P-2}^B < H \leq H_{P-1}^B \\
&= H^P \quad \text{if } H > H_{P-1}^B,
\end{aligned}
\tag{7.4}
$$

giving $P$ alternative values for $H_{(.)}$. Household net incomes may then be calculated for the set of discrete hours combinations $H_{(.)}$ as:

$$Y[H_{(.)}] = W H_{(.)} + V - T(H_{(.)}, W, V; X) \tag{7.5}$$

for $H_{(.)} \in \{H^1, H^2, .., H^P\}$. The household is assumed to maximise:

$$U(Y[H_{(.)}], T - H_{(.)}) \tag{7.6}$$

for $H_{(.)} \in \{H^1, H^2, .., H^P\}$. This approach removes from the optimisation problem many of the complexities of a nonlinear tax schedule, but at the cost of introducing rounding errors in the hours levels used for estimation.

The degree of aggregation may therefore have a potentially detrimental effect on the authenticity of the parameters estimated under a discrete regime, and ought at the very least to be subjected to sensitivity analysis.

## 7.1.2   A Reduced Form Approach to Estimation

To operationalise the discrete choice model requires a specification both of the preference function and of the stochastic structure. A popular approach specifies directly a series of state-specific utilities to be enjoyed in each discrete hours regime $H_{(\cdot)} \in \{H^1, H^2, .., H^P\}$. Let state specific utilities be represented by:

$$U_{H(\cdot)} = U_H(Y_{H(\cdot)}; Z, X) \tag{7.7}$$

where $Y_{H(\cdot)}$ represents the net household income that would be enjoyed at $H_{(\cdot)}$. Often, (7.7) is specified as a linear combination of state-specific incomes and household characteristics, such that $U_{H(\cdot)} = X'\beta_{H(\cdot)} + \gamma Y_{H(\cdot)}$. Random disturbances are added to utilities in each state of the world, leading to a stochastic utility specification of the form:

$$U^*_{H(\cdot)} = X'\beta_{H(\cdot)} + \gamma Y_{H(\cdot)} + \varepsilon_{H(\cdot)} \tag{7.8}$$

for $H(\cdot) = H^1, H^2, .., H^P$. By introducing stochastic structure, we are in a position to derive probabilistic expressions for the likelihood of choosing any labour market regime by application of the maximum utility criterion (7.6). That is to say, the probability that the individual works $H^j \in \{H^1, H^2, .., H^P\}$ hours is:

$$
\begin{aligned}
\Pr(H_{(\cdot)} = H^j) &= \Pr[U^*_{H^j} > U^*_{H^p} \text{ for all } j \neq p, p \in \{1, .., P\}] \\
&= \Pr[X'\beta_{H^j} + \gamma.Y_{H^j} + \varepsilon_{H^j} > X'\beta_{H^p} + \gamma.Y_{H^p} + \varepsilon_{H^p}] \\
&= \Pr[\varepsilon_{H^p} - \varepsilon_{H^j} < X'_i(\beta_{H^j} - \beta_{H^p}) - \gamma.(Y_{H^p} + Y_{H^j})] (7.9)
\end{aligned}
$$

The parameters of (7.8) may be estimated using a likelihood function formed from probabilities (7.9) for a sample of data, once assumptions are made about the distribution of random components $\varepsilon_{H(.)}$. Only $P-1$ sets of parameters $\beta_{H(.)}$ can be identified. Typically, a reference state of the world is chosen for which $\beta_0 = 0$. If, as is common, the $\varepsilon_{H^j}$ in (7.8) are assumed to follow a Type I Extreme Value distribution, a standard Multinomial Logit Model results. The probability (7.9) depends both on state-invariant individual characteristics and state-varying characteristics, specifically, net income at different hours levels.

One problem with this approach is the difficulty with which the statistical model may be tested against economic theory. Since the parameters of the utilities in each state are estimated independently, one cannot easily confirm that the preference function is consistent with theory. Hence, the use of such models in simulation is likely to be unreliable. For this reason a more structural approach is adopted.

### 7.1.3    A Basic Structural Model

Preferences are modelled as a quadratic direct translog function, and the estimation strategy allows both for random preference heterogeneity and state-specific errors in perception. Let:

$$U_{H(.)} = U(T - H_{(.)}, Y_{H(.)}; X) \qquad (7.10)$$

for $H_{(.)} \in \{H^1, H^2, .., H^P\}$, where the unified preference function now depends both on (discrete) hours $H_{(.)}$ and income $Y_{H(.)}$. Compared with the discrete approach, this method is parsimonious in its parameterisation and preserves the same preference structure over the whole range of hours. Random disturbances specific are added to utilities in each state $H_{(.)} \in \{H^1, H^2, .., H^P\}$, to give random utilities:

$$U_{H(.)}^* = U(T - H_{(.)}, Y_{H(.)}; X) + \varepsilon_{H(.)} \qquad (7.11)$$

Each $\varepsilon_{H(.)}, H_{(.)} \in \{H^1, H^2, .., H^P\}$ are assumed to be independently distributed, yielding probabilities of choosing state $H_{(.)} = H^j$, for all $j \neq p$,

$p \in \{1, .., P\}$, as:

$$
\begin{aligned}
\Pr[H_{(.)} \; = \; H^j)] &= \Pr[U^*_{H^j} > U^*_{H^p}] \\
&= \frac{\exp[U(T - H^j, Y_{H^j}; X)]}{\sum_{k=1}^{P} \exp[U(T - H^k, Y_{H^k}; X)]}
\end{aligned}
\tag{7.12}
$$

For the empirical analysis the quadratic direct utility function is chosen:

$$
U(H, Y) = \alpha_{YY} Y^2 + \alpha_{HH} H^2 + \alpha_{YH} YH + \beta.Y + \beta_H H
\tag{7.13}
$$

For parameters $\phi = \{\alpha_{YY}, \alpha_{HH}, \alpha_{YH}, \beta_Y, \beta_H\}$ this function is tractable, yet permits a wide range of possible behavioural responses. Observed heterogeneity is introduced linearly through parameters $\beta_Y$ and $\beta_H$ thus

$$
\beta_Y \; = \; \beta_{y0} + \beta'_y X
\tag{7.14}
$$

$$
\beta_H \; = \; \beta_{h0} + \beta'_h X
\tag{7.15}
$$

The characteristics we include in the empirical estimates include dummies for the age of the youngest child, age and education. For the basic structural model, the likelihood contribution corresponding to (7.13) is:

$$
L(\phi|X) = \sum_{j=1}^{P} d_j \ln \Pr[H_{(.)} = H^j)]
\tag{7.16}
$$

where $d_j = 1(H_{(.)} = H^j)$.

To incorporate random preference heterogeneity, error terms can be added to equations 7.14 and 7.15 such that:

$$
\beta^*_Y \; = \; \beta_{y0} + \beta'_y X + v_Y
\tag{7.17}
$$

$$
\beta^*_H \; = \; \beta_{h0} + \beta'_h X + v_H,
\tag{7.18}
$$

where $\{v_Y, v_H\}$ are assumed jointly normal with variances $\sigma_Y, \sigma_H$. However, although now the likelihood function has no analytical closed form, estimation can be undertaken via the method of Simulated Maximum Likelihood.

### 7.1.4 Modelling Participation

There are numerous observationally equivalent reasons why individuals are observed to be not working. They may be involuntary unemployed, not in the labour force or discouraged workers. Superficially, it would appear preferable to accommodate all of these states in model estimation. The Australian Income Distribuion Survey only enables identification of three labour force states: these are employed, unemployed and not in the labour force.

$$\Pr[NP|X, Z] = \Pr\{U^*(T, Y_0|X)$$
$$> \max_{H(.)>0} [U(T - H(.), Y_{H(.)}|X]\}$$
$$\Pr[US|X, Z] = \{1 - \Phi(Z.\delta)\} \Pr\{U^*(T, Y_0|X)$$
$$< \max_{H(.)>0} [U(T - H(.), Y_{H(.)}|X]\}$$
$$\Pr[H^j|X, Z] = \Phi(Z.\delta) \Pr\{U^*(H^j, Y_{H^j}|X)$$
$$< \max_{H(.)\neq H^j} [U(T - H(.), Y_{H(.)}|X]\}$$

However, this strategy is not used here as it introduces an asymmetry into the analysis. That is, it only allows for individuals to be not at their optimal level of hours, if their observed level of hours is zero.

Fixed costs can be introduced in estimation using the specification:

$$FC = X_{FC}.\gamma + v_f \tag{7.19}$$

The unobserved fixed cost component $v_f$ is distributed normally around a zero mean and $X_{FC}$ are instruments to proxy fixed costs; $v_f$ is allowed to be potentially correlated with the random preference parameters $\varepsilon_Y$ and $\varepsilon_H$. Fixed costs are incorporated into estimation. As they only have an impact on workers, the utilities $U(T - H, Y_H; X)$ entering the likelihood function of (8.12) become $U(T - H, Y_H - FC; X)$ for all states $H^j > 0$. To observe a worker in the presence of fixed costs therefore requires that:

$$\max_{H(.)\neq 0} U(T - H_{(.)}, Y_{H_{(.)}} - FC; X) > U(Y_0, T; X) \tag{7.20}$$

## 7.2   Empirical Results

### 7.2.1   The Data

The data are taken from the pooled three Income Distribution Surveys (IDSs) for the years 1994-95 to 1996-97. This is the same database utilised by MITTS. From the total sample, self-employed and retired households are excluded, as are extreme outliers and missing values. This leaves a working sample of 8,624 sole parent households, of whom 7,040 were employed, 864 unemployed and 720 not in the labour force. To generate net incomes, MITTS was used. For the workers, their current wage was assumed to remain unchanged, and for the non-workers, wages were imputed based on their personal characteristics as described in chapter 3 above.

### 7.2.2   Model Estimates for Sole Parents

A range of estimates for the labour supply behaviour of lone parent households are report in Table 8.1. Eleven discrete hours levels were used, with the following allocation rule:

$$
\begin{aligned}
H_{(.)} &= & 0 \text{ if } H \leq 2.5 \\
&= & 5 \text{ if } 2.5 < H \leq 7.5 \\
&= & 10 \text{ if } 7.5 < H \leq 12.5 \\
&= & 15 \text{ if } 12.5 < H \leq 17.5 \\
&= & 20 \text{ if } 17.5 < H \leq 22.5 \\
&= & 25 \text{ if } 22.5 < H \leq 27.5 \\
&= & 30 \text{ if } 27.5 < H \leq 32.5 \\
&= & 35 \text{ if } 32.5 < H \leq 37.5 \\
&= & 40 \text{ if } 37.5 < H \leq 42.5 \\
&= & 45 \text{ if } 42.5 < H \leq 47.5 \\
&= & 50 \text{ if } H > 47.5
\end{aligned}
$$

Table 7.1: Utility Function Only, Observed Heterogeneity and Constant Fixed Costs

| | (1) | | (2) | | (3) | |
|---|---|---|---|---|---|---|
| $\alpha_{YY} \times 100$ | -0.335 | (0.206) | -0.484 | (0.257)* | -0.129 | (0.308) |
| ×1 (youngest child 0-2) | - | - | 0.024 | (0.764) | 0.438 | (1.136) |
| ×1 (youngest child 3-4) | - | - | 0.467 | (0.370) | -0.811 | (0.750) |
| ×1 (youngest child 5-9) | - | - | -0.217 | (0.404) | 0.136 | (0.446) |
| $\alpha_{HH} \times 100$ | 0.316 | (0.021)** | 0.152 | (0.032)** | -0.052 | (0.049) |
| ×1 (youngest child 0-2) | - | - | 0.184 | (0.060)** | -0.001 | (0.096) |
| ×1 (youngest child 3-4) | - | - | 0.117 | (0.051)** | -0.030 | (0.082) |
| ×1 (youngest child 5-9) | - | - | 0.056 | (0.036) | -0.079 | (0.063) |
| $\alpha_{YH}$ | 0.157 | (0.358) | 1.136 | (0.510)** | -0.596 | (0.556) |
| $\beta_Y$ | 0.913 | (0.159)** | 0.667 | (0.258)** | 0.933 | (0.203)** |
| ×1 (youngest child 0-2) | - | - | -1.934 | (0.987)** | 0.136 | (0.548) |
| ×1 (youngest child 3-4) | - | - | -0.806 | (0.556) | 0.668 | (0.584) |
| ×1 (youngest child 5-9) | - | - | 0.576 | (0.549) | 0.104 | (0.331) |
| × # children | - | - | -0.201 | (0.087)** | 0.131 | (0.084) |
| ×1 aged over 40 | - | - | -0.084 | (0.138) | 0.006 | (0.095) |
| ×1 qualification | - | - | 0.257 | (0.136)* | 0.001 | (0.087) |
| $\beta_H$ | -0.225 | (0.013)** | -0.163 | (0.018)** | 0.007 | (0.022) |
| ×1 (youngest child 0-2) | - | - | -0.057 | (0.050) | -0.043 | (0.044) |
| ×1 (youngest child 3-4) | - | - | -0.069 | (0.033)** | -0.015 | (0.038) |
| ×1 (youngest child 5-9) | - | - | -0.070 | (0.025)** | 0.014 | (0.028) |
| × # children | - | - | 0.004 | (0.005) | 0.002 | (0.003) |
| ×1 aged over 40 | - | - | 0.003 | (0.009) | -0.005 | (0.005) |
| ×1 qualification | - | - | 0.015 | (0.008)* | 0.024 | (0.004)** |
| Fixed Costs/100 | - | - | - | - | 2.77 | (0.731)** |
| Log-Likelihood | -3956 | | -3822 | | -3611 | |

** and * significant at 5 and 10 per cent respectively (two-sided).

The specifications are considered sequentially. In (1), only the parameters of the utility function are estimated; in (2), allowance is made for observed heterogeneity on the linear and quadratic terms of the basic utility function parameters; finally, in (3) fixed costs are added. The instruments chosen to account for variation in tastes for work include dummies for the age of the youngest child (0-2, 3-4 and 5-9) for the quadratic terms and, in addition for the linear terms, the total number of children, whether the individual was aged 40 or over and whether the the individual possessed a formal qualification.

In Table 7.2 the specification is further augmented; (4) allows fixed costs to vary across demographic groups and (5) incorporates random preference heterogeneity. The instruments chosen to allow for variation in fixed costs include a dummy for residing in a capital city, the number of pre-school and school-aged children and a dummy for residing in New South Wales.

In terms of the simpler specifications, use of the Likelihood Ratio criteria, clearly suggests the superiority of the more flexible functional form of model (3), although the parameters of this specification do not appear to have been estimated with as much precision individually, as in model (1) or (2). The introduction of variable fixed costs in model (4) (Table 7.2), appears to be an improvement, based on the Likelihood Ratio criterion. Average shadow fixed costs are estimated to be around $220 per week, as opposed to around $280. It also suggests that there is a significant increase in fixed costs arising from living in New South Wales, although the effect of the number of children on fixed costs appears to be imprecisely estimated. However, when random preference heterogeneity is introduced, as in specification (5), none of the variance or covariance terms is significantly different from zero. Indeed, it cannot be concluded that jointly these terms contribute statistically to the model. In the light of these findings, the preferred specification is specification (4).

Table 7.2: Controlling for Fixed Costs and Random Preference Heterogeneity

|  | (4) | | (5) | |
|---|---|---|---|---|
| $\alpha_{YY} \times 100$ | -0.073 | (0.320) | -0.081 | (0.330) |
| $\times 1$ (youngest child 0-2) | 0.204 | (0.694) | 0.214 | (0.707) |
| $\times 1$ (youngest child 3-4) | -0.498 | (0.846) | -0.493 | (0.859) |
| $\times 1$ (youngest child 5-9) | 0.104 | (0.534) | 0.040 | (0.576) |
| $\alpha_{HH} \times 100$ | -0.031 | (0.048) | -0.034 | (0.050) |
| $\times 1$ (youngest child 0-2) | -0.052 | (0.095) | -0.046 | (0.095) |
| $\times 1$ (youngest child 3-4) | -0.077 | (0.086) | -0.082 | (0.086) |
| $\times 1$ (youngest child 5-9) | -0.080 | (0.058) | -0.081 | (0.059) |
| $\alpha_{YH}$ | -0.755 | (0.564) | -0.7428 | (0.583) |
| $\beta_Y$ | 1.012 | (0.201)** | 1.028 | (0.206)** |
| $\times 1$ (youngest child 0-2) | -0.104 | (0.496) | -0.155 | (0.484) |
| $\times 1$ (youngest child 3-4) | 0.112 | (0.728) | 0.078 | (0.732) |
| $\times 1$ (youngest child 5-9) | 0.175 | (0.426) | 0.209 | (0.456) |
| $\times$ # children | 0.146 | (0.083) | 0.148 | (0.085)* |
| $\times 1$ aged over 40 | 0.028 | (0.100)* | 0.028 | (0.101) |
| $\times 1$ qualification | -0.063 | (0.094) | -0.067 | (0.093) |
| $\beta_H$ | -0.006 | (0.021) | -0.005 | (0.022) |
| $\times 1$ (youngest child 0-2) | -0.002 | (0.045) | -0.004 | (0.046) |
| $\times 1$ (youngest child 3-4) | 0.024 | (0.046) | 0.027 | (0.045) |
| $\times 1$ (youngest child 5-9) | 0.013 | (0.025) | 0.013 | (0.025) |
| $\times$ # children | 0.003 | (0.003) | 0.003 | (0.003) |
| $\times 1$ aged over 40 | -0.004 | (0.005) | -0.004 | (0.005) |
| $\times 1$ qualification | 0.023 | (0.004)** | 0.023 | (0.004)** |
| Fixed Costs/100 | 2.275 | (0.540)** | 2.263 | (0.540)** |
| $\times 1$ capital city | 0.132 | (0.130) | 0.133 | (0.131) |
| $\times$ # pre-school children | 1.156 | (1.307) | 1.266 | (1.353) |
| $\times$ # school-aged children | -0.063 | (0.270) | -0.047 | (0.275) |
| $\times 1$ New South Wales | 0.414 | (0.170)** | 0.402 | (0.170)** |
| $\sigma_Y^2$ | - | - | 0.002 | (0.0179) |
| $\sigma_H^2$ | - | - | 3e-05 | (1e-04) |
| $\sigma_{FC}^2$ | - | - | 0.076 | (0.152) |
| $\sigma_{YH}$ | - | - | 2e-04 | (9e-04) |
| $\sigma_{YFC}$ | - | - | 1e-04 | (0.015) |
| $\sigma_{HFC}$ | - | - | 9e-04 | (0.004) |
| Log-Likelihood | -3604 | | -3603 | |

### 7.2.3   Some Model Evaluations

Given the complexities of the model specifications involved, it is not obvious how one might evaluate and interpret the above results. One attractive option is to consider how well the model predicts in terms of 'hit and miss' tables. That is, the model estimates are used to predict the probability of an individual being in a particular state, and is said to predict that outcome which yields the maximum probability. Comparing these predictions with the actual states yields the usual 'hit and miss' tables.

However, if standard techniques are used to do this, based on the maximum probability rule stated above, discrete hours models generally tend to over-predict the empirically most frequently chosen outcome. This result stems from the fact that the random elements of the model are explicitly ignored in its subsequent evaluation.

An alternative method of evaluating such models, is to utilise the underlying economic model, in this case equation (7.11), and to simulate it by repeated draws of the unobserved random variates. That is, it is necessary to draw from a Type I Extreme Value distribution. For each such random draw, the probabilistic expressions are evaluated and the outcome which yields the maximum probability, is the one predicted for that repetition. Each separate hit and miss table is collected, and the simulated hit and miss table is simply the average of all of these independent ones. The results of this are presented in Table 7.3 for all of the model specifications.

As Table 7.3 illustrates, the models which allow for varying fixed costs predict better than those which do not. The major reason for this is that if fixed costs of employment are ignored, the probability of working zero hours is underestimated. As indicated by the Likelihood ratio tests, the performance of models (4) and (5) is close, both being marginally more accurate than model (3), which assumes constant fixed costs.

Another method of model evaluation is to obtain predicted indifference

Table 7.3: Percentage Model Predictions: 1,000 Random Draws

|  | | Predicted | | | | |
| --- | --- | --- | --- | --- | --- | --- |
|  | Actual | (1) | (2) | (3) | (4) | (5) |
| $H \leq 2.5$ | 57.0 | 36.0 | 39.2 | 47.3 | 51.1 | 51.0 |
| $2.5 < H \leq 7.5$ | 2.8 | 19.0 | 15.0 | 5.9 | 2.8 | 2.9 |
| $7.5 < H \leq 12.5$ | 3.6 | 9.2 | 8.1 | 5.9 | 3.6 | 3.7 |
| $12.5 < H \leq 17.5$ | 3.3 | 5.0 | 5.1 | 4.3 | 3.9 | 3.9 |
| $17.5 < H \leq 22.5$ | 3.5 | 3.3 | 3.7 | 4.0 | 4.3 | 4.3 |
| $22.5 < H \leq 27.5$ | 2.8 | 2.7 | 3.1 | 4.2 | 4.9 | 4.9 |
| $27.5 < H \leq 32.5$ | 3.0 | 2.5 | 2.9 | 4.6 | 5.4 | 5.4 |
| $32.5 < H \leq 37.5$ | 5.1 | 2.8 | 3.3 | 5.0 | 5.8 | 5.8 |
| $37.5 < H \leq 42.5$ | 11.0 | 3.8 | 4.1 | 5.5 | 6.1 | 6.1 |
| $42.5 < H \leq 47.5$ | 3.1 | 5.8 | 5.8 | 6.2 | 6.1 | 6.1 |
| $H > 47.5$ | 4.3 | 10.0 | 9.6 | 7.1 | 5.9 | 6.0 |
| Per cent correctly predicted | | 25.0 | 29.7 | 36.2 | 37.5 | 37.7 |

curves maps from the model estimates for respective demographics. The different demographic groups were found to exhibit differing amounts of curvature in their indifference curves. However, all are consistent with economic theory, increasing with hours of work and concave over the feasible range of hours and income levels. For both qualified and unqualified sole parents with an only child, the indifference curve surfaces are at their steepest when the child is between three and four years of age. This implies that the parent's wage elasticities are at their lowest when their only child is at this age.

## 7.2.4 Single Persons

The same basic approach can be applied to single individuals without children, simply by omitting the variables relating to children. In addition, fixed costs of employment were excluded. The results for single persons are shown in Tables 7.4 and 7.5.

Table 7.4: Single Men: Utility Function Only and Observed Heterogeneity

|  | (1) | | (2) | |
|---|---|---|---|---|
| $\alpha_{YY} \times 100$ | -0.831 | $(0.129)^{**}$ | -0.819 | $(0.148)^{**}$ |
| $\alpha_{HH} \times 100$ | -0.209 | $(0.025)^{**}$ | -0.229 | $(0.029)^{**}$ |
| $\alpha_{YH}$ | 3.472 | $(0.307)^{**}$ | 3.510 | $(0.362)^{**}$ |
| | | | | |
| $\beta_Y$ | -1.261 | $(0.082)^{**}$ | -1.511 | $(0.107)^{**}$ |
| $\times 1$ aged over 40 | - | - | -0.150 | $(0.092)^{*}$ |
| $\times 1$ qualification | - | - | 0.407 | $(0.087)^{**}$ |
| | | | | |
| $\beta_H$ | 0.139 | $(0.013)^{**}$ | 0.160 | $(0.015)^{**}$ |
| $\times 1$ aged over 40 | - | - | 0.015 | $(0.011)$ |
| $\times 1$ qualification | - | - | -0.014 | $(0.010)$ |
| | | | | |
| Log-Likelihood | | | | |
| Likelihood Ratio Test, $\chi^2_{df}$ | | | (2) $vs$ (1) | |

** and * significant at 5 and 10 per cent respectively (two-sided).

Table 7.5: Single Women: Utility Function Only and Observed Heterogeneity

|  | (1) | | (2) | |
|---|---|---|---|---|
| $\alpha_{YY} \times 100$ | 0.2576 | $(0.124)^{**}$ | -0.1087 | $(0.157)$ |
| $\alpha_{HH} \times 100$ | 0.1681 | $(0.015)^{**}$ | 0.1245 | $(0.016)^{**}$ |
| $\alpha_{YH}$ | -1.0545 | $(0.235)^{**}$ | -0.3764 | $(0.284)$ |
| | | | | |
| $\beta_Y$ | -0.1234 | $(0.063)^{**}$ | -0.2643 | $(0.074)^{**}$ |
| $\times 1$ aged over 40 | - | | -0.1433 | $(0.070)^{**}$ |
| $\times 1$ qualification | - | | 0.4285 | $(0.073)^{**}$ |
| | | | | |
| $\beta_H$ | -0.0171 | $(0.006)^{**}$ | -0.0053 | $(0.007)$ |
| $\times 1$ aged over 40 | - | | -0.0083 | $(0.006)$ |
| $\times 1$ qualification | - | | -0.0062 | $(0.006)$ |
| | | | | |
| Log-Likelihood | | | | |
| Likelihood Ratio Test, $\chi^2_{df}$ | | | (2) $vs$ (1) | |

** and * significant at 5 and 10 per cent respectively (two-sided).

## 7.3 Conclusions

In this chapter, the labour supply of sole parents and single individuals was modelled as the outcome of choice among a set of discrete hours levels. A direct quadratic utility function was used and allowance was made for random preference heterogeneity, and fixed costs were included for sole parents. Net incomes were generated by the MITTS model. The results for sole parents indicated that if fixed costs were not included, the probability that individuals do not work is underestimated. The results produced indifference maps that conform to expected properties.

# Chapter 8

# Household Labour Supply

This chapter extends the treatment of labour supply used in the previous chapter, in order to deal with households. Section 8.1 describes the basic structural discrete choice model and its extension to allow differentiation among non-working household heads and spouses. The data are described briefly in section 8.2. Section 8.3 describes the empirical estimates.

## 8.1 The Framework of Analysis

In the traditional approach to modelling household labour supply, individuals derive utility from net household income $Y$ and leisure. Hours worked are denoted $\mathbf{H} = \{H_1, H_2\}$, where subscripts 1 and 2 denote head of household and spouse respectively. In this simple extension of the single-person model, the household maximises utility, which is considered to be a function of net household income and total household leisure. The household utility function can be written:

$$U = U(Y, H_1, H_2; X) \qquad (8.1)$$

where $X$ represents household and individual characteristics. The budget constraint for the household is defined by gross wage rates $\mathbf{W}$, total household unearned income, $V$, from assets and other sources, and the tax and transfer system. If $\mathbf{H}$ is the vector of hours worked, and net tax payments are denoted

113

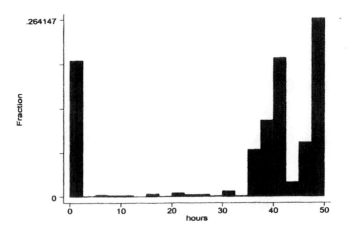

Figure 8.1: Married Male Hours Worked

by $T(\mathbf{H}, \mathbf{W}, V; X)$, the budget set is given by:

$$Y = \sum_{i=1}^{2} W_i H_i + V - T(\mathbf{H}, \mathbf{W}, V; X) - \sum_{i=1}^{2} FC_i(Z_i) \qquad (8.2)$$

where $FC_i(Z_i)$ denotes the fixed cost of employment for the $i$th individual in the household with characteristics $Z_i$. Households are assumed to maximise $U(Y, H_1, H_2)$, subject to (8.2) over a continuum of hours, to give desired hours $\mathbf{H}^*$.

It has been suggested that labour market participation usually takes the form of fixed wage and hours contracts, with individuals choosing from among a discrete set of hours combinations (most often at part-time levels of around 20 hours, and at full-time levels of between 38 and 40 hours per week). In particular, for prime-aged married men the decision is likely to be between working full-time and not working. This is shown in Figure 8.1, which refers to the data used in the empirical application. Of the working married males, there is a clustering of observations at the usual working week of 40-50 hours.

The strategy adopted in the discrete approach is to replace the budget set with a finite number of points, and optimise only over those discrete points. The procedure supposes that hours choices can be approximated by the discrete hours level $H_{i(.)} \in \{H^1, H^2, .., H^P\}$ according to the grouping rule:

$$
\begin{aligned}
H_{i(.)} \ &= \ H^1 \quad \text{if } H_i \leq H_1^B \\
&= \ H^2 \quad \text{if } H_1^B < H_i \leq H_2^B \\
&\qquad \dots\dots\dots \\
&= \ H^{P-1} \text{ if } H_{P-2}^B < H_i \leq H_{P-1}^B \\
&= \ H^P \quad \text{if } H_i > H_{P-1}^B
\end{aligned}
$$

giving $P$ alternative values for $H_{i(.)}$. The following analysis uses the choice set $H_{2(.)} = \{0, 10, 20, 30, 40\}$ where $H_1^B = 5$, $H_2^B = 15$, $H_3^B = 25$ and $H_4^B = 35$ for females and $H_{1(.)} = \{0, 40\}$ where $H_1^B = 20$ for males. Household net incomes may then be calculated for the set of discrete hours combinations $\mathbf{H}_{(.)} = \{H_{1(.)}, H_{2(.)}\}$ as:

$$
Y[\mathbf{H}_{(.)}] = Y\left[H_{1(.)}, H_{2(.)}\right] = \sum_{i=1}^{2} W_i H_i + V - T(\mathbf{H}_{(.)}, \mathbf{W}, V; X)
$$

for $H_{1(.)}, H_{2(.)} \in \{H^1, H^2, .., H^P\}$. The household is assumed to maximise

$$
U(Y[H_{1(.)}, H_{2(.)}], H_{1(.)}, H_{2(.)}) \tag{8.3}
$$

This approach removes from the optimisation problem many of the complexities of a nonlinear tax schedule. However, it does so at the cost of introducing rounding errors in the hours levels used for estimation.

## 8.1.1    A Reduced Form Approach to Estimation

The discrete choice model requires a specification of the preference function and the stochastic structure. One approach specifies directly a series of state-specific utilities in each combination of discrete hours $H_{i(.)} \in$

$\{H^1, H^2, .., H^P\}$. Let combined state-specific utilities be represented by:

$$U_{\mathbf{H}(.)} = U(Y_{\mathbf{H}(.)}, H_{1(.)}, H_{2(.)}; Z, X), \qquad (8.4)$$

for $H_{i(.)} \in \{H^1, H^2, .., H^P\}$, such that the joint utility function depends on the discrete hours set $\mathbf{H}_{(.)}$ and total household net income $Y_{\mathbf{H}(.)}$, which would be enjoyed at $\mathbf{H}_{(.)}$. To derive probabilistic expressions, add random disturbances to utilities in each state of the world, giving a stochastic utility specification of the form:

$$U^*_{\mathbf{H}(.)} = U(Y_{\mathbf{H}(.)}, H_{1(.)}, H_{2(.)}; Z, X) + \varepsilon_{\mathbf{H}(.)} \qquad (8.5)$$

for $H_{i(.)} = H^1, H^2, .., H^P$. If the $\varepsilon_{\mathbf{H}(.)}$ in (8.5) are assumed to follow a Type I Extreme Value distribution, standard Multinomial Logit probabilities result. That is, the probability that the household in total works $H_{1(.)} = H^j$ and $H_{2(.)} = H^k$ hours for all $j \neq p_1, k \neq p_2, \{p_1, p_2\} \in \{1, .., P\}$, is:

$$\Pr(H_{1(.)} = H^j, H_{2(.)} = H^k) = \Pr\left[U_{\{H^j, H^k\}} > U^*_{\{H^{p_1}, H^{p_2}\}}\right] \qquad (8.6)$$

The right hand side can be written as:

$$\frac{\exp[U(Y_{\{H^j, H^k\}}, H^j, H^k; X)]}{\sum_{p_1=1}^{P} \sum_{p_2=1}^{P} \exp[U(Y_{\{H^j, H^k\}}, H^{p_1}, H^{p_2}; X)]} \qquad (8.7)$$

To complete this structural approach, a functional form for the utility function is required. For the quadratic direct utility function:

$$
\begin{aligned}
U(Y, \mathbf{H}) = \ & \alpha_{YY} Y^2 + \alpha_{H_1 H_1} H_1^2 + \alpha_{H_2 H_2} H_2^2 \\
& + \alpha_{Y H_1} Y H_1 + \alpha_{Y H_2} Y H_2 + \alpha_{H_1 H_2} H_1 H_2 \\
& + \beta_Y Y + \beta_{H_1} H_1 + \beta_{H_2} H_2
\end{aligned} \qquad (8.8)
$$

For $\phi = \{\alpha_{YY}, \alpha_{H_1 H_1}, \alpha_{H_2 H_2}, \alpha_{Y H_1}, \alpha_{Y H_2}, \alpha_{H_1 H_2}, \beta_Y, \beta_{H_1}, \beta_{H_2}\}$. this function is tractable, yet permits a wide range of possible behavioural responses. Observed heterogeneity is introduced linearly through the three parameters in

$\beta = \left(\beta_Y, \beta_{H_1}, \beta_{H_2}\right)'$ thus:

$$\beta_Y = \beta_{y0} + \beta'_y X \tag{8.9}$$

$$\beta_{H_1} = \beta^1_{h0} + \beta^{1'}_h X \tag{8.10}$$

$$\beta_{H_2} = \beta^2_{h0} + \beta^{2'}_h X \tag{8.11}$$

The characteristics included in the empirical estimates include dummies for the age of the youngest child, age and education. For the structural model, the likelihood contribution corresponding to (8.8) is:

$$L(\phi|X) = \sum_{j=1}^{P}\sum_{k=1}^{P} d_{jk} \ln \Pr[H_{1(.)} = H^j, H_{2(.)} = H^k] \tag{8.12}$$

where $d_{jk} = \mathbf{1}[H_{1(.)} = H^j, H_{2(.)} = H^k]$.

To additionally incorporate random preference heterogeneity, error terms can be added to equations (8.9), (8.10) and (8.11) such that:

$$\beta^*_Y = \beta_y + \upsilon_Y \tag{8.13}$$

$$\beta^*_{H_1} = \beta_{H_1} + \upsilon_{H_1} \tag{8.14}$$

$$\beta^*_{H_2} = \beta_{H_2} + \upsilon_{H_2} \tag{8.15}$$

where $\upsilon = (\upsilon_Y, \upsilon_{H_1}, \upsilon_{H_2})'$ are assumed to be jointly normal with variance-covariance matrix $\Sigma_\upsilon$. However, although the likelihood function has no analytical closed form, estimation can be undertaken using the method of Simulated Maximum Likelihood.

## 8.1.2 Modelling Participation

Individuals observed not to be working may be involuntarily unemployed, not in the labour force or discouraged workers. It is preferable to accommodate all of these states in model estimation. The Income Distribution Survey only enables identification of three labour force states: employed, unemployed and not in the labour force.

For married males, the hours decision is essentially a binary one; married males tend to be either non-participants/unemployed or they work full-time. Therefore, effectively it is impossible to separately identify the effects of personal characteristics on the fixed costs and involuntary unemployment equations in addition to those on the taste parameters. Consequently, these further equations are introduced only for the married women.

Modelling the involuntarily unemployed is achieved by specifying an index of employability as:

$$I^* = Z'\delta + v_I \tag{8.16}$$

where $\delta$ represents a parameter vector, $Z$ denotes a vector of characteristics thought to influence the probability of obtaining employment and $v_I$ an error term assumed to be independently distributed as a standard normal variate. The probability of getting a job is accordingly $\Pr(I^* > 0|Z) = \Phi(Z'\delta)$.

Introducing the involuntarily unemployed into estimation requires a modification to the likelihood function. First, let $d_e$ represent an indicator variable for which $d_e = 1$ if a labour market participant finds a job, 0 otherwise. Conditioning on the male's labour market status, the probability of observing a non-participant spouse, $\Pr[H_{1(.)}, NP|X, Z, \phi]$, is:

$$
\Pr\{U^*(Y_{\{H_{1(.)},0\}}, H_{1(.)}|X, \phi)
$$
$$
> \max_{H_{2(.)}>0}[U(Y_{\{H_{1(.)},H_{2(.)}\}}, H_{1(.)}, H_{2(.)}|X, \phi)]\}
$$

The probability, $\Pr[H_{1(.)}, US|X, Z, \phi]$, of observing an unemployed job-seeker spouse is:

$$
\{1 - \Phi(Z\delta)\} \Pr\{U^*(Y_{\{H_{1(.)},0\}}, H_{1(.)}|X, \phi)
$$
$$
< \max_{H_{2(.)}>0}[U(Y_{\{H_{1(.)},H_{2(.)}\}}, H_{1(.)}, H_{2(.)}|X, \phi)]\}
$$

The probability, $\Pr[H_{1(.)}, H_{2(.)} = H^j|X, Z, \phi]$, of observing a working spouse is:

$$\Phi(Z\delta)\Pr\{U^*(Y_{\{H_{1(.)},H^j\}}, H_{1(.)}, H^j | X, \phi)$$
$$> \max_{H_{2(.)}\neq H^j}[U(Y_{\{H_{1(.)},H_{2(.)}\}} H_{1(.)}, | X, \phi]\}$$

A fixed costs equation is specified as:

$$FC = X_{FC}\gamma + v_f \tag{8.17}$$

where the unobserved fixed cost component $v_f$ is distributed normally around zero mean, $X_{FC}$ are instruments to proxy fixed costs, and $v_f$ is allowed to be potentially correlated with the random preference parameters, $v_Y$, $v_{H_1}$ and $v_{H_2}$. Fixed costs are easily incorporated into estimation. As they only have an impact on workers, the utilities $U^*(Y_{\{H_{1(.)},H_{2(.)}\}}, H_{1(.)}, H_{2(.)} | X, \phi)$ entering the likelihood function of (8.12) become $U^*(Y_{\{H_{1(.)},H_{2(.)}\}} - FC, H_{1(.)}, H_{2(.)} | X, \phi)$ for all states $H^j > 0$. To observe a worker in the presence of fixed costs therefore requires that

$$\max_{H_{2(.)}>0} U^*(Y_{\{H_{1(.)},H_{2(.)}\}} - FC, H_{1(.)}, H_{2(.)} | X, \phi) \tag{8.18}$$

exceeds:

$$U^*(Y_{\{H_{1(.)},0\}} - FC, H_{1(.)}, 0 | X, \phi) \tag{8.19}$$

Although this potentially adds a fourth labour market state to the likelihood, that of discouraged worker, these cannot be identified within the Income Distribution Survey. Therefore, all fixed costs are attributed to the involuntarily unemployed.

## 8.2 The Data

The data are taken from the pooled Income Distribution Surveys 1994 to 1996. Self-employed and retired households were excluded, as are outliers and missing values, leaving a working sample of 8,624 households. Of the household heads, just over 7,000 were in employment. Of the spouses, nearly 5,000 were in employment.

The net incomes were obtained using MITTS. The financial returns for each working age individual to employment at all possible hours are calculated using gross and net incomes at these levels. For workers, the current wage is assumed to remain unchanged, and for non-workers, a level is imputed as described in chapter 3.

## 8.3   Empirical Results

Several sets of estimates for the labour supply behaviour of households are reported in Table 8.1. The first series of estimates uses an eleven-hour labour supply regime for the spouse, $H_{(.)} = \{0, 5, 10, 15, 20, 25, 30, 35, 40, 45, 50\}$, using the following allocation rule:

$$
\begin{aligned}
H_{(.)} &= & 0 \text{ if } H \leq 2.5 \\
&= & 5 \text{ if } 2.5 < H \leq 7.5 \\
&= & 10 \text{ if } 7.5 < H \leq 12.5 \\
&= & 15 \text{ if } 12.5 < H \leq 17.5 \\
&= & 20 \text{ if } 17.5 < H \leq 22.5 \\
&= & 25 \text{ if } 22.5 < H \leq 27.5 \\
&= & 30 \text{ if } 27.5 < H \leq 32.5 \\
&= & 35 \text{ if } 32.5 < H \leq 37.5 \\
&= & 40 \text{ if } 37.5 < H \leq 42.5 \\
&= & 45 \text{ if } 42.5 < H \leq 47.5 \\
&= & 50 \text{ if } H > 47.5
\end{aligned}
$$

For the household heads, the allocation was effectively a binary one of 0 or forty hours, given by the allocation rule $H_{(.)} = 0$ if $H \leq 2.5$ and 40 otherwise.

The specifications are considered sequentially: in (1), the parameters of the utility function only are estimated; then in (2) allowance is made for

Table 8.1: Utility Function Only; Observed Heterogeniety and Constant Fixed Costs

| | (1) | | (2) | | (3) |
|---|---|---|---|---|---|
| $\alpha_{YY} \times 100$ | -0.042 | $(0.010)^{**}$ | 0.055 | $(0.014)^{**}$ | -0.194 |
| $\times 1$ (youngest child 0-2) | - | - | -0.236 | $(0.047)^{**}$ | 0.012 |
| $\times 1$ (youngest child 3-4) | - | - | -0.297 | $(0.066)^{**}$ | -0.074 |
| $\times 1$ (youngest child 5-9) | - | - | -0.133 | $(0.038)^{**}$ | -0.026 |
| $\alpha_{H_2 H_2} \times 100$ | 0.240 | $(0.006)^{**}$ | 0.166 | $(0.008)^{**}$ | -0.116 |
| $\times 1$ (youngest child 0-2) | - | - | 0.166 | $(0.018)^{**}$ | 0.085 |
| $\times 1$ (youngest child 3-4) | - | - | 0.082 | $(0.024)^{**}$ | 0.076 |
| $\times 1$ (youngest child 5-9) | - | - | 0.020 | $(0.016)$ | -0.003 |
| $\alpha_{Y H_2}$ | -0.013 | $(0.037)^{**}$ | 0.139 | $(0.045)^{**}$ | -0.320 |
| $\beta_Y$ | 0.302 | $(0.026)^{**}$ | -0.062 | $(0.046)$ | 0.613 |
| $\times 1$ (youngest child 0-2) | - | - | 0.646 | $(0.121)^{**}$ | 0.147 |
| $\times 1$ (youngest child 3-4) | - | - | 0.678 | $(0.169)^{**}$ | 0.158 |
| $\times 1$ (youngest child 5-9) | - | - | 0.276 | $(0.103)^{**}$ | 0.093 |
| $\times$ # children | - | - | 0.030 | $(0.015)^{**}$ | 0.001 |
| $\times 1$ aged over 40 | - | - | 0.016 | $(0.043)$ | 0.026 |
| $\times 1$ partner aged over 40 | | | 0.029 | $(0.042)$ | 0.009 |
| $\times 1$ qualification | - | - | -0.095 | $(0.030)^{**}$ | -0.026 |
| $\times 1$ partner qualified | | | 0.072 | $(0.028)^{**}$ | 0.021 |
| $\beta_{H_1}$ | 0.019 | $(0.001)^{**}$ | 0.032 | $(0.004)^{**}$ | 0.002 |
| $\times 1$ (youngest child 0-2) | - | - | -0.022 | $(0.005)^{**}$ | -0.005 |
| $\times 1$ (youngest child 3-4) | - | - | -0.020 | $(0.007)^{**}$ | -0.004 |
| $\times 1$ (youngest child 5-9) | - | - | -0.007 | $(0.005)$ | -0.003 |
| $\times$ # children | - | - | 0.000 | $(0.001)$ | 0.004 |
| $\times 1$ aged over 40 | - | - | -0.011 | $(0.004)^{**}$ | -0.010 |
| $\times 1$ partner aged over 40 | | | -0.008 | $(0.004)^{**}$ | -0.009 |
| $\times 1$ qualification | - | - | 0.020 | $(0.003)^{**}$ | 0.011 |
| $\times 1$ partner qualified | | | 0.001 | $(0.003)$ | 0.004 |
| $\beta_{H_2}$ | -0.161 | $(0.003)^{**}$ | -0.103 | $(0.005)^{**}$ | 0.072 |
| $\times 1$ (youngest child 0-2) | | | -0.149 | $(0.010)^{**}$ | -0.099 |
| $\times 1$ (youngest child 3-4) | | | -0.088 | $(0.013)^{**}$ | -0.080 |
| $\times 1$ (youngest child 5-9) | | | -0.032 | $(0.009)^{**}$ | -0.022 |
| $\times$ # children | | | -0.008 | $(0.002)^{**}$ | -0.005 |
| $\times 1$ aged over 40 | | | -0.010 | $(0.005)^{**}$ | -0.009 |
| $\times 1$ partner aged over 40 | | | -0.013 | $(0.004)^{**}$ | -0.008 |
| $\times 1$ qualification | | | 0.012 | $(0.003)^{**}$ | 0.001 |
| $\times 1$ partner qualified | | | 0.011 | $(0.003)^{**}$ | 0.017 |
| Fixed Costs$_2$/100 | - | - | - | - | 6.995 |
| $\times 1$ capital city | | | | | -0.074 |
| $\times$ # pre-school children | | | | | -2.183 |
| $\times$ # school-aged children | | | | | -0.915 |
| $\times 1$ New South Wales | | | | | 0.003 |
| Log-Likelihood | -22,501 | | -21,708 | | -20,019 |

$^{**}$ and $^{*}$ significant at 5 and 10 per cent respectively (two-sided).

observed heterogeneity on the linear and quadratic terms of the basic utility function parameters, and finally additionally parameterised fixed costs are included in (3). The instruments chosen to account for variation in tastes for work include dummies for the age of the youngest child (0-2, 3-4 and 5-9) only for the quadratic terms. In addition, for the linear terms, instruments included the total number of children; whether the individual was aged 40 or over and; whether or not they possessed any formal qualification. The instruments used to proxy fixed costs were residence in a capital city, number of pre-school-aged children, number of school-aged children and residence in New South Wales.

## 8.4   Conclusion

This chapter has extended the approach of the previous chapter in order to estimate preference functions for households. These results form the basis of behavioural simulations in MITTS.

# Chapter 9

# The Quadratic Direct Utility Function

The previous two chapters have reported estimates of quadratic direct utility functions for various demographic groups. This chapter examines the basic properties of such utility functions in more detail. The quadratic direct utility function has a long history in economics. It was used in the first derivation of supply and demand curves, using specific assumptions about the form of the utility function. Using the exchange model of Jevons and Walras, Launhardt (1885) examined supply and demand curves for two traders, each holding stocks of one good before trade, expressed in terms of the relative price of the two goods. Launhardt argued, following Jevons, that marginal utility decreases steadily as consumption increases. His derivation showed that backward bending supply curves can easily arise in such an exchange context. Further use was made of the quadratic direct utility function by Allen and Bowley (1935). They showed that for any form whereby the marginal rate of substitution is a linear function of the two goods, the expenditure on each good is a linear function of total expenditure, with coefficients depending on prices.

In using specific functional forms, either in theoretical or empirical studies, the quadratic was largely neglected until more recently, when it has been used in empirical analyses of labour supply. The use in MITTS follows the examples of Keane and Moffitt (1998), Duncan and Weeks (1997, 1998), Duncan and Giles (1998), which were designed to examine the effects of changes in tax and transfer systems within behavioural microsimulation models.[1] The advantages of using the quadratic (and corresponding translog) form of utility function outweigh the disadvantages mentioned by Stern (1986), in a survey of functional forms for empirical labour supply analysis. Stern (1986, pp. 171-172) commented that they have 'rather inconvenient or opaque labour supply functions and, further, satisfy appropriate monotonicity and concavity conditions only over certain ranges'.

In this application, where leisure is given up in order to obtain consumption goods, there is an obvious similarity with Launhardt's context of exchange. None of the above studies reported welfare changes measured in terms of compensating or equivalent variations. Indeed, Stern (1986) suggested that it is not possible to obtain analytical expressions for welfare changes when using the quadratic utility function.

This chapter shows how welfare changes can be produced using quadratic direct utility in the context of the analysis of labour supply. Convenient expressions for the associated indirect utility function and the expenditure function are presented, and the use of the latter function in the computation of welfare changes is discussed. The basic model of labour supply is presented in section 9.1. The Slutsky condition is derived in section 9.2. Section 9.3 is concerned with the derivation of the expenditure function and the analysis of welfare changes.

---

[1] Van Soest (1995), Callan and Van Soest (1996) and Van Soest and Das (2000) use the translog form of quadratic utility in which utility is expressed as a quadratic function of the logarithms of the square of consumption, and so on. The logarithmic transformation can be awkward where fixed costs of working are included, since circumstances exist where consumption can be negative.

## 9.1  Labour Supply

Let $h$ denote the number of hours devoted to labour supply, and let $c$ denote an index of consumption, with the price index normalised to unity. The framework of analysis is one in which individuals are allowed to vary their hours of work continuously. The quadratic direct utility function can be written as:

$$U(h, c) = \alpha c^2 + \beta h^2 + \gamma ch + \delta c + \varepsilon h \qquad (9.1)$$

In empirical work, the parameters can be specified as functions of a variety of personal characteristics. The form in (9.1) is more convenient than expressing utility in terms of leisure, $T - h$, where $T$ is the total number of hours available for work and leisure. This approach means that $\varepsilon < 0$.

For decreasing marginal utility, it is required to have $\alpha < 0$ and $\beta < 0$. However, further restrictions on the range of $c$ and $h$ for which (9.1) is applicable are needed for marginal utility to be positive and (more importantly) to have decreasing marginal rates of substitution along indifference curves. The parameters of (9.1) are also affected by the units of measurement of $c$ and $h$. Suppose, for example, that a change of units means that all prices, income tax thresholds and the wage rate facing the individual increase by a proportion, $\theta$. For the optimal choice of hours to remain unchanged, new values $\alpha'$, and so on, are required whereby: $\alpha' = \alpha / (1 + \theta)^2$; $\delta' = \delta / (1 + \theta)$; $\gamma' = \gamma / (1 + \theta)$; $\varepsilon' = \varepsilon$; $\beta' = \beta$.

Unlike the standard commodity demand model in which prices are constant irrespective of the amount of each good consumed, the individual faces a variety of net wage rates. Although the gross wage is assumed to remain constant (independent of the number of hours worked), varying effective marginal tax rates associated with the piecewise linear nature of the budget constraint means that the net wage varies with $h$. The actual net wage depends on the chosen position on the budget constraint and is therefore, like the number of hours worked, endogenous.

With a piecewise-linear budget constraint any interior (tangency) solution or corner solution can be regarded as being generated by a simple linear constraint of the form:

$$c = wh + \mu \tag{9.2}$$

In the case of such tangency solutions, $w$ and $\mu$ represent the appropriate net wage rate and virtual income respectively. Virtual income is the intercept (where $h = 0$) corresponding to the relevant segment of the budget constraint and associated net wage; it is therefore distinct from actual non-wage income. In the case of a corner solution, the appropriate virtual income is defined as the value generated by a linear constraint having a net wage, the virtual wage, equal to the slope of the indifference curve at the kink. The concept of the virtual wage is the same as that of the virtual price used in the theory of rationing.

The marginal rate of substitution is given by:

$$\left.\frac{dc}{dh}\right|_U = -\frac{\partial U/\partial h}{\partial U/\partial c} = -\left\{\frac{2\beta h + \gamma c + \varepsilon}{2\alpha c + \gamma h + \delta}\right\} \tag{9.3}$$

Equate the marginal rate of substitution and the slope of the budget constraint, given by:

$$\frac{dc}{dh} = w \tag{9.4}$$

Then substitute for $c$ using (12.31) and solve for $h$, giving:[2]

$$h = \frac{2\alpha\mu w + \delta w + \gamma\mu + \varepsilon}{-2\left(\alpha w^2 + \gamma w + \beta\right)} \tag{9.5}$$

It is convenient to write:

$$
\begin{aligned}
A &= \alpha w^2 + \gamma w + \beta \\
B &= 2\alpha w + \gamma \\
C &= \delta w + \varepsilon
\end{aligned}
\tag{9.6}
$$

---

[2] There is a typographical error in Stern (1986), where the minus sign is missing.

Rewrite (9.5) as:

$$h = \frac{B\mu + C}{-2A} \tag{9.7}$$

This is clearly a special case of the general Allen and Bowley result mentioned above, that expenditure is a linear function of total expenditure (in the present context the latter can be represented either by virtual income or by full income).

It may be tempting to think of (9.7) as a labour supply function; it shows, for example, how $h$ varies as $w$ varies, for given $\mu$. However, the relationship between $h$ and the gross wage, say $w_g$, is much more complicated. This is because $w$ and $\mu$, like $h$, are endogenous and vary as the gross wage varies, since budget constraints are generally piecewise-linear. Also, at a kink in the budget constraint where the marginal effective tax rate falls, net income remains constant as $w_g$ rises, so that $h$ falls along a rectangular hyperbola.[3]

## 9.2 The Slutsky Condition

The values of the parameters, $\alpha$, $\beta$, and so on must ensure that the integrability conditions are satisfied. These require (for necessity and sufficiency) the Slutsky matrix to be symmetric and negative semi-definite; for further discussion in the context of labour supply, see Deaton and Muellbauer (1980, pp.89-93) and Stern (1986, pp.145-146). The Slutsky condition requires the wage response of the compensated labour supply to be non-negative, that is:

$$\frac{\partial h}{\partial w} - h\frac{\partial h}{\partial \mu} \geq 0 \tag{9.8}$$

In the case of the quadratic direct utility function, Stern (1986, p.183) stated only that, if $\alpha \neq 0$, the 'expression [for the Slutsky condition] is messy'. However, a convenient result can be obtained as follows. Differentiation of

---

[3] For further discussion of these complexities, and illustrations using Cobb-Douglas and CES utility functions, see Creedy (2001b).

(9.5) with respect to the net wage gives:

$$\frac{\partial h}{\partial w} = \frac{2\alpha\mu + \delta}{-2A} + \frac{(B\mu + C)\,B}{2A^2} \tag{9.9}$$

Let $D = 2\alpha\mu + \delta$, so that further rearrangement of (9.9) gives:

$$\frac{\partial h}{\partial w} = \frac{AD - (B\mu + C)\,B}{-2A^2} \tag{9.10}$$

Differentiation of (9.5) with respect to virtual income gives:

$$\frac{\partial h}{\partial \mu} = \frac{B}{-2A} \tag{9.11}$$

so that:

$$h\frac{\partial h}{\partial \mu} = \frac{(B\mu + C)\,B}{4A^2} \tag{9.12}$$

Substitution into (9.8) gives:

$$\frac{B\,(B\mu + C) - 2AD}{4A^2} \geq 0 \tag{9.13}$$

and further rearrangement gives:

$$\frac{Bh + D}{-2A} \geq 0 \tag{9.14}$$

In view of the complexities associated with the signs of the terms in (9.14), it is best to leave it in the form shown.

## 9.3    Welfare Changes

This section derives the expenditure function corresponding to the quadratic direct utility function, and shows how this can be used to obtain welfare changes measured in terms of compensating and equivalent variations.

### 9.3.1    The Expenditure Function

The evaluation of welfare changes requires an expression for the expenditure function, which is obtained by inverting the indirect utility function. Stern

(1986, p.183) reported that the expenditure function is 'less straightforward since indirect utility function is quartic in $m$'. The following treatment shows that this is incorrect and that a relatively simple form can be derived.

To obtain the indirect utility function, first substitute for $c = wh + \mu$ into the direct utility function in (9.1), giving:

$$U = h^2 A + \mu h B + hC + \alpha \mu^2 + \delta \mu \qquad (9.15)$$

Secondly, substituting for $h$, from (9.7), into (9.15) and rearranging gives the indirect utility function:

$$U(w, \mu) = \mu^2 \left( \alpha - \frac{B^2}{4A} \right) + \mu \left( \delta - \frac{BC}{2A} \right) - \frac{C^2}{4A} \qquad (9.16)$$

To invert (9.16), rewrite it as:

$$\mu^2 q_1 + \mu q_2 + q_3 = 0 \qquad (9.17)$$

where:

$$
\begin{aligned}
q_1 &= \alpha - \frac{B^2}{4A} \\
q_2 &= \delta - \frac{BC}{2A} \\
q_3 &= -\left( U + \frac{C^2}{4A} \right)
\end{aligned}
\qquad (9.18)
$$

Hence, the expenditure function, expressed in terms of virtual income, is obtained as the appropriate root of the quadratic in (9.17):

$$\mu(w, U) = \frac{-q_2 \pm \sqrt{q_2^2 - 4q_1 q_3}}{2q_1} \qquad (9.19)$$

It is found that the positive root, giving the lower value of $\mu(w, U)$, is appropriate. This can be used to find welfare changes, as shown in the following subsection.

## 9.3.2   Compensating and Equivalent Variations

In terms of the expenditure function defined in terms of virtual income, compensating and equivalent variations are given, where superscripts refer to tax systems 0 and 1, by:

$$CV = \mu\left(w^1, U^0\right) - \mu^1 \tag{9.20}$$

$$EV = \mu^0 - \mu\left(w^0, U^1\right) \tag{9.21}$$

In the case of corner solutions the net wage is replaced by the appropriate virtual wage, $w^*$, and income, $\mu^*$, corresponding to the values that generate $c$ and $h$ as interior solutions to the virtual linear constraint. Hence, from (9.3)

$$w^* = -\left\{\frac{2\beta h + \gamma c + \varepsilon}{2\alpha c + \gamma h + \delta}\right\} \tag{9.22}$$

and

$$\mu^* = c - w^* h \tag{9.23}$$

In the present context a change in the net or virtual wage has two effects on welfare. It represents both a change in the effective price of leisure and has an income effect. It is therefore convenient to decompose the welfare changes into these price and income effects. This requires the changes to be expressed in terms of full income, $M$, rather than virtual income. Letting $T$ denote the total available number of hours, full income is given by:

$$M = \mu + wT \tag{9.24}$$

This represents the total resources which can be used to purchase goods and leisure. Hence the expenditure function, expressed in terms of full income, is:

$$E\left(w, U\right) = \mu\left(w, U\right) + wT \tag{9.25}$$

The welfare changes can be expressed as:

$$CV = \left\{E\left(w^1, U^0\right) - M^0\right\} + \left(M^0 - M^1\right) \tag{9.26}$$

$$EV = \left\{ M^1 - E\left(w^0, U^1\right)\right\} + \left(M^0 - M^1\right) \qquad (9.27)$$

The absolute value of the term in curly brackets in each of the above expressions corresponds to an area to the left of a compensated leisure demand curve between appropriate prices. A fall in the wage rate, so that $w^1 < w^0$, lowers the price of leisure, so that the welfare reduction from the price effect is negative, while reducing full income.

## 9.4 Conclusions

This chapter has examined the use of the quadratic direct utility function in modelling labour supply behaviour, as a special application of a more general model of exchange. The quadratic was indeed used in the first derivation, by Launhardt, of explicit demand and supply functions expressed in terms of relative prices. Although this utility function has been used in empirical studies of labour supply, welfare changes have not been reported, perhaps as a result of the earlier suggestion by Stern that the expenditure function is intractable. For this reason, emphasis has been given to the treatment of welfare changes, involving the derivation of the expenditure function. A convenient expression for the Slutsky condition was also obtained.

# Part III

# The MITTS Model

# Chapter 10

# Outline of MITTS

This chapter describes the basic structure of the Melbourne Institute Tax and Transfer Simulator – MITTS. This microsimulation model was designed to examine the effects on individuals and households in Australia of policy changes to any component of the income tax and transfer payments system. A brief description of the functions performed by MITTS is given in section 10.1. Its structure is described in section 10.2. Further details of its installation and use are given in chapters 10 and 11.

MITTS actually consists of two closely integrated simulation models. First, an arithmetic model, MITTS-A, examines the effects of a specified change in the direct tax and transfer system, assuming that the labour supply, and hence pre-tax and transfer income, of each individual remains fixed. Second, a behavioural model, MITTS-B, allows for the effects of labour supply variations in response to changes in the tax and transfer system.

When using MITTS, it should be borne in mind that it is a supply-side partial equilibrium model. In particular, the behavioural component, MITTS-B, concentrates on examining the effects of changes in the tax structure on variations in the hours of work that individuals wish to supply. No allowance is made for the demand for labour. Hence, in interpreting the output from MITTS, it should be recognised that, depending on what happens to the demand for labour, individuals may not in reality be able to work their desired number of hours; they may be constrained as a result of demand-side considerations. Large changes in the tax structure, designed for example to increase the labour force participation of benefit recipients, may also have effects on the demand for labour. In addition, changes in the tax and transfer system are assumed to have no effect on individuals' wage rates, so that general equilibrium considerations are ignored.

## 10.1   The Main Features of MITTS

The main features of MITTS can be listed as follows.

1. MITTS is operated via a user-friendly 'front end' which provides a series of menus. Choices are available for selecting alternative tax systems, data sets, and analyses.

2. Tax reforms can be examined using a choice of Australian Bureau of Statistics Confidential Unit Record Files (CURFs). MITTS contains the Income Distribution Surveys for 1994, 1995, 1996 and 1997.[1] The interview period for the IDS is the twelve months running from July to the following June. Hence, reference to IDS survey, IDS$t$, means that weekly incomes are based on financial year $t$ to $t+1$. However, annual incomes are for the financial year $t-1$ to $t$.

3. When using MITTS, two tax and transfer systems must be selected for analysis. These are referred to as pre-reform and post-reform systems, and can be selected in two basic ways, as follows.

   (a) The tax systems can be selected from a range of previously stored systems.

   (b) It is possible to modify an existing tax and transfer system interactively using a set of menus. Considerable flexibility in altering the

---

[1] The 1997 survey was, at the time of writing, the latest available.

tax system is allowed. Hence substantial reforms can be examind without the need to alter the basic programming code.

4. For each tax system, MITTS calculates the gross and net incomes of each individual, household and tax unit in the data base. Two options are available. First, MITTS-A produces an arithmetic calculation of changes in net incomes on the assumption that all gross earnings are fixed. Second, MITTS-B can allow for the probable variations in labour supply of each individual, using the econometric estimates of preference functions (as described in Part II).

5. Government expenditures on benefits, and tax revenues, can be updated to specified years.

6. For individuals who are not working during the sample period, and for whom a wage rate is therefore not observed, MITTS assigns a wage rate, based on econometric estimates of wage functions (as described in Part II, chapter 3). Individuals are assumed to work in a single job, at which they are paid a fixed wage rate, irrespective of the number of hours worked.

7. MITTS-B uses econometric estimates of quadratic direct utility functions defined in terms of consumption (net income) and leisure.

8. MITTS provides details of the effects of changing the tax system on the benefit levels and net incomes of individuals.

9. MITTS produces, for each individual, the precise nature of the budget constraint, in terms of relationship between the number of hours worked and net income (consumption). Given the individual's observed or imputed wage rate, it provides details of the variation in net income as the number of hours of work increases, under each specified tax system.

The algorithm used to obtain budget constraints is described in Part II.

10. Details are provided of the reasons for each discontinuity and kink in each individual's budget constraint.

11. MITTS allows individual budget constraints to be printed. Detailed breakdowns of the components of net income at each point in the budget constraints are also provided in bar charts.

12. It is possible to examine, for each tax system, the relationship between hours worked and net income for particular hypothetical types of household, according to specified demographic characteristics and wage rates.

13. MITTS contains a user-friendly 'back end' which allows, through a set of menus, the calculation of summary measures of distributional changes. These include Lorenz curves of net income, changes in a variety of inequality measures, a range of poverty measures and diagrams showing the incidence and intensity of poverty.

14. MITTS produces, using a set of menus, a wide variety of summary tables showing the characteristics of gainers and losers from the specified tax structure change.

15. It is possible to move directly from a cell of each summary table (for example, of gainers and losers from a tax reform) to an examination of those individuals and households who appear in the cell. The characteristics of these individuals and households can be changed interactively to study the effect of a change on the net income and benefit payments.

16. MITTS calculates the overall tax revenue and expenditure effects of a tax policy change.

17. Diagrams and tables can be printed or pasted into documents. MITTS also enables the tables to be written to other files for further analysis using other software, such as spreadsheets.

## 10.2 The Structure of MITTS

This section provides a broad description of the basic structure of MITTS.

### 10.2.1 Data Input Files

1. MITTS is based on the (Australian) Income Distribution Survey (IDS). The surveys for the four years 1994, 1995, 1996 and 1997 are available in MITTS. The IDS is the only Australian cross-sectional survey containing hours of work in a continuous form. This information is required both for the simulations and the labour supply estimation of the model.

2. The IDS surveys have been transformed so that the data can be read by MITTS along with all the variable names.

3. Most of the variables have been re-coded so that they have names instead of code numbers. This makes it possible to present the output in a form that is more easily read.

### 10.2.2 Data Transformations

The data contained in the Data Input File (the modified IDS file) undergo a series of transformations in preparation for modelling. The data transformations use several inputs, as follows:

1. Weighting factors provide information about the number of each type of household in the population. This means that, for example, the aggregate revenue and expenditure values reflect national aggregates and the distributional analysis represents the Australian population rather than the sample characteristics.

2. Uprating factors make it possible to examine values corresponding to the current calendar year, although the basic Data Input File inevitably contains information relating to an earlier year (1994, 1995, 1996 and 1997). For example, wage indexation rates are used along with appropriate rates for adjusting tax and benefit thresholds.

3. Data imputations are required. The most important of these concerns the wages of non-workers.

## 10.2.3   Wage Equations

It is necessary to assign an appropriate wage rate to those individuals in the sample who did not work during the sample period. This is because no observed wage rate is directly available. The required rates are obtained by estimating wage equations using the observed wages of workers; the procedure used is described in detail in chapter 3. For those who do work, wage rates can be obtained directly from information about gross earnings and hours worked in the IDS. Allowance is made for selectivity bias arising from the use of a sample consisting only of workers.

The demographic information about each non-working individual is used in order to produce an appropriate imputed wage. The imputed wages provide an input into the behavioural model, the estimation of labour supply behaviour, and the production of the budget constraints for non-workers.

Estimation of wages of non-workers includes:

1. Division of the IDS population into five demographic groups. These are sole parents; single males; single females; married males; married females.

2. Estimation, for each demographic group, of probit equations whereby employment status is determined as a function of individual characteristics, such as education, location, and age.

3. Estimation of wage functions for each demographic group. The wage rate for each individual is expressed as a function of a number of characteristics. These wage functions allow for any bias arising from the use of a sample containing only those who work, and whose wage rate is known. This is achieved by the addition of a variable for each individual, the 'inverse Mills ratio', calculated from the probit equations.

4. In imputing the wages of non-workers, extraneous information about the industry and occupation characteristics of non-workers are used. These are, on average, different from those of workers.

### 10.2.4 The Tax System

The Tax System component of MITTS contains the procedures for applying each type of tax and benefit. Each tax structure has a data file containing the required tax and benefit rates, benefit levels, and income thresholds used in means testing. In view of the data limitations of the IDS, it is not possible to include within MITTS all of the complexity of the tax and transfer system.

Changes to the tax and benefit structure, including the introduction of additional taxes, can be modelled by editing this component. MITTS stores several previous Australian tax and transfer systems which can be used as bases for the analysis of policy changes.

It is also possible to generate a new tax system by introducing various types of policy change interactively when using MITTS. This enables new tax structures to be generated without the need for additional programming.

### 10.2.5 Take-up Rates

Ideally, it would be useful to model take-up rates for each of the types of benefit at the same time as labour supply behaviour is modelled. Take-up rates may depend on the level of the benefit for which the individual is eligible, along with the income level and demographic structure of the household. This is considerably complicated by the fact that take-up rates are in general expected to depend on the levels and conditions applying to benefits. MITTS obtains the benefits to which all individuals are entitled, rather than using actual benefits received. It therefore assumes 100 per cent take-up of benefits. Further work is planned on this aspect of MITTS in future.

## 10.2.6   Budget Constraints

A crucial ingredient of the labour supply analysis, in addition to the information on preferences from the behavioural model component, consists of the budget constraints for each individual. These constraints in turn require output generated by the arithmetic component, MITTS-A. Regarding budget constraints, MITTS contains the following features.

1. MITTS contains an algorithm for constructing the exact form of the budget constraint in an efficient manner. The algorithm used is superior to an alternative approach consisting of numerically evaluating the relationship between gross and net income for a specified range of hours worked. Such an approch would be more cumbersome and may not identify the precise location of kinks in the budget constraint. The algorithm is described in chapter 4.

2. MITTS provides the ability to produce a detailed description of each individual's budget constraint, providing graphs of net income against hours worked under alternative tax structures.

3. A description of the reason for each kink or discontinuity in the budget constraint is provided in tabular form for both tax structures examined.

### 10.2.7 MITTS-A

MITTS-A is the arithmetic tax and benefit modelling component of the analysis of the effects of a specified tax reform. It assumes that labour supplies are fixed. This component also provides, using the wage rate of each individual, the information needed for the construction of the budget constraints that are crucial for the analysis of behavioural responses to tax changes.

The Tax System component is directly linked to MITTS-A, and *vice versa*. MITTS assembles the various components of the tax and benefit structure in the required way in order to work out the transformation between hours worked and net income for each individual under each tax system. For example, some benefits are taxable while others are not, so the order in which taxes and transfers are evaluated is important. MITTS-A contains the following facilities.

1. It is possible to examine each household, income unit and individual in the selected IDS in turn, and to display major relevant demographic characteristics along with taxes and benefits received. This component of MITTS also allows comparisons to be made with results obtained from other Australian non-behavioural tax-benefit models.

2. MITTS-A allows the production of net incomes for each individual in the IDS, at the given hourly wage rate, for variations in the number of hours worked. The facility to examine budget constraints and net incomes for hypothetical households.

3. Distributions of effective marginal tax rates, for a variety of demographic groups, are produced for pre-reform and post-reform tax systems.

4. Distributions of gainers and losers, for various demographic characteristics, can be produced. It is possible to move from cells of these tables to identify specific individuals.

## 10.2.8   MITTS-B

MITTS-B is the behavioural component of MITTS. It examines the effects of a specified tax reform, allowing individuals to adjust their labour supply behaviour where appropriate. The behavioural responses generated by MITTS-B are based on the use of quadratic preference functions whereby the parameters are allowed to vary with an individual's characteristics. These parameters have been estimated for five demographic groups, which include married or partnered men and women, single men and women, and sole parents (as described in chapters 7 and 8). The joint labour supply of couples is estimated simultaneously, contrary to the popular approach in which female labour supply is estimated with the spouse's labour supply taken as exogenous. The framework is one in which individuals are considered as being constrained to select from a discrete set of hours levels, rather than being able to vary labour supply continuously. Different sets of discrete hours points are used for each demographic group.

For those individuals in the data set who are not working, and who therefore do not report a wage rate, an imputed wage is obtained. This imputed wage is based on estimated wage functions, which allow for possible selectivity bias, by first estimating probit equations for labour market participation (as described in chapter 3 above). However, some individuals are excluded from the database if their imputed wage or their observed wage (obtained by dividing total earnings by the number of hours worked) is unrealistic.

The simulation is essentially probabilistic. That is, it does not identify a particular level of hours worked for each individual after the policy change, but generates a probability distribution over the discrete hours levels used. For this reason the present version of MITTS-B does not produce distributional analyses of the effects of tax reforms on net incomes. Some individuals, such as the self employed, the disabled, students and those over 65 have their labour supply fixed at their observed hours.

The behavioural simulations begin by taking the discrete hours level for each individual that is closest to the observed hours level. Then, given the parameter estimates of the quadratic preference function (which vary according to a range of characteristics), a random draw is taken from the distribution of the 'error' term. This draw is rejected if it results in an optimal hours level that differs from the discretised value observed. The accepted drawings are then used in the determination of the optimal hours level after the policy change. A user-specified total number of 'successful draws' (that is, drawings which generate the observed hours as the optimal value under the base system for the individual) are produced. This gives rise to a probability distribution over the set of discrete hours for each individual under the new tax and transfer structure. In computing the transition matrices showing probabilities of movement between hours levels, the labour supply of each individual before the policy change is fixed at the discretised value, and a number of transitions are produced for each individual, equal to the number of successful draws specified.

When examining average hours in MITTS-B, the labour supply after the change for each individual is based on the average value over the successful draws, for which the error term leads to the correct predicted hours before the change. This is equivalent to calculating the expected hours of labour supply after the change, conditional on starting from the observed hours before the change. In computing the tax and revenue levels, an expected value is also obtained after the policy change. That is, the tax and revenue for each of the accepted draws are computed for each individual, and the average of these is taken.

In some cases, the required number of successful random draws producing observed hours as the optimal hours cannot be generated from the model within a reasonable number of total drawings. The number of random draws tried, like the number of successful draws required, is specified by the user. If after the total draws from the error term distribution, the model fails to predict the observed labour supply a sufficient number of times, the individual is dropped from the simulation. For example, the total number of attempts may be specified as 5,000, where the required number of successful draws may be 100. The use of such a probabilistic approach means that the run-time of MITTS-B is substantially longer than that of MITTS-A.

## 10.3    Conclusions

This chapter has provided a generation introduction to, and description of, the MITTS simulation model. The installation of MITTS is described in the next chapter.

# Chapter 11

# Installing MITTS

This chapter describes the installation of the MITTS package and the associated data files. The file structure is also provided.

MITTS is written in GAUSS and requires the DOS version 3.2.14, or later, of GAUSS. In the following description it is assumed that GAUSS is placed in a directory c:\gauss. First it is necessary to edit (using an ASCII editor) the file GAUSS.CFG to ensure that there is sufficient memory allocated. Change the appropriate line so that it reads: max_workspace = 50.

Installation of MITTS involves preparation of the basic IDS data files and the program itself. In most cases Windows software, such as Windows Explorer and WinZip can be used. However, appropriate DOS commands are also given.

Computer keys to be pressed are indicated using italics. Commands which need to be typed, following the DOS command prompt, after which the *enter* key must be pressed, are indicated within rectangular boxes.

## 11.1 Data Installation

Analyses using MITTS can be based on one of several Australian Income Distribution Surveys (IDS). The present version of MITTS allows for the use of surveys for 1994, 1995, 1996 and 1997. The following instructions are for the 1995 survey. In order to install the other IDSs, simply replace 95 with the appropriate date (either 94, 96 or 97) at each stage.

1. From the root directory, make a directory called IDS95. This can be achieved using the DOS command $\boxed{\text{mkdir ids95}}$. Then move to this directory, using the DOS command $\boxed{\text{cd\textbackslash ids95}}$.

2. Insert the disk marked IDS95 into the floppy disk drive and copy the file IDS95.ZIP into the IDS95 directory, using $\boxed{\text{copy a:ids95.zip}}$.

3. Unzip the file. This can be done using either WinZip or the DOS version, PKUNZIP, using the command $\boxed{\text{pkunzip ids95.zip}}$. This produces the three files:

   (a) IDS95URT.DAT

   (b) IDS_VARS.TXT

   (c) READ_IDS.E.

4. The first file contains the basic IDS data for 1995; the second file contains a list of variable names for use by MITTS; the third file contains a program to carry out the required data transformation.

## 11.1.1   Data Preparation

1. Start GAUSS, and go to the directory IDS95. To change the directory in GAUSS, enter the command $\boxed{\text{dos cd\textbackslash ids95}}$. The current directory in GAUSS is indicated in the bottom right hand corner of the screen.

2. Run the program READ_IDS.E by entering command $\boxed{\text{run read\_ids.e}}$. This program takes several minutes to run. It creates four files, as follows:

   (a) IDS95_IN.DAT

    (b) IDS95_IN.DHT

    (c) IDS95_PR.DAT

    (d) IDS95_PR.DHT.

3. Files with the extension .DHT are GAUSS data files of the corresponding ASCII files, with a .DAT extension.

## 11.2 Installing MITTS

1. Create a sub-directory of the C:\GAUSS directory, called MITTS. If using DOS, from the c:\gauss directory enter the command $\boxed{\text{mkdir mitts}}$. Move to this directory, using the DOS command $\boxed{\text{cd mitts}}$.

2. Insert the disk market MITTS into the floppy disk drive and copy the file MITTS.ZIP into the MITTS directory. The DOS command is $\boxed{\text{copy a:mitts.zip}}$.

3. Unzip the MITTS.ZIP file. If WinZip is being used, ensure that that the option 'retain folders' is selected. Alternatively, use the DOS command $\boxed{\text{pkunzip -d mitts.zip}}$. The option to retain folders is necessary because a number of separate folders are created, containing different groups of files. Details are given in the following section.

## 11.3 The MITTS File Structure

This section provides further details of the MITTS file structure. On installation, the MITTS.ZIP file is placed in the c:\gauss\mitts subdirectory. When MITTS is run, a further set of subdirectories is created, leading from the c:\gauss\mitts directory. These contain groups of data files or procedures and are described as follows.

### 11.3.1   Mitts

1. Mitts.e is the main file needed to runs MITTS

2. Mitts is the default file containing simulation results concerning government revenues and costs

3. Graphic.tkf contains the output of the last diagram produced when running MITTS. It can be loaded into other software that is capable of handling or converting graphics files.

### 11.3.2   Benefits

This subdirectory (c:\gauss\mitts\benefits) contains the gauss procedures used to compute benefits.

1. AgePen.prc - Age pension

2. Allow.prc - Allocates individuals to particular allowances. It also calls the particular allowance procedure and determines entitlements.

3. Austudy.prc - AUSTUDY (post-July 2000)

4. AusYTA.prc - AUSTUDY (pre-July 2000)

5. CarerPay.prc - Carer Payment

6. DSPen.prc - Disability Support Pension

7. DVADis.prc - Department of Veterans Affairs Disability Pension

8. DVAPen.prc - Allocates individuals to particular Department of Veterans Affairs pensions. It also calls the particular DVA pension procedure and determines entitlements.

9. DVAServ.prc - Department of Veterans Affairs Service Pension

10. DVAWWP.prc - Department of Veterans Affairs War Widows Pension and Income Support Supplement.

11. Family.prc - Determining whether Family Allowance or Family Tax Benefit is to be called.

12. FamPay.prc - Family Allowance/Payment. It also calculates Family Tax Payment/Assistance entitlements.

13. FamTBen.prc - Family Tax Benefit Parts (A) and (B)

14. FlatTax.prc - Negative Income Tax

15. MatAge.prc - Mature Age Allowance

16. Newstart.prc - Newstart Allowance

17. ParntPay.prc - Parenting Payment

18. Partner.prc - Partner Allowance

19. Pension.prc - Allocating individuals to particular pensions. It also calls the particular pension procedure and determines entitlements.

20. RentAss.prc - Determines maximum entitlements to Rent Assistance based on family circumstances and rent paid.

21. ResAllow.prc - Allocating individuals to residual allowances, that is, Special Benefit or Partner Allowance. It also calls the particular allowance procedure and determines entitlements.

22. Sickness.prc - Sickness Allowance

23. SpecBen.prc - Special Benefit

24. WidBPen.prc - Widow B Pension

25. Widow.prc - Widow Allowance

26. WifePen.prc - Wife Pension

27. YouthAll.prc - Youth Allowance

28. YthTrain.prc - Youth Training Allowance

### 11.3.3   Data

This subdirectory (c:\gauss\mitts\data) contains the various data files used by MITTS.

1. B_hh5.fmt - Labour supply parameters

2. B_sm2.fmt - Labour supply parameters

3. B_sp5.fmt - Labour supply parameters

4. B_sw2.fmt - Labour supply parameters

5. Betas.dat/dht - Wage equation parameters needed for imputing wages for non-workers.

6. Deflate.dat/dht - Average weekly wage deflators

7. Femawe.dat/dht - Female average weekly wage deflators needed for uprating.

8. Gammas.dat/dht - Selection equation parameters needed for imputing wages.

9. Maleawe.dat/dht - Male average weekly earnings deflators needed for uprating.

10. Mind.dat/dht - Average proportion of employed persons in each industry (needed for imputing wages of non-workers).

11. Mindur.dat/dht - Average proportion of unemployed persons in each industry taken from labour force data (needed for imputing wages of non-workers).

12. Mocc.dat/dht - Average proportion of employed persons in each occupation group (needed for imputing wages of non-workers).

13. Moccur.dat/dht - Average proportion of unemployed persons in each occupation group taken from labour force data (needed for imputing wages of non-workers).

14. Xx_in.fmt

15. Xx_pr.fmt

### 11.3.4 NetInc

This subdirectory (c:\gauss\mitts\netinc) contains the Gauss procedure used to compute net incomes. There is just one file.

1. NetInc.prc - Calculates net incomes

### 11.3.5 Programs

This subdirectory (c:\gauss\mitts\programs) contains a range of Gauss procedures used when running MITTS.

1. Assets.prc - Imputes household assets (currently returns zeros)

2. Back_end.prc - Calculates winners and losers, inequality measures, poverty measure and marginal effective tax rate results.

3. ClearSys - Clears parameters needed for tax systems.

4. Data.prc - Defines openfile procedure, seekhh procedure. Also defines data transformation procedures (datatran performs the transformations and tranfile applies them using seekhh). Data transformations include uprating, imputing certain information such as assets and parental income, recoding numeric variables to string variables, and generating equivalence scale information.

5. DTran.prc - Performs data transformations needed for imputing wages

6. Equiv1.prc - Equivalence scales

7. FindKink.prc - Algorithm to find kinks in individuals budget constraints.

8. Frontend.prc - Presents all tax system information to screen enabling user to run simulations interactively.

9. Hours.prc - Defines the range of discrete hours over which labour supply behaviour is simulated.

10. IneqMenu.prc - Sets up menu for inequality and poverty measure settings.

11. Input.inc - Creates menus to enable interactive use of MITTS.

12. List.prc - Adjusts parameters of the tax system

13. Pickyear.prc - Opens data file depending on year chosen by user

14. Pincome.prc - Imputes parental income for dependent students living away from home, needed for Youth Allowance.

15. PredWage.prc - Calculates imputed wages for non-workers.

16. PrintBC.prc - Plots budget constraints.

17. ReadSys - Reads tax system parameters for simulation RiteMain.prc

18. RunMitts.prc - Runs simulation of MITTS-A. Specifies variables to be written to data file (note that this data file is what is called when generating split groups for results whether it be winners and losers, inequality, marginal effective tax rates or poverty measures.

19. RunSim.prc - Runs simulation of MITTS-B.

20. ShowHH.prc - Generates household information to be written to screen. This includes calculation of net incomes; that is, it calls MittCalc procedure found in NetInc.prc

21. Sysset.prc - Determines tax systems to be used in simulation

22. Tabulate.prc - Defines many procedures used in back_end.prc. Defines tabulate procedure which is a called when output needs to be tabulated; Bar_Diff procedure which is called when bar charts average income changes are graphed; GenCount procedure which generates information for tables of winners and losers; MetrTab which is used to generate tables of METR differences and; a range of procedures which generate various inequality and poverty measures which are all used in the Inequal procedure.

23. Uprate.prc - Defines procedure uprating all income data in base file

24. Utility.prc - Household utility specifications for behavioural simulations

25. Virtual.prg - Generates virtual incomes and net marginal effective wage rates.

26. WriteSys - Writes tax systems updated interactively to file

### 11.3.6   Rebates

This subdirectory (c:\gauss\mitts\rebates) contains the Gauss procedures used to compute rebates.

1. BenReb.prc - Beneficiary Rebate

2. DSRReb.prc - Dependent Spouse Rebate

3. LIRebate.prc - Low Income Rebate

4. Prebate.prc - Pension rebate

5. SPPReb.prc - Sole Parent Pensioner rebate

6. SPRebate.prc - Sole Parent Rebate

### 11.3.7   Results

This subdirectory (c:\gauss\mitts\results) contains any files saved during the running of MITTS.

### 11.3.8   Systems

This subdirectory (c:\gauss\mitts\systems) contains various tax system parameter files. These include, for example:

1. ANTS.tbp - A New Tax System (July 2000)

2. Jan00.tbp - January 2000

3. July98.tbp - July 1998 (Youth Allowance introduced)

4. March98.tbp - March 1998

5. March99.tbp - March 1999

## 11.3.9 Tax&ML

This subdirectory (c:\gauss\mitts\tax&ml) contains the Gauss procedures used to compute income taxation and the Medicare Levy.

1. AssessI.prc - Calculates assessable income needed to determine eligibility for allowances

2. IncomTax.prc - Income Tax procedure

3. Medicare.prc - Medicare Levy procedure

# Chapter 12

# Using MITTS

This chapter describes the way in which MITTS can be used to examine a policy change. In designing MITTS, ease of use has been a primary objective. MITTS is operated by moving between a series of menus. Choices are available for selecting alternative tax systems, data sets and types of analysis.

Section 12.1 describes the basic method of starting MITTS. A broad description of the general sequence of operations and the way in which MITTS may be used is given in section 12.1.2. The choice of alternative tax systems and modification of tax structures is described in section 12.2. The procedures involved in running MITTS-A and producing summary results of tax reforms are described in section 12.3. MITTS-B is described in section 12.4. The selection of individuals and households from the data file, or the examination of hypothetical households, is described in section 12.5. Further comments on handling the output from MITTS are made in section 12.6.

## 12.1 Starting MITTS

1. Start GAUSS, and go to the directory C:\GAUSS\MITTS, using the command $\boxed{\text{dos cd mitts}}$.

2. Start the main program MITTS.E by entering the GAUSS command $\boxed{\text{run mitts.e}}$.

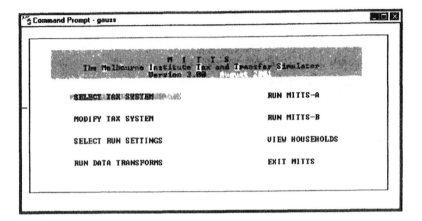

Figure 12.1: The Main Menu

After a few seconds the main menu appears. This is shown in Figure 12.1. MITTS should now be ready for use.

When running GAUSS, it may be shown within a separate window or occupy the full screen: simultaneously hitting the keys *alt* and *enter* toggles between a window and full screen.[1]

If MITTS crashes for any reason, simultaneously pressing the *ctrl* and *home* keys returns control to the GAUSS command prompt, allowing MITTS to be run again. Then enter the command | mainmenu | to use the set-up when the crash took place, or restart entirely.

Movement between menu items is achieved using the standard direction keys. Operating the highlighted menu choice is achieved by hitting the *enter* key.

---

[1] The size of the window can be adjusted as required: click on the right mouse button and use the options available under 'properties'.

### 12.1.1  Data Transforms

After first installing MITTS it is necessary to prepare each of the IDS datasets for further analysis. For each of the IDS surveys in turn, use the 'Select run settings' option to select the required year and then select the 'Run data transforms' option from the main menu. This takes several minutes to cycle through the data. After the transforms have been run for each year of data, it is not necessary to use this option again.

### 12.1.2  The General Procedure

The first thing to do when using MITTS is to select two tax and transfer systems for analysis, as described in the following section. These are referred to as the 'first system' (pre-reform) and 'second system' (post-reform). If an attempt is made to run MITTS-A or MITTS-B or to examine households before the tax structures are specified, MITTS requests details.

After selecting the two tax systems, the cost and distributional implications of the alternative systems, along with various effects of the reform, can be examined. It is possible to examine, first, the aggregate revenue and distributional effects of a policy change using either MITTS-A or MITTS-B and, second, the effects on particular individuals and households (including specific households contained in the IDS and hypothetical households). These facilities are described in turn below.

## 12.2  Alternative Tax Systems

### 12.2.1  Selecting Tax Systems

The option 'Select Tax System' from the main menu gives the choices shown in Figure 12.2. On highlighting 'select first system' and hitting *enter*, a choice of several Australian tax systems is displayed. After selecting one of these, the second tax system must then be chosen. It is possible to select one of

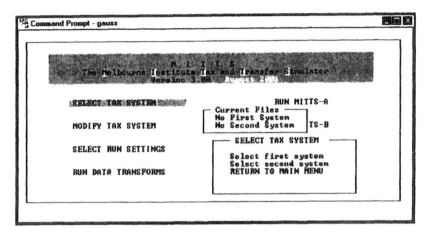

Figure 12.2: Selecting Tax Systems

the systems that are already programmed or to copy the first system. A tax reform can then be examined by suitably modifying the second tax system, using the options described in the following subsection.

The tax systems from which selections can be made include the following: March 1998, July 1998 (Youth Allowance introduced), March 1999, January 2000, ANTS (A New Tax System, July 2000).

## 12.2.2   Modifying Tax Systems

It is possible to make a large number of modifications to the selected tax and transfer systems using the choices available under the 'Modify Tax System' option in the main menu. Selecting this option gives rise to the menu shown in Figure 12.3.

For example, selection of the option, income taxes and rebates, gives the window shown in 12.4. To make alterations, use the direction keys to move to the different features. Then hit *enter*, and a box will appear round the items that can be modified. Moving to each item in turn, using the direction

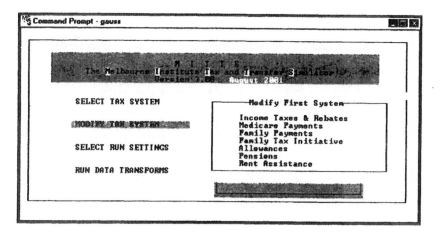

Figure 12.3: Modifying Tax Systems

keys, gives rise to a description of that item in the bottom left hand corner of the screen. To make a change, highlight the item, hit *enter*, and then type the new value. Press *esc* and then respond to the invitation to save the change, which appears in the bottom left hand corner of the window. After responding (y/n), press *esc* to return to the 'modify first system' window. Further changes can then be made as required.

If it is required to delete a row of rates and thresholds, move to the relevant row and press *del*. In order to add a row, move to the required position, hit *insert* and then enter the values as required. Again, after making the changes, press *esc* and follow the invitation to save the changes.

A large variety of changes to a tax and benefit system can be carried out, involving a large number of features of the tax system, by repeatedly carrying out the procedures outlined in the previous subsection. The changes may be made to either the first or second tax system chosen.

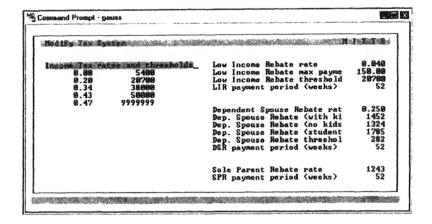

Figure 12.4: Modifying Income Taxation

## 12.2.3   Saving New Systems

For some purposes it is desired to save the generated tax system for future analysis. This is done as follows. Suppose the first tax system has been changed. After returning to the 'modify first system' window, pressing *esc* displays a window with the invitation to 'save first system'. If it is not required to save the system for future use, press *esc* again, and a message 'system not saved' is displayed.

By responding positively, an invitation is given to name the new system. Simply type in a name without a file extension, and press *enter*. MITTS automatically adds the required extension (.TBP) and places the file in the c:\gauss\mitts\systems subdirectory. Then, enter a brief description of the new system. This description appears at the head of the new .tbp file as a reminder.

## 12.3 Running MITTS-A

### 12.3.1 Run Settings

Before actually running MITTS-A it is necessary to specify a range of run settings, using the 'Run Settings' option in the main menu. The selections are as follows:

1. Choice of IDS

2. Upratings setting

3. Equivalence scales

Select the required item and press *enter* for further options. The first item allows for choice of the required IDS survey (1994, 1995, 1996 or 1997).

When 'uprating settings' is chosen, the menu shown in Figure 12.5 is displayed. The choice is given to uprate the data: select yes or no by pressing the space bar. The answer 'yes' means that the data are adjusted to the same year as the tax and transfer system selected. The final costs can then be adjusted to a specified year and quarter. These adjustments use the retail price index. The choice of an index for uprating wage rates can also be made.

The equivalence scales option gives a choice of Whiteford or OECD scales, as shown in Table 12.1. Alternatively, an option is available to specify user-defined equivalence scales.

Table 12.1: Equivalence Scales

| Scale | Head | Spouse | Other Adult | Child |
|-------|------|--------|-------------|-------|
| Whiteford | 1 | 0.52 | 0.52 | 0.32 |
| OECD | 1 | 0.70 | 0.5 | 0.5 |

These scales are used in the distributional analyses.

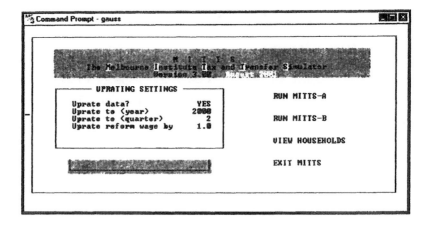

Figure 12.5:  Upratings Settings

## 12.3.2   Run MITTS-A

Selection of the menu option Run MITTS-A produces a further set of menu choices shown in Figure 12.6. When the Run MITTS-A option is selected, a box is displayed indicating the simulation file. This file is given the default name of 'mitts', and is placed in the subdirectory c:\gauss\mitts\results. It contains the results relating to the costs of a simulation run. If desired, a user-specified output filename can be given by selecting the option 'Simulation file name'. Follow the instruction to type a file name (limited to a maximum of eight characters). This named file is placed in the subdirectory c:\gauss\mitts\results.

The 'simulation settings' option produces the choice shown in Figure 12.7. This allows for the choice of range of households to examine from the IDS. The default values cover all households in the survey. A further choice involves the decision to weight the cost and revenue information using the IDS weights, so that they represent population values rather than sample values.

It is possible to run MITTS-A for a specified population group. Selection

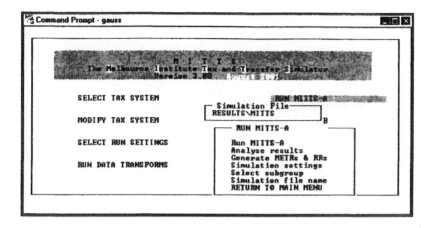

Figure 12.6: MITTS-A Menu

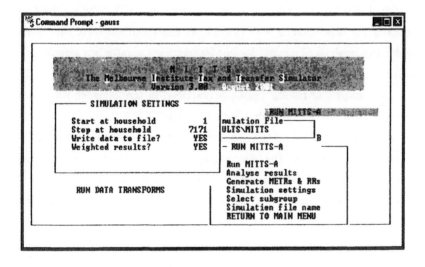

Figure 12.7: Simulation Settings

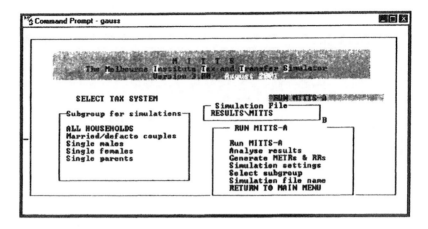

Figure 12.8: Selection of Simulation Group

of the option 'select subgroup' gives the options shown in Figure 12.8.

The 'Generate METRs and RRs' option generates information about marginal effective tax rates and replacement rates. This option must be selected if it is later required to examine various distributions of these rates under the 'analysis of results' option. Generating the rates is a lengthy procedure.

The 'analysis of results' option is described in the following subsection below and can be selected only after running MITTS-A.

To begin the analysis of the specified tax reform, select the 'Run MITTS-A' option. This provides the basic aggregate effects of the tax reform examined. This takes several minutes, depending on the speed of the computer being used. An indication is given of the estimated running time and costs, as shown in the screen illustrated in Figure 12.9.

The costs are given in $millions, and are aggregates based on weighting factors given in the IDS. During the running time, it is possible to view details of Allowances, Pensions, and Rebates by hitting the $a$, $p$ and $r$ keys respectively. To return to the Main Costings, hit the $m$ key.

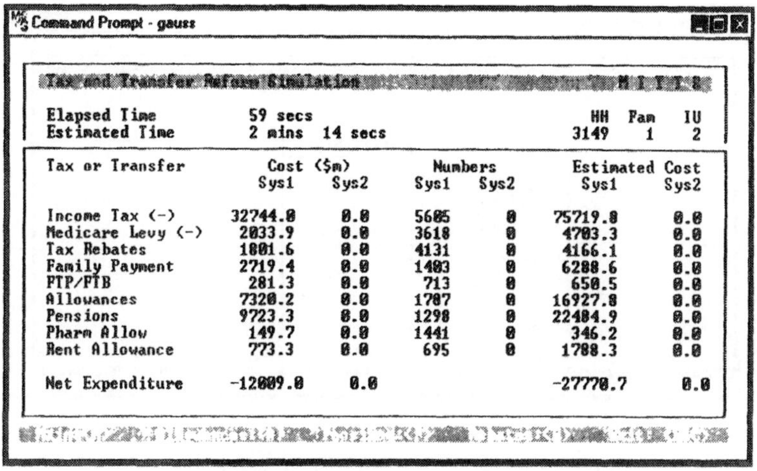

Figure 12.9: A MITTS-A Run

The run can be stopped at any time by pressing *esc*. This causes the run to stop: it does not cause MITTS-A simply to pause.

When the run is complete, hit any key to return to the menu. After pressing *esc* or when the run is complete, tables are automatically written to the simulation file (either the default or the named file).

## 12.3.3  Analysis of Results

Selection of the 'Analyse Results' option from the Run MITTS-A sub-menu displays the further choices shown in Figure 12.10. The items indicated along the bottom of the screen include the choice of

1. Winners and losers

2. Income changes

3. Inequality

4. METRs and Rep Rates

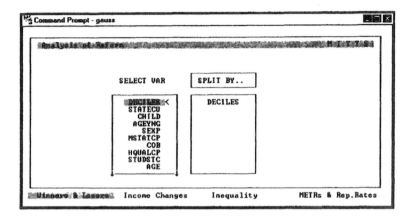

Figure 12.10: Selection of Categories for Analysis

In each case the analyses can be carried out for a range of characteristics. When selecting one of these options, a range of income unit categories and individual characteristics of the income unit head is listed, as also shown in Figure 12.10.

The choice of categories to be examined is achieved by moving through the list of options displayed in the left-hand window shown in Figure 12.10, using the direction keys, and then making the selection of the highlighted option by pressing the *space bar*. The categories are listed using the abbreviations provided by the IDS. These are defined in Table 12.2 and, where relevant, refer to the characteristics of the head of the income unit.

The selected categories move into the right-hand window. After selecting the required categories, press *enter*. The results for the first category selected are then displayed. To move to the next table on the list, press *esc*.

When selecting 'income differences', charts such as that in Figure 12.11, for deciles, are given.

Figure 12.12 gives an example of a table of Gainers and Losers, divided into age groups. This type of table can be saved using the Alt-S option given

Table 12.2: Categories

| No. | Item | Description |
|---|---|---|
| 1 | DECILES | Household income decile |
| 2 | IUTYPEP | Income unit type |
| 3 | HHTYPEC | Household type |
| 4 | FAMTYPE | Family type |
| 5 | STATECU | State of residence |
| 6 | CHILD | No. of dep children in unit |
| 7 | AGEYNG | Age of youngest child |
| 8 | SEXP | Gender |
| 9 | TENURECU | Tenure type |
| 10 | MSTATCP | Marital status |
| 11 | COB | Country of birth |
| 12 | HQUALCP | Highest educational qualification |
| 13 | STUDSTC | Study status |
| 14 | AGE | Age |
| 15 | EMPSTAT | Employment status |
| 16 | AREAU | Resident in capital city |
| 17 | OCCCP | Occupation in major job |
| 18 | INDCP | Industry of major job |
| 19 | DWELLCU | Dwelling type |

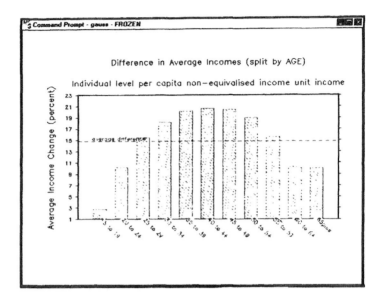

Figure 12.11: Income Changes

on the bottom of the window, as shown in Figure 12.12. After this option
is selected, follow the instruction to name the file. This file is automatically
placed in the c:\gauss\mitts\results subdirectory with other output files.
Then follow the instruction to provide a file description: this is placed at
the head of the file as a convenient reminder. The file automatically adds
information about which tax systems are used.

### From Cells to Households

It is possible to examine specific households falling into each of the cells of the
table. For example, in the case of the table shown in Figure 12.12, pressing
the *F7* key produces a screen in which the selected cell is indicated along
the bottom of the screen. In order to select the desired row (in this case the
age group, that is, whichever household characteristic is relevant), use the
up and down direction keys. In order to select the column of the table, use

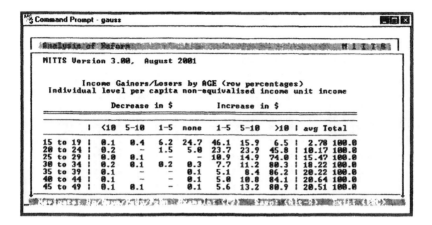

Figure 12.12: Gainers and Losers

the left and right direction keys.

After selecting the cell, hit the *enter* key. The screen will then display the details for one of the households in that cell. To view other households, press the *n* or *p* keys, for 'next' and 'previous' respectively; up to 20 households from each cell may be viewed in this way. Further analysis of each specific household is described in more detail in section 12.5 below. To return to the original table, hit *esc*.

**Marginal Tax Rates and Replacement Rates**

If the 'generate METRs and RRs' option has previously been selected from the 'Run MITTS-A' submenu, it is possible to obtain a large variety of distributions of marginal effective tax and replacement rates. Selecting the 'METRs and Rep Rates' option from the 'Analyse Results' submenu gives the choice of the following:

1. METRs (system 1)

2. METRs (system 2)

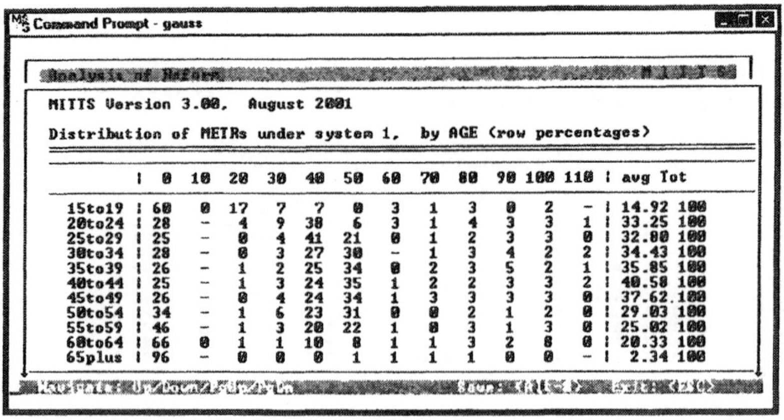

*CHAPTER 12.  USING MITTS*

Figure 12.13:  An Example of METRs

3. RRs (system 1)

4. RRs (system 2)

5. METRs (diffs)

6. RRs (diffs)

For each of these choices, tables can be obtained for the categories listed in Table 12.2 above. Selection is carried out as before, using the direction keys to highlight a category and then pressing the space bar. Hitting *enter* produces the required tables. An example of a table of distributions of effective marginal tax rates for each age group is shown in Table 12.13. Similarly, an example of distributions of replacement rates for each age group are shown in Table 12.14. The term 'diffs' in the last two options refers to distributions of changes in the rates as a result of a policy change.

```
Command Prompt - gauss                                                    _ □ ✕

  Analysis of Reform                                                    M I T T S

  MITTS Version 3.00,   August 2001

  Distribution of RRs under system 1,  by AGE (percent)
  ══════════════════════════════════════════════════════════════════════════

             I  0  10  20  30  40  50  60  70  80  90 100 110 I avg Tot
  15to19  I   -   -   6  24  36  12  11   8   2   1   -   - I 38.35 100
  20to24  I   -   -   6   8  15   8  10  25  24   3   0   - I 54.83 100
  25to29  I   -   -   0   4   8   7  13  30  20   9   0   - I 62.46 100
  30to34  I   -   -   1   4   7   6  10  22  32  17   1   - I 65.35 100
  35to39  I   -   -   0   4   5   6   8  22  30  23   2   - I 60.04 100
  40to44  I   -   -   1   2   5   8  10  22  30  20   2   - I 66.90 100
  45to49  I   -   -   0   3   6   9  13  22  29  15   2   - I 64.77 100
  50to54  I   -   -   0   4   6   7  15  29  30   8   1   - I 63.84 100
  55to59  I   -   -   0   2   6   8  10  25  32   7   1   - I 63.44 100
  60to64  I   -   -   0   9   5  17  13  27  24   5   0   - I 58.73 100
  65plus  I   -   -   0   8   0  16  26  39   3   0   0   - I 54.00 100
```

Figure 12.14: Replacement Rates

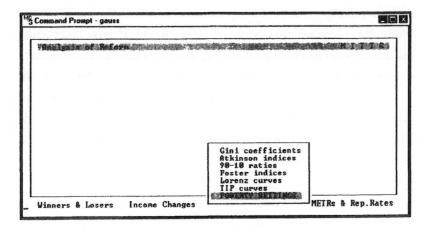

Figure 12.15: Inequality Measures

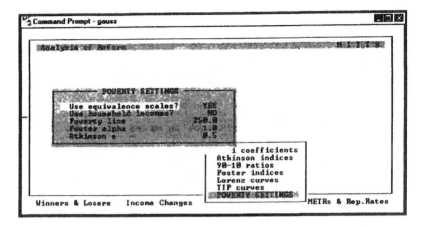

Figure 12.16: Settings for Inequality Measures

**Inequality Measures**

If 'inequality' is selected the options are displayed as in Figure 12.15. Before selecting measures, the 'poverty settings' should be specified. The choices are shown in Figure 12.16. The space bar is used for selecting yes/no and values of the required parameters are set in the usual way. Selection of equivalence scales and individual incomes gives individual level analyses with each individual given the household income per equivalent adult. Selection of equivalence scales and household incomes produces analyses using one observation per household, having the household income per equivalent adult. Selecting no equivalence scales and individual incomes produces analyses at the individual level, with each individual receiving an equal share of the household income.

Definitions of these measures are as follows. This discussion refers to the unit of analysis as the individual, but MITTS allows for households or individuals. For the Lorenz curve, individuals are first ranked in ascending order according to their incomes, $y_i$, for individuals $i = 1, ..., N$, so that

$y_i > y_j$ for $i > j$. As $i$ is increased from 1 to $N$, the Lorenz curve is defined as the relationship between the proportion of people with income less than or equal to $y_i$, and the associated proportion of total income obtained by those individuals.

The Gini inequality measure is twice the area contained by the Lorenz curve and the line of equality. The area is doubled simply to ensure that the maximum value that the Gini measure can take is 1. For the distribution of $y$, where incomes are arranged in ascending order and $\bar{y}$ is the arithmetic mean, the Gini measure, $G_y$, can be calculated directly using:

$$G_y = 1 + \frac{1}{N} - \frac{2}{N^2} \sum_{i=1}^{N} (N + 1 - i) \left( \frac{y_i}{\bar{y}} \right) \tag{12.1}$$

Suppose $y_p$ is the poverty level and let $g(y_i | y_p)$ take the value of 1 if $y_i \leq y_p$, and 0 otherwise. The headcount poverty measure, $H$, is:

$$H = \frac{1}{N} \sum_{i=1}^{N} g(y_i | y_p) \tag{12.2}$$

and is the proportion of the population found on or below the poverty line. The TIP curve refers to three characteristics of poverty (the 'Three "I"s of Poverty') - its incidence, intensity and inequality. In defining the TIP curve, redefine $g(y_i | y_p)$, so that it indicates not only whether an individual is below the poverty line, $y_p$, but also the absolute poverty gap, or the extent to which $y_i$ falls below $y_p$. Thus let:

$$
\begin{aligned}
g(y_i | y_p) &= y_p - y_i \quad \text{for } y_i \leq y_p \\
&= 0 \quad \quad \text{for } y_i > y_p
\end{aligned}
\tag{12.3}
$$

Suppose, as before, that individuals are ranked in ascending order. The TIP curve is obtained by plotting the total poverty gap per capita against the corresponding proportion of people. In other words:

$$\text{plot} \quad \frac{1}{N} \sum_{i=1}^{k} g(y_i | y_p) \quad \text{against} \quad \frac{k}{N} \quad \text{for } k = 1, ..., N \tag{12.4}$$

The slope of the non-horizontal section of the curve at any point is the poverty gap at that point. The extent to which the poverty gap falls as income rises is therefore reflected in the flattening of the TIP curve, so the extent of inequality among the poor is shown by the concavity of the TIP curve.

The Foster poverty measures are the set, $P_\alpha$:

$$P_\alpha = \frac{1}{N} \sum_{y_i \le y_p} \left( \frac{y_p - y_i}{y_p} \right)^\alpha \tag{12.5}$$

where $\alpha$ is a parameter to be set by the user. When $\alpha = 0$, the poverty measure, $P_0$, is equal to the headcount measure. When $\alpha = 1$, the corresponding poverty measure is equal to the headcount measure multiplied by $G = 1 - \mu_p / y_p$, where $\mu_p$ is the arithmetic mean income of those in poverty. Hence $P_1 = P_0 G$ depends on both the proportion of people in poverty and the extent to which, on average, those people fall below the poverty line. When $\alpha = 2$, the poverty measure depends also on the inequality of those in poverty, as measured by the coefficient of variation, $\eta_p^2$. It can be shown that $P_2 = P_0 \left\{ G^2 + (1 - G)^2 \eta_p^2 \right\}$.

Atkinson's inequality measure is linked to a social welfare function, $W$, defined as:

$$W = \sum H(y_i) = NH(y_e) \tag{12.6}$$

The function, $H(y)$, is given by:

$$H(y) = \frac{y^{1-\varepsilon}}{1-\varepsilon} \qquad \text{for } \varepsilon \neq 1$$

$$H(y) = \log y \qquad \text{for } \varepsilon = 1 \tag{12.7}$$

where $\varepsilon$ is a measure of relative inequality aversion. Combining (12.6) and (12.7) gives:

$$y_e = \left\{ \frac{1}{N} \sum_{i=1}^{N} y_i^{1-\varepsilon} \right\}^{1/(1-\varepsilon)} \tag{12.8}$$

The term $y_e$ is the equally distributed equivalent income and is that level which, if obtained by everyone, produces the same social welfare as the actual distribution. The Atkinson inequality measure, $A$, is the proportional difference between arithmetic mean income and the equally distributed equivalent level. Hence:

$$A = \frac{\overline{y} - y_e}{\overline{y}} \qquad (12.9)$$

The inequality aversion parameter required can be selected as described above.

**Saving Simulations Runs**

It may be required to run MITTS-A for a specified policy change and then to return to MITTS at a later date in order to carry out further analyses of the results. This can be achieved without having to re-run the simulation, as follows.

After carrying out the simulation, go to the c:\gauss\mitts\results directory. Copy the file MITTS.DAT to another file where you wish to store the results for future use. For example, to copy to a file named MRUN1.SAV, use the DOS command $\boxed{\text{copy mitts.dat mrun1.sav}}$. When it is required to return to these results to obtain further distributional and summary analyses, simply copy the stored file back to MITTS.DAT, using the DOS command $\boxed{\text{copy mrun1.sav mitts.dat}}$.

Similarly, the details of marginal effective tax rates and replacement rates under the two tax systems may be stored by copying the files METR1.DAT and METR2.DAT to other files.

Figure 12.17: MITTS-B Menu

## 12.4   Running MITTS-B

A behavioural microsimulation analysis of a tax reform can be carried out by
selecting the Run MITTS-B option in the main menu. This displays another
sub-menu, shown in Figure 12.17. The simulation settings are chosen as in
Figure 12.18, and the choice of population group to be considered is shown
in Figure 12.19. The last option regarding hours data is used only for the
estimation of preference functions and can be ignored by MITTS users.

MITTS-B is a discrete hours simulation model, in contrast with a continuous hours model. Behavioural responses are based on estimated preference functions for individuals in several demographic groups; these include
married (or partnered) men and women, single men and women, and single
parents. Hours worked are limited to a set of discrete hours that are chosen
under the option 'simulation settings' (described below). The simulations are

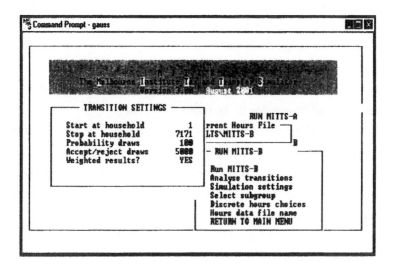

Figure 12.18: MITTS-B Simulation Settings

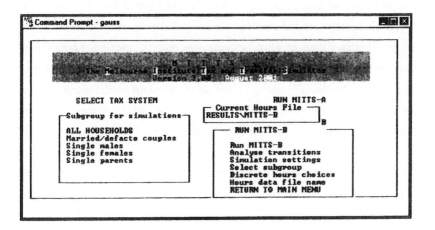

Figure 12.19: MITTS-B Selection of Groups

essentially probabilistic, in that they are not based on identification of a particular level of hours for each individual, but on the probability distribution over the discrete hours levels used.

It is first necessary to select the 'simulation settings' option. This provides a choice of household number at which to start and end the simulation (the default being all households in the chosen IDS).

In addition, the simulation settings include an option 'Simulation draws'. This refers to the fact, mentioned above, that simulation results are based on probabilities of working at specified hours levels. These probabilities are obtained by selecting observations at random from the relevant distributions underlying the estimates of preference functions, for each individual. The number chosen under 'Simulation draws' refers to the number of random draws required; the default is 100 draws. A higher number of draws increases the required running time.

Before running MITTS-B it is also necessary to set the discrete hours choices. This enables the discrete hours levels to be chosen for each of the five demographic groups distinguished. As MITTS uses discrete simulation, rather than assuming that individuals are able to choose over a continuous range of hours, a decision must be made regarding the particular hours levels that are feasible. Selection of this option gives the screen displayed in Figure 12.20, with the default values. These settings relate to the discrete hours levels assumed to be available for working. The default values shown are those used in estimation of respective preference functions.

To change the hours levels from the default values, use the up and down direction keys to move between demographic groups. When the desired group is highlighted, hit the *enter* key. Then use the direction keys to highlight a level to be changed. Press *enter* and respond to the invitation to make the change. After typing the new value, press *esc* and respond to the request to save the new level.

To delete an hours level, highlight the selection and press *del*. To insert

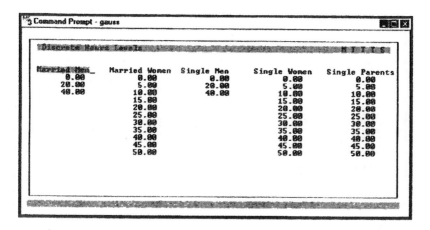

Figure 12.20: Hours Selection for MITTS-B

an additional level of hours, highlight the level before which the new one is to be inserted and hit *ins*. To add higher levels than the existing maximum, highlight it and press both *ctrl* and *ins*. As many hours levels as required can be used.

## 12.4.1 Run MITTS-B

The desired behavioural simulation can be carried out by selecting the Run MITTS-B option in the sub-menu. This takes substantially longer than the corresponding static simulation of MITTS-A. The time required, and summary information about labour supply responses to the reform, are displayed in a screen similar to Figure 12.21. The run can be stopped at any time by pressing *esc*. Information about costs can be obtained by pressing *r*. Pressing *h* returns to the window displaying details of changes in hours worked.

The summary information about changes in revenue, shown in Figure 12.21, are weighted average costings based on the conditional distribution of hours (over the discrete range specified) for each individual. Instead of assigning a single level of hours to each individual, the probability distributions

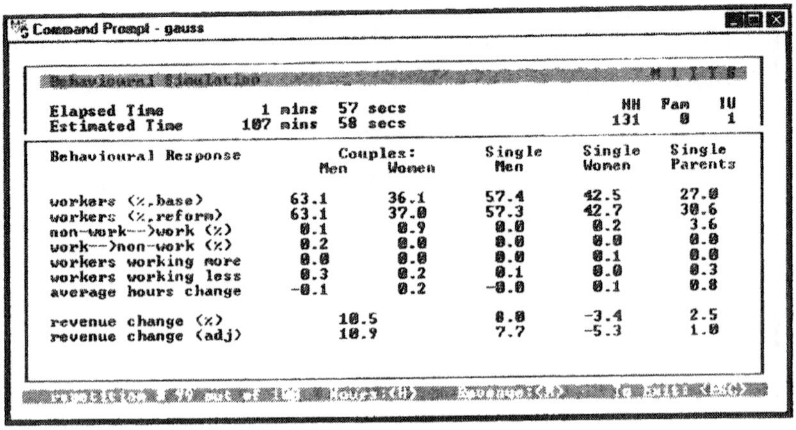

Figure 12.21: A MITTS-B Summary Table

of hours worked for the two tax systems are obtained, along with the costs
and revenues at all hours levels, for each individual. These are used to generate the weighted average costs. The non-adjusted change in revenue uses
the pre-reform discrete hours for both tax systems. However, the adjusted
change in revenue uses the post-reform conditional probability distributions
of hours resulting from the new tax structure in order to obtain the post-
reform revenues. Hence the non-adjusted change in revenue corresponds to
a tax change that assumes no changes in the conditional hours distributions
and is effectively a non-behavioural simulation. However, this uses the discretised hours rather than the actual hours observed in the data. Hence it
gives results that differ from those reported by MITTS-A.

On completion (or termination) of the simulation run, control returns to
the Run MITTS-B submenu. The results can be examined by selecting the
'Analyse transitions' option. This gives rise to the further choices shown in
Figure 12.22.

Selection of 'Summary' gives the summary information regarding the cost
and revenue implications of the tax reform, along with aggregate information

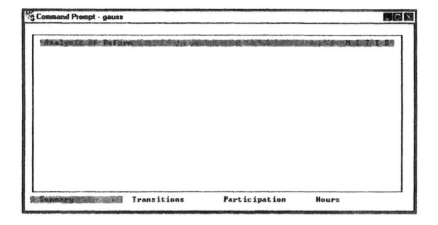

Figure 12.22: MITTS-B Analysis Options

about hours. These tables, as with all others in MITTS-B, can be saved by using the Alt-S option provided at the bottom of the window.

Selection of 'Transitions' produces the transition matrices which show probabilities of movement between the selected hours levels, for each of the demographic groups in turn. An example of a transition matrix for married men is illustrated in Figure 12.23.

Selection of the 'Participation' option gives results regarding the labour force participation effects of the simulated tax reform, for a range of categories, listed in Table 12.2 above. An example of changes in the probability of participation in different age groups is given in Figure 12.24. As with various MITTS-A tables, it is possible to examine specific individuals and households included in any element of the table, using the F7 key.

Distributions of changes in hours, for various categories, are obtained by selecting the 'Hours' option. An example is provided in Figures 12.25. Using the F7 key, it is possible to examine specific individuals from the basic dataset.

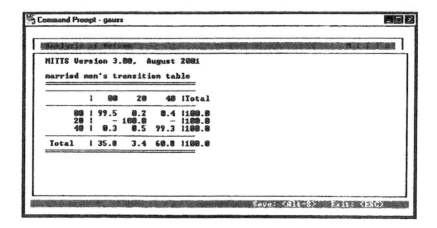

Figure 12.23: A Transition Table

Command Prompt - gauss

Analysis of Reform                                                    M I T T S

MITTS Version 3.00,  August 2001

Change in Work Probability by AGE (row percentages)

|          | >50 | 10-50 | 2-10 | none | 2-10 | 10-50 | >50 | avg | Total |
|----------|-----|-------|------|------|------|-------|-----|------|-------|
| 15 to 19 | -   | -     | -    | 93   | 4    | 3     | -   | 0.42 | 100   |
| 20 to 24 | -   | -     | --   | 93   | 4    | 3     | -   | 0.52 | 100   |
| 25 to 29 | -   | -     | 4    | 84   | 11   | -     | -   | 0.52 | 100   |
| 30 to 34 | --- | --    | -    | 67   | 30   | 3     | -   | 1.51 | 100   |
| 35 to 39 | -   | -     | -    | 88   | 12   | -     | -   | 0.61 | 100   |
| 40 to 44 | -   | -     | -    | 78   | 19   | 3     | -   | 0.92 | 100   |
| 45 to 49 | -   | -     | 1    | 94   | 5    | -     | -   | 0.31 | 100   |
| 50 to 54 | -   | -     | -    | 87   | 13   | -     | -   | 0.32 | 100   |
| 55 to 59 | -   | -     | 3    | 92   | 5    | -     | -   | 0.26 | 100   |
| 60 to 64 | -   | -     | -    | 87   | 13   | -     | -   | 0.30 | 100   |
| 65plus   | -   | -     | -    | 100  | -    | -     | -   | 0.00 | 100   |

Figure 12.24: Labour Market Particiption

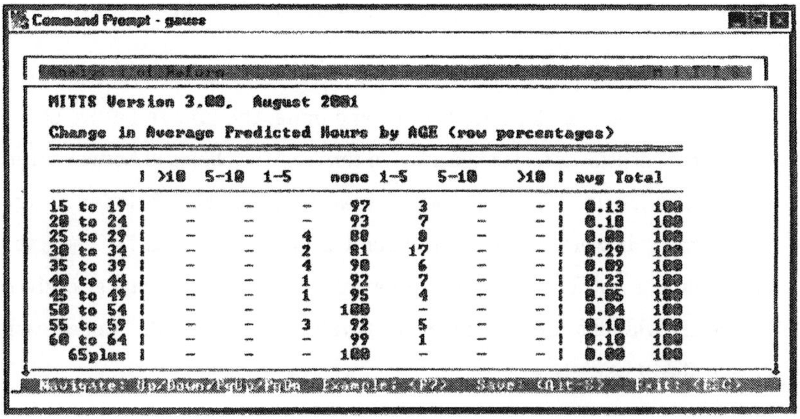

Command Prompt - gauss

MITTS Version 3.00, August 2001

Change in Average Predicted Hours by AGE (row percentages)

| | >10 | 5-10 | 1-5 | none | 1-5 | 5-10 | >10 | avg | Total |
|---|---|---|---|---|---|---|---|---|---|
| 15 to 19 | - | - | - | 97 | 3 | - | - | 0.13 | 100 |
| 20 to 24 | - | - | - | 93 | 7 | - | - | 0.10 | 100 |
| 25 to 29 | - | - | 4 | 88 | 8 | - | - | 0.00 | 100 |
| 30 to 34 | - | - | 2 | 81 | 17 | - | - | 0.29 | 100 |
| 35 to 39 | - | - | 4 | 90 | 6 | - | - | 0.09 | 100 |
| 40 to 44 | - | - | 1 | 92 | 7 | - | - | 0.23 | 100 |
| 45 to 49 | - | - | 1 | 95 | 4 | - | - | 0.05 | 100 |
| 50 to 54 | - | - | - | 100 | - | - | - | 0.04 | 100 |
| 55 to 59 | - | - | 3 | 92 | 5 | - | - | 0.10 | 100 |
| 60 to 64 | - | - | - | 99 | 1 | - | - | 0.10 | 100 |
| 65plus | - | - | - | 100 | - | - | - | 0.00 | 100 |

Figure 12.25: Changes in Hours Worked

# 12.5 Selecting Households

MITTS can also be used to produce a variety of analyses for particular individuals and tax units. Furthermore, after running MITTS-A or MITTS-B, it is possible to examine a sample of households who fall into any specified cell in a summary table. The available options are described in this section.

For information about particular households in the selected data set, or hypothetical types of household, select the option 'View Households' from the Main Menu. Then select the desired choice of 'households from the dataset' or 'hypothetical households' from the resulting sub-menu. Choice of hypothetical household gives the options shown in Figure 12.26; the details of the selected type can then be modified.

This component of MITTS can carry out the following analyses.

1. MITTS calculates the gross and net incomes of specified individuals and tax unit in the IDS data base.

2. MITTS provides details of the effects of changing the tax system on

all benefit levels and net incomes of specified individuals and income units.

3. MITTS produces, for specified income units, the precise nature of the budget constraint facing the unit, in terms of the choice of hours worked and net income. That is, it provides details of the variation in the income unit's net income as the number of hours worked by a selected individual (either the reference person or the spouse) changes, given the individual's and partner's wage rate, where relevant, under each specified tax system.

4. MITTS provides details of the reasons for each discontinuity and kink in each budget constraint.

After selecting the menu option, 'Households from Dataset', it is necessary to select household number, family number and income unit number in turn, as shown in Figure 12.27. Hit *enter* after typing each desired number. MITTS then lists the amounts of various taxes and transfers pre- and post-reform, along with the differences. An example is shown in Figure 12.28. Further information about the income unit can be obtained by selecting from the sub-menu along the bottom of the screen. An example of income unit information is shown in Figure 12.29.

Moving between the reference person and the spouse is achieved using *pgup* and *pgdn* keys. Moving to the next and previous income unit is achieved using the *n* and *p* keys respectively.

It is possible to examine the effects of variations in some of the characteristics of the income unit, such as the wage rate or hours worked. Hit the *F10* key. Then use the direction keys to highlight the variable to be changed. Pressing *enter* produces a dialogue box, allowing a new value to be entered. The new tax and transfer levels are automatically provided.

The abbreviations used are described in Table 12.3. Where two values

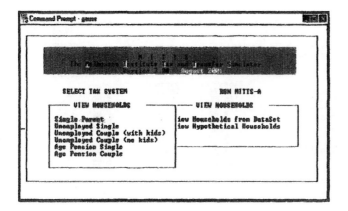

Figure 12.26: View Hypothetical Household

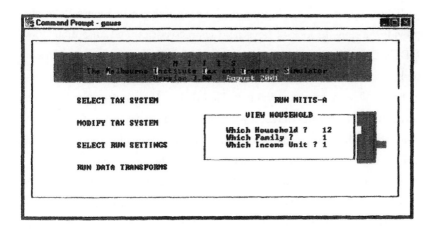

Figure 12.27: View Households Selection

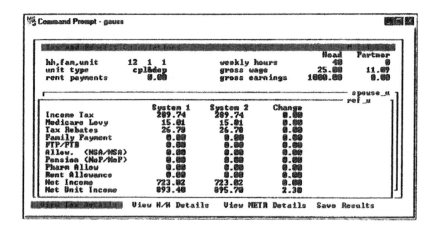

Figure 12.28: Tax and Benefit Details for Selected Unit

are given using, for example, (DSP/WP), the first term refers to the tax and transfer system 1 while the second term refers to tax system 2. The abbreviations used to describe the individuals are described in Table 12.3.

The sub-menu on the bottom of the screen shown in Figure 12.28 also provides options to look at household characteristics, and an option 'View METR Details'. On selecting this option, MITTS then computes the exact budget constraint. This gives the net income of the income unit for variations in hours of work by the individual displayed in the window (for the given actual number of hours worked by the spouse, where relevant). First, details of all the kinks in the constraint, and probable reasons for those kinks and discontinuities, are given in tabular form for the pre-reform system. An example is shown in Figure 12.30. This table may be saved to a named file by selecting the *alt-s* option and following the prompts, as before.

Pressing *esc* then provides a further sub-menu for the choice of tax system to be examined, along with 'graph options'. Selecting 'graph options' then allows a choice of either the budget constraint or the profile of marginal effective tax rates. Profiles for both tax systems are placed on a single di-

Table 12.3: Abbreviations

| Allowances | |
|---|---|
| PPs | Parenting payment (single) |
| PPp | Parenting payment (couple) |
| SA | Sickness allowance |
| WA | Widow's allowance |
| AUS | Austudy |
| NSA | Newstart allowance |
| MAA | Mature age allowance |
| YA | Youth allowance |
| SpB | Special benefit |
| PA | Partner allowance |
| NoA | No allowance |
| **Pension** | |
| AP | Age pension |
| DSP | Disability support pension |
| WP | Wife's pension |
| WBP | Widow B pension |
| CP | Carer's payment |
| VSP | Veteran pension |
| VDP | Veteran's Disability pension |
| WWP | War Widow's pension |
| NoP | No pension |
| **Demographic Group** | |
| ref_h | Reference person |
| spouse_h | Spouse of reference person |
| depkid_h | Dependent child of reference person |
| ndkid_h | Non-dependent child |
| non_fam | Non-family member |

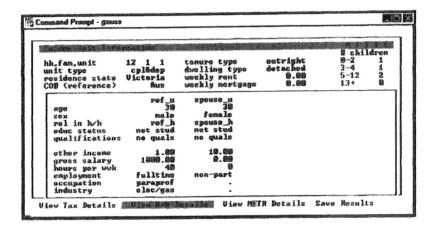

Figure 12.29:  Income Unit Information

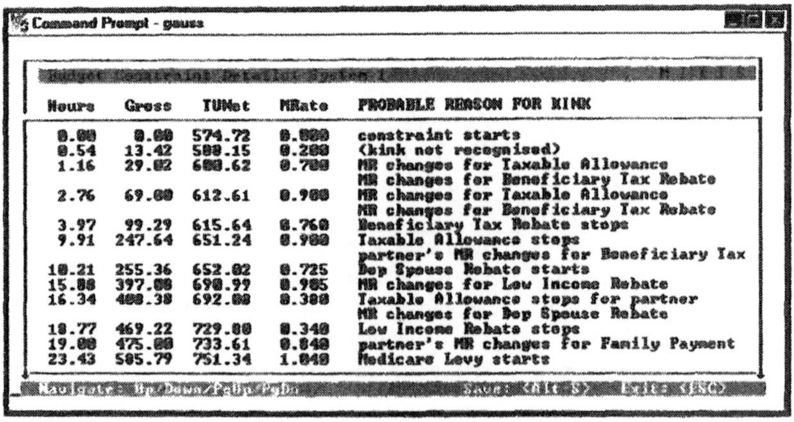

Figure 12.30:  A Budget Constraint

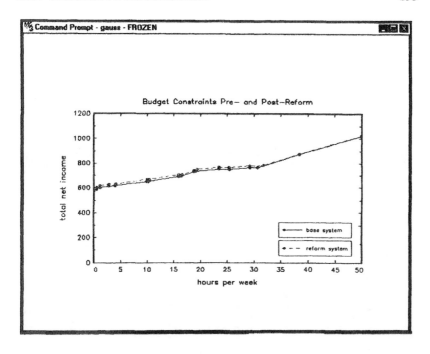

Figure 12.31: A Budget Constraint

agram. In order to return to the menu after viewing the figure, press *esc*. Examples are given in Figures 12.31 and 12.32.

Other graph options include the ability to examine replacement rates at different hours levels and average marginal tax rates. These are actually obtained as continuous functions, having derived the exact form of each budget constraint in terms of hours thresholds, net wages and virtual incomes. In addition, a breakdown of the budget constraint, in terms of the source of income, is available in the form of bar charts; an example is shown in Figure 12.33. The bar charts are actually displayed in colour, and are therefore clearer than the monochrome figures shown here.

The examination of 'hypothetical households' proceeds as for households from the dataset, except that it is possible to set wage rates, hours worked

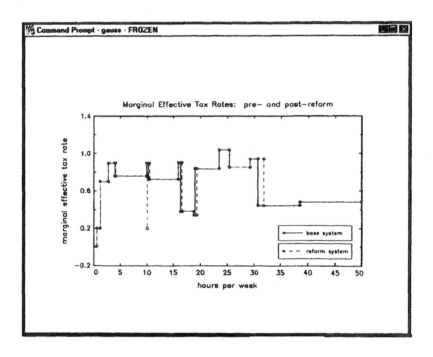

Figure 12.32: Marginal Effective Tax Rates

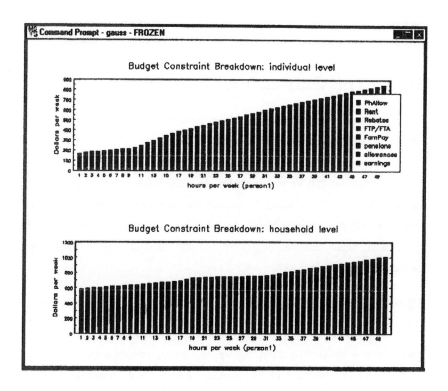

Figure 12.33: Breakdown of Budget Constraints

and number and ages of dependent children. After making the choice from the main menu, press the *F10* key in order to make changes to the default values displayed. Moving between reference person and spouse is achieved as before by pressing *pgup* and *pgdn*. Again, after selecting 'view METR details', press *esc* for graph options. This gives the options discussed above, including plots of net incomes and METRs, along with replacement rates and average marginal effective rates, corresponding to hours worked.

## 12.6   The Output from MITTS

The generation of files containing tables produced by MITTS has been described at the appropriate points above. These files, placed in the subdirectory c:\gauss\mitts\results, are in ASCII form. They can be loaded into other software for further manipulation. In some cases, for example importing into Excel, it is necessary to change the filename so that it has a .txt extension. On loading into Excel, the information can be converted into an Excel table, which can then be pasted into MS-Word as a table. Figures can be handled as follows.

### 12.6.1   Printing Figures

Several alternative procedures may be used in order to save or print any figures produced by MITTS. First, figures may be pasted into a wordprocessor. With the figure displayed on the screen, simultaneously press the *alt* and *pr scr* keys. Then open a word processor (such as MS-Word, or Scientific Word) and place the cursor where the figure is required. Then simultaneously press the *shift* and *insert* keys. The figure will appear and can be scaled to the required size using the word processor. When using this method, Gauss should be displayed within a window, rather than taking up the full screen, otherwise memory problems arise. This method was used to produce the figures in the present document.

An alternative procedure involves, when viewing the figure, hitting any key; this produces a list of options. The most useful of these options are 'zoom' (select this option and then use the direction keys to select the area, and hit *enter*), and 'Convert File Format'. After making the latter choice by pressing *c*, select *e* for 'Encapsulated postscript'. This writes the figure to a file in the c:\gauss\mitts directory and gives the file an .out extension. The name of the file is displayed briefly on the screen. In order to print this file, change the name so that it has a .ps extension.[2] Finally, use the DOS command $\boxed{\text{copy filename.ps LPT1}}$, or whichever printer is required. This has the effect of printing a full page landscape copy of the figure. Importing the .ps file into a wordprocessor also produces a landscape figure.

## 12.6.2 Using PlayW.exe

An alternative, and preferred, method of importing a figure into a wordprocessor makes use of a Gauss utility called PlayW.exe. This software converts files into alternative formats. It can be downloaded from the web site: http://www.aptech.com/download.html. After downloading the PlayW.zip file, use Windows Explorer to unzip it and follow the instructions for installation. The installation produces a convenient short cut and icon.

When a figure is being displayed by MITTS, Gauss produces a file called graphic.tkf which is placed in the c:\gauss\mitts subdirectory. With the file displayed, go into PlayW, import the graphic.tkf file and select the convert option from the menu. Select the postscript option and follow the instruction to name the file.[3] The resulting file can then be loaded into the word processor. Figure 12.34 was produced in this way.

More flexibility is available if the file is converted into a bitmap. Select bitmap, and leave the options as the default value. Name the file and place

---

[2]This can be carried out using the DOS command $\boxed{\text{rename oldname newname}}$.

[3]Selection of the wmf (MetaFile) option produces a figure with the same colour scheme as that displayed by MITTS, which is not optimal for documents.

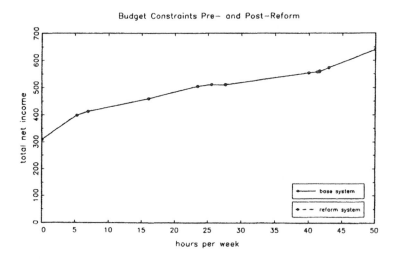

Figure 12.34: A Figure Obtained using PlayW.exe

it in the desired directory. After this, open Windows Explorer, go to the directory and double click to open the file (in MS Paint). From the Image menu on the toolbar, select Invert Colors in order to change the background colour to white. Then click on the dotted rectangular icon from the tool bar: it is then possible to drag the cursor in order to frame the required area of the graph that you wish to save (for example, you may wish to omit the title). Other editing of the figure can be carried out using the other facilities provided (such as erasing sections or adding text).

From the Edit menu, select Copy. It is then possible to paste the figure into a word document. Simply open the word processor, place the cursor at the required point and press *shift+ins*. Alternatively, if using MS Word, use Edit and then Paste. If using Scientific Word, the alternative to *shift+ins* is to use Edit and Paste Special.

## 12.7 Conclusions

This chapter has provided a detailed guide to the way in which MITTS can be used to examine a wide range of types of policy change.

# Chapter 13

# Taxes And Benefits: March 1998

MITTS has a number of tax and benefit systems programmed, as mentioned in chapter 11. To provide an indication of the basic form of the structure in Australia, and to illustrate its complexity, this chapter describes the structure of taxes and benefits in Australia at March 1998. Some features are not modelled in MITTS, as indicated.

## 13.1   Income Taxation

Income taxation consists of the standard form of income tax schedule plus a Medicare Levy which is also payable by individuals earning above a minimum threshold taxable income. Tax assistance for families is available through Family Tax Assistance (FTA). Alternatively, Family Tax Payment (FTP) is available through the social security system for families paying only small, or zero, amounts of income tax. Several tax rebates are also available, as described in the next section.

### Income Tax

Define $y_i$ as individual $i$'s taxable income over the financial year. The income tax schedule takes the familiar multi-step form, defined in terms of a series of income thresholds, $a_k$, and marginal tax rates, $t_k$. The tax paid, $T(y_i)$, is defined by:

$$
\begin{aligned}
T(y_i) &= \quad\quad 0 & 0 < y_i \le a_1 \\
&= \; t_1(y_i - a_1) & a_1 < y_i \le a_2 \quad\quad (13.1) \\
&= \; t_1(a_2 - a_1) \; + \; t_2(y_i - a_2) & a_2 < y_i \le a_3
\end{aligned}
$$

and so on. Hence if $y_i$ falls into the $k$th tax bracket, so that $a_k < y_i \le a_{k+1}$, and $a_0 = t_0 = 0$, $T(y_i)$ can be written for $k \ge 1$ as:

$$
T(y_i) = t_k(y_i - a_k) + \sum_{j=0}^{k-1} t_j(a_{j+1} - a_j) \quad\quad (13.2)
$$

This function clearly displays increasing average tax rates that are characteristic of a progressive structure. The expression for $T(y_i)$ in (13.2) can be rewritten as:

$$
T(y_i) = t_k y_i - \sum_{j=1}^{k} a_j(t_j - t_{j-1}) \quad\quad (13.3)
$$

Hence:

$$
T(y_i) = t_k(y_i - a_k') \quad\quad (13.4)
$$

where:

$$
\begin{aligned}
a_k' &= \; a_k - \sum_{j=0}^{k-1} \left(\frac{t_j}{t_k}\right)(a_{j+1} - a_j) \\
&= \; \sum_{j=1}^{k} a_j\left(\frac{t_j - t_{j-1}}{t_k}\right) \quad\quad (13.5)
\end{aligned}
$$

The annual earnings thresholds and corresponding marginal tax rates applying to individual taxable incomes over the financial year are shown in Table 13.1.

## Medicare Levy

An additional income tax is imposed in the form of a Medicare Levy. The rate is 1.5 per cent of taxable income, and is payable above a threshold level of

Table 13.1: Tax Thresholds and Rates: March 1998

| Earnings | Threshold | Marginal Tax Rate |
|---|---|---|
| 0 | 5400 | 0.00 |
| 5401 | 20700 | 0.20 |
| 20701 | 38000 | 0.34 |
| 38001 | 50000 | 0.43 |
| 50001 | ∞ | 0.47 |

Table 13.2: Medicare Levy Thresholds

| Demographic Characteristics | Shade-in starts: $ | Surcharge starts: $ |
|---|---|---|
| Single (no dependents) | 13,389 | 50,000 |
| Single (with dependents) | 22,594 | 100,000 |
| Couple | 22,594 | 100,000 |
| Threshold add-on per child | 2,100 | 1,500 |

taxable income. Once this threshold level of income is reached the Medicare Levy is shaded-in at a rate of 20 per cent of the excess above the threshold income. The threshold amount increases by $2100 for each dependent child or student for whom the taxpayer or taxpayer's spouse is entitled to a notional dependents' rebate. For high levels of taxable income a surcharge of 1 per cent is payable if the taxpayer is not a member of a private health insurance scheme. The annual thresholds where the Medicare Levy shade-in starts and where the surcharge is payable are presented in Table 13.2.

To qualify for the add-on to the surcharge income threshold, taxpayers must have the care of at least two children under the age of 17 years.

Thus, let amount of Medicare Levy paid by an individual taxpayer per financial year is equivalent be denoted by $M$. Also, let $y$ refer to individual taxable income, $y_h$ the shade-in threshold and $y_u$ the surcharge thresholds.

Then $M$ is given by:

$$
\begin{aligned}
M &= (0.01 + 0.015)y & \text{if } y \geq y_u \\
&= \min[0.015y, 0.2(y - y_h)] & \text{if } y_h \geq y > y_u \qquad (13.6)\\
&= 0 & \text{if } y < y_h
\end{aligned}
$$

### Family Tax Assistance

If the taxpayer is entitled to Family Tax Assistance (FTA), the standard tax-free threshold is increased. There is a Part A benefit, and a Part B benefit. If family income is less than $70,000 (plus $3,000 for each dependent child after the first), the family may be entitled to FTA (A). This increases the tax-free threshold for one parent by $1,000 for each dependent child. Part B benefit further increases the threshold by $2,500 for single-income families with at least one dependent child under 5 years old. In addition, family income must be below $65,000 plus $4,573 for each dependent child below age 5, after the first child.

For low income families who do not pay sufficient tax to enjoy the full benefits of tax assistance, Family Tax Assistance is mirrored as a payment through the social security system in the Family Tax Payment, described below. Any FTA benefits are reduced if FTPs are received by the taxpayer or the taxpayer's spouse. The amount of the reduction is calculated as the amount of the FTP divided by the lowest marginal tax rate (of 20 per cent) and rounded up to the nearest dollar.

## 13.2   Income Tax Rebates

### Pensioner Rebate

All recipients of taxable social security and Veterans Affairs service pensions, including the parenting payment (single), may be eligible for the pensioner rebate. Once taxable income reaches a threshold of $y_T$ the rebate is shaded out at 12.5 cents for each dollar above the threshold. The maximum rebate level is calculated as the difference between the threshold level of income, $y_T$, and the tax-free threshold (of \$5400) multiplied by the lowest marginal tax rate (20 per cent). Thus the maximum rebate, max $PR$, is given by:

$$\max PR = 0.2(y_T - 5,400) \tag{13.7}$$

The threshold amount is the sum of the maximum annual base pension payable, $P_B$, plus the income-free area for the pension per person, $P_F/n$. Thus:

$$y_T = P_B + P_F/n \tag{13.8}$$

The pensioner rebate is thus calculated as:

$$PR \quad = \max PR \qquad\qquad\qquad \text{if } y < y_T$$
$$= \max[0, \max PR - 0.125(y - y_T)] \quad \text{if } y \geq y_T \tag{13.9}$$

Partnered pensioners can transfer the unused portion of their rebate to their partner if the partner has a tax liability.

## Beneficiary Rebate

Recipients of taxable allowances are entitled to the beneficiary rebate below a certain level of taxable income. The maximum beneficiary rebate for which a person is eligible depends, unlike the pensioner rebate, on the benefit paid and not the maximum benefit payable. Where 20 per cent is the lowest marginal tax rate and \$5,400 is the tax free threshold, the beneficiary rebate is calculated using:

$$BR = 0.20(\text{Benefit Paid} - \$5,400) \tag{13.10}$$

## Sole Parent Rebate

A maximum rebate of \$1,243 per financial year is available to people with sole care of children under 16 years or dependent full time students. The rebate is reduced by 25 cents for each dollar the child's 'Seperate Net Income' exceeds $282 a year. Seperate Net Income is equal to gross income minus expenses, where expenses may include items that are not tax deductable.

## Sole Parent Pensioner Rebate

See Pensioner Rebate below.

## Low Income Rebate

Individuals with annual taxable income below $20,000 are entitled to the Low Income Rebate (LIR). The maximum level of the rebate is $150 per year and is reduced by 4 cents for every dollar of taxable income above the threshold. Let $y$ denote the individual's income, and $y_T = \$20,000$ the threshold level of income, with $\max LIR = \$150$. The annual amount of Low Income Rebate is calculated as:

$$
\begin{aligned}
LIR \quad &= \max LIR && \text{if } y < y_T \\
&= \max[0, \max LIR - 0.04(y - y_T)] && \text{if } y \geq y_T
\end{aligned}
\tag{13.11}
$$

## Dependent Spouse Rebate

The Dependent Spouse Rebate is available to individuals who have a dependent spouse, a child housekeeper, an invalid relative, a dependent parent or a spouse's dependent parent. Previously, there were basically two forms of dependent spouse rebate, 'with child' and 'without child'. The dependent's Seperate Net Income (SNI) decreases the rebate level at 25 cents for each dollar of SNI exceeding $282. The maximum rebate available for those 'with child' is $1,452 per year, 'without child' is $1,324 per year and for those with the care of dependent students it is $1,785.

Table 13.3: Maximum Rent Assistance

| Demographic Characteristics | Max Per Fortnight | Min Rent |
|---|---|---|
| Single, no dependent children | 70.60 | 71.60 |
| Single, sharer, no dependent children | 49.80 | 71.60 |
| Couple, no dependent children | 70.60 | 116.60 |
| Couple (each), separated due to illness, no child | 74.80 | 71.60 |
| Couple (each), temporarily separated, no child | 70.60 | 71.60 |
| Single, 1 or 2 children | 87.40 | 94.20 |
| Single, 3 or more children | 98.80 | 94.20 |
| Couple, 1 or 2 children | 87.40 | 139.20 |
| Couple, 3 or more children | 98.80 | 139.20 |

## 13.3 Rent Assistance

Rent Assistance is available with Centrelink or DVA payments to persons in private rental accommodation. It is paid with the Family Allowance for those with dependents and with the basic pension or allowance for those without dependents. The amount of Rent Assistance paid depends on the amount of rent paid and fortnightly income. The maximum rate of rent assistance available depends on the fortnightly amount of rent paid. Once the maximum amount of rent assistance payable has been determined it is added onto the maximum basic pension or allowance (family tax benefit (Part A) if dependent children are present). It is income tested according to the relevant income test applicable to that particular benefit (see above). Thus Rent Assistance increases the amount of fortnightly benefit received and increases the amount of income where the benefit cuts out.

The maximum annual amount of rent assistance available to particular individuals is set out in Table 13.3.

Once the amount of rent paid is above the amounts shown in Table 13.3, the maximum amount of Rent Assistance available to persons is 75 cents for each dollar of rent paid above the threshold until the maximum possible pay-

Table 13.4: Age Pension Qualifying Age: Women

| Date of Birth Between: | Age |
|---|---|
| 1 July 1935 and 31 December 1936 | $60\frac{1}{2}$ |
| 1 January 1937 and 30 June 1938 | 61 |
| 1 July 1938 and 31 December 1939 | $61\frac{1}{2}$ |
| 1 January 1940 and 30 June 1941 | 62 |
| 1 July 1941 and 31 December 1942 | $62\frac{1}{2}$ |
| 1 January 1943 and 30 June 1944 | 63 |
| 1 July 1944 and 31 December 1945 | $63\frac{1}{2}$ |
| 1 January 1946 and 30 June 1947 | 63 |
| 1 July 1947 and 31 December 1948 | $64\frac{1}{2}$ |
| 1 July 1949 and later | 65 |

ment per fortnight is reached. Let max $RA$ denote the maximum amount of rent assistance payable, $RPaid$ is the amount of rent paid per fortnight, and $R_T$ is the threshold amount of rent needed to be paid in order to receive any rent assistance. The maximum rate of rent assistance available is calculated as:

$$RA \quad = \quad \min[\max RA, \min[0, 0.75(RPaid - R_T)]] \qquad (13.12)$$

Rent Assistance is not paid to people in public housing, to residents of Commonwealth funded nursing homes and hostels, to single disability support pensioners under 25 who are living with their parents, to other single people under 25 living with their parents and to students without dependents receiving Austudy.

## 13.4   Pension and Benefit Rates

### Age Pension

#### Conditions of Eligibility

The Age Pension is paid to males aged 65 and over. The qualifying age for women is given in Table 13.4.

The individual must be an Australian resident and have been an Australian resident for at least 10 years.

## Basic Rates per Fortnight

The basic rates are \$354.60 for singles and \$295.80 each for couples.

## Income Test

Let $Y_R$ denote the reference person's income, $Y_S$ the spouse's income, $Y = Y_R + Y_S$ the combined income, and $RA$ Rent Assistance. The reduction in age pension per fortnight is given by:

$$
\begin{aligned}
\text{Singles:} \quad AP_1 &= AP_B + RA + 5.40 \quad - \max[0, 0.5(Y - 100)] \\
AP &= \quad \max[0, AP_1]
\end{aligned}
$$

$$(13.13)$$

$$
\begin{aligned}
\text{Couples:} \quad AP_1 &= AP_B + RA + \tfrac{5.40}{2} \quad - \max[0, 0.25(Y - 176)] \\
AP &= \quad \max[0, AP_1]
\end{aligned}
$$

For couples, this relates to combined income and pension per person. The \$5.40 refers to the Pharmaceutical Allowance. For each additional child, add \$24 per child to the threshold. Half of the married rate is payable to one of a couple if the partner is not receiving a pension, benefit or allowance.

# Disability Support Pension

## Conditions of Eligibility

To be eligible for the Disability Support Pension, individuals must:

1. be aged over 16 and under age pension age at the date of claim lodgement;

2. have a physical, intellectual or psychiatric impairment of 20% or more;

3. be unable to work for at least the next two years as a result of the impairment;

4. be unable, as a result of the impairment, to undertake educational or vocational training which would equip the person for work within the next 2 years, or;

5. be permanently blind.

## Basic Rates

The basic rates of payment are the same as that of Age Pension, unless single and under 21.

1. DSP is not subject to parental income or assets tests.

2. Youth Disability Supplement of $76.40 per fortnight is payable to DSP beneficiaries under 21.

3. The rate payable to those age under 21 cannot exceed the rate payable to those aged over 21.

The Pharmaceutical Allowance is paid to all DSP beneficiaries. An Employment Entry payment of $300 may be available, and an Education Entry payment of $200 may be available.

## Income Test

See under Age Pension. There are no income or assets tests for Disability Support Pensioners who are permanently blind.

# Wife Pension

## Conditions of Eligibility

A qualifying individual must be the wife of an Age or Disability Support Pensioner, or a recipient of Disability Wage Supplement, who is not receiving a pension in her own right. From 1 July 1995, no new grants of Wife Pension were given.

### Basic Rates of Payment and Income Test

See Age Pension for couples. The Education Entry payment of $200 may be available.

# Bereavement Allowance

The Bereavement Allowance is not modelled in MITTS.

## Conditions of Eligibility

The Bereavement Allowance can be received by a person whose partner has died, and who was living with the partner immediately before death and has no dependent children for purposes of Parenting Payment (single). It is paid for a maximum of 14 weeks from the date of death of the partner, but can be extended if the widow is pregnant.

## Basic Rates of Payment and Income Test

See Age Pension single

# Widow 'B' Pension

From 20 March 1997, no new grants of Widow 'B' Pension. Current recipients continue to receive this pension until they are transferred to the Age Pension.

## Basic Rates of Payment and Income Test

See Age Pension for singles.

# Carer Payment

This is paid to a full-time carer of a person who has a physical, intellectual or psychiatric disability, who needs care permanently or for an extended period. The carer is not required to live with or adjacent to the person being cared for, but must be providing constant care.

## Conditions of Eligibility

1. Individuals cannot receive the Carer Payment if they are already receiving another income support payment

2. The individual being cared for must receive Social Security Income Support or a DVA service pension; or not have met the qualifying residence condition for a pension; or meet the special care receiver income and assets limits.

## Basic Rates of Payment and Income Test

See Age Pension. For income and assets tests, if the person being cared for is not an Income Support Pension or Service Pension recipient, then the special care receiver income and assets test apply.

## 13.5   Newstart Allowance

Newstart (NSA) is an unemployment benefit available to individuals from 18 years of age until the time at which they become eligible for the Age Pension, which occurs at age 65 for men. The benefit may be received by both spouses. Recipients must be capable of, available for, and actively seeking employment, or be temporarily incapacitated. Recipients may do training and voluntary work, and must be willing to enter into an Activity Agreement if required. There are also Australian residence requirements.

Table 13.5: Basic Newstart Rates

| Demographic Characteristics | $NSA_B$ |
|---|---|
| Single, 18 or over, with children | 347.80 |
| Single 21 or over, no children | 321.50 |
| Single, under 21, no children, at home | 176.00 |
| Single, under 21, no children, away from home | 265.50 |
| Single, aged 60 or over, after 9 months | 347.80 |
| Single, with children | 347.80 |
| Couple, under 21, no children | 265.50 |
| Couple (each), 21 or over or with children | 290.10 |

For couples where one partner receives Newstart, the partner typically receives either the Parenting Allowance or the Partner Allowance, depending on the presence of dependent children. The Partner Allowance has the same income test and benefits as Newstart, but does not require the recipient to be in the labour force. For this reason the Partner Allowance has not been modelled separately in MITTS. The Parenting Allowance is described in detail below.

The basic newstart rate, $NSA_B$ per fortnight, depends on demographic characteristics such as age and family status. Maximum payments are shown in Table 13.5.

## Income Test

The income test relating to newstart is as follows. Let the unemployed person's fortnightly income be $Y_R$ and the income of the spouse, where relevant, be $Y_S$. The basic rate, $NSA_B$, is given if $Y_R \leq \$60$ and $Y_S \leq \$Y_C$ per fortnight, where $Y_C$ is referred to as the cut-out income, which also depends on demographic characteristics. The cut out points $Y_C$ are calculated by the following equation:

$$Y_C = 140 + (NSA_B - (140 - 60)50)/70 \qquad (13.14)$$

Table 13.6: Basic Rates of Youth Training Allowance

| Demographic Characteristics | $YA_B$ |
|---|---|
| Single, at home - max rate | 145.40 |
| Single, away from home - max rate | 240.00 |
| Single, with children | 347.80 |
| Partnered, no children | 240.00 |
| Partnered, with children | 290.10 |

The newstart allowance is calculated as follows. Define:

$$NSA_1 = NSA_B + RA \quad - \max\left[0, 0.5\left(Y_R - 60\right)\right]$$
$$- \max\left[0, 0.2\left(Y_R - 140\right)\right] \quad (13.15)$$
$$- \max\left[0, 0.7\left(Y_S - Y_C\right)\right]$$

Then:

$$NSA = \max\left[0, NSA_1\right] \quad (13.16)$$

The Newstart Allowance is taxable.

## 13.6  Youth Training Allowance

The Youth Training Allowance (YTA) is similar in structure to the NSA for unemployed persons aged 16-17 years. Rent assistance is generally not available for YTA recipients, unless they are receiving the independent rate.

### Basic Rates of Payment

The basic rates of YTA payment are shown in Table 13.6.

### Income Test

A parental income test also applies to Youth Training Allowance recipients. Let $Y_P$ denote annual combined parental income, $k$ the additional number of dependent children under 16 in parents' care, with $k_1 = 1$ if $k > 0$. Let

$s$ denote the number of dependent students aged 16-21. If $YTA_A$ is the maximum yearly payment of YTA available, then the parental income test reduces YTA payment by (in terms of annual income):

$$YTA_1 = \max[0, YTA_A] \quad -\max[0, 0.25Y_P - (23,400 + 1,200k_1$$
$$+2,500(k - k_1) + 3,700s)] \tag{13.17}$$

The personal income test, for all YTA recipients, reduces YTA payment (in terms of fortnightly income) as follows:

$$YA_1 = YA_B + RA \quad -\max[0, 0.5(Y_R - 60)]$$
$$-\max[0, 0.2(Y_R - 140)] \tag{13.18}$$
$$-\max[0, 0.7(Y_S - Y_C)]$$
$$Y_C = 140 + (YA_B - (140 - 60)50)/70 \tag{13.19}$$

**Assets Test**

If the young person is not independent, a parental assets test also applies. For personal assets test see general assets test for all pensions and allowances. However, assets tests are not currently modelled in MITTS.

# 13.7 Mature Age Allowance

## Conditions of Eligibility

If the Mature Age Allowance, MAA, was granted before August 1996, individuals must be:

1. unemployed and registered as unemployed for the past 12 months,

2. aged 60 or over but less than Age Pension age, and

3. in receipt of DSS or DVA income support payment for the preceding 12 months.

If MAA was granted after 1/7/96, individuals must:

1. have no recent workforce experience,

2. be aged 60 or over but less than Age Pension age, and

3. be in receipt of DSS or DVA income support payment for the preceding 9 months and on NSA at time of claim, OR have received a payment of a pension or a non-activity tested allowance in the 13 weeks preceding the claim OR have previously received MAA at any time.

### Basic Rates of Payment

If granted before August 1996, See Age Pension.

If granted after August 1996, See NSA.

Employment Entry payment of $100 may be available.

Education Entry payment of $200 may be available.

### Income Test

If granted before 1/7/96, See Age Pension.

If granted after 1/7/96, See NSA.

## Sickness Allowance

### Conditions of Eligibility

To receive the Sickness Allowance, SA, individuals must be under Age Pension age, and temporarily incapacitated for work (or be in full time study or in receipt of Austudy or Abstudy).

In addition, individuals must have a job or full time study to which to return, and a medical certificate from a qualified medical practitioner.

SA may be paid up to 4 years, without medical certificates, if undertaking a Commonwealth Rehabilitation Service programme.

Table 13.7: Basic Rates of Sickness Allowance

| Family Characteristics | $NSA_B$ |
|---|---|
| Single, 16-17 years, at home | 145.40 |
| Single, 16-17 years, away from home | 240.00 |
| Single 21 or over, no children | 321.50 |
| Single, 18-21 years, no children, at home | 176.00 |
| Single, 18-21 years, no children, away from home | 265.50 |
| Single, aged 60 or over, after 9 months | 347.80 |
| Single, with children | 347.80 |
| Couple, 16-17 years, no children | 240.00 |
| Couple, 18-21 years, no children | 265.50 |
| Couple, 21 or over or with children (each) | 290.10 |

## Basic Rates of Payment

The basic rates are the same as for NSA or YTA and are shown in Table 13.7.

A Pharmaceutical Allowance of $5.40 per fortnight is paid (to single or couple combined).

## Income Test

Let $Y_C$ denote the gross income level where the basic payment cuts out completely (see NSA). Let $n = 1$ for singles, and $n = 2$ for couples. Where:

$$
\begin{aligned}
SA_1 = \quad & SA_B + RA + 5.40/n \quad - \max[0, 0.5(Y_R - 60)] \\
& - \max[0, 0.2(Y_R - 140)] \\
& - \max[0, 0.7(Y_S - Y_C)]
\end{aligned}
\tag{13.20}
$$

then the Sickness Allowance is given by:

$$
SA = \max[0, SA_1]
\tag{13.21}
$$

## 13.8   Widow Allowance

### Conditions of Eligibility

The Widow Allowance is paid to a woman aged 50 or over, who is not a member of a couple, or widowed, divorced or separated (including separated de facto) since turning 40, with no recent workforce experience. Recent workforce experience means work of at least 20 hours a week, for at least 13 weeks during the last 12 months.

### Basic Payment Rate

See NSA. A Pharmaceutical Allowance of $5.40 is also payable to recipients aged 60 years or over. An Employment Entry payment of $50 or $100 may be available. An Education Entry payment of $200 may be available.

### Income Test

See NSA.

## 13.9   AUSTUDY

### Conditions of Eligibility

Individuals must be full-time students aged 16 years or over.

### Basic Rates of Payment

The basic rates of payment are shown in Table 13.8.

A pensioner education supplement of $60 per fortnight is available for students receiving a Department of Veteran's Affairs income support payment because they are disabled, sole parents or carers. AUSTUDY is not means-tested.

No rent assistance is payable to AUSTUDY recipients living at home.

Table 13.8: AUSTUDY Basic Payments Rates

| Demographic Characteristics | $NSA_B$ |
|---|---|
| Single, 16-17 years, at home | 145.41 |
| Single, 16-17 years, away from home | 240.07 |
| Single 21 or over, no children | 265.39 |
| Single, 18-21 years, no children, at home | 174.90 |
| Single, 18-21 years, no children, away from home | 265.39 |
| Single, with children | 342.79 |
| Couple, 16-21 years, no children | 240.07 |
| Couple, 21 or over or with children (each partner) | 265.39 |

## Income Test

Defining $AUS_B, Y_R$ and $Y_S$ in annual terms, the amount received is given by:

$$AUS = \max[0, AUS_B - \max[0, 0.5(Y_R - 6000)] - \max[0, 0.5(Y_S - 14,750)]] \quad (13.22)$$

A parental income test such as that for YTA is also applied for Austudy recipients who are deemed dependants. Annual payment is reduced by 25 cents in the dollar for parental income over $23,400 (see YTA income test for details).

# 13.10  Special Benefit

## Conditions of Eligibility

The Special Benefit is for individuals who are in financial hardship and are unable to earn a sufficient livelihood for themselves and their dependents for reasons beyond their control. Recipients are not able to get any other income support pension. For a short-term payment, available funds must not be more than the applicable fortnightly Newstart or Youth Training Allowance rate. For a long-term payment available funds must be no more than $5,000.

## Basic Rates of Payment

The basic rates are the same as for NSA or YA. The Special Benefit may be reduced if the beneficiary is in receipt of free board and/or lodgings or is receiving other forms of support. Individuals may be eligible for the Education Entry payment of $200.

## Income Test

The Special Benefit is withdrawn dollar for dollar for any earned income. Hence:

$$SB = \max[0, SB_B + RA - Y] \tag{13.23}$$

# 13.11   Partner Allowance

## Conditions of Eligibility

Individuals must be: born on or before 1/7/1955; a member of a couple where the partner is on a pension, allowance or Austudy/Abstudy at time of PA claim; have no recent workforce experience and; no dependent children under 16 years.

## Basic Rates of Payment

The maximum rate of Partner Allowance is $290.10 per fortnight. An Employment Entry payment of $100 may be available and Education Entry payment of $200 may be available.

## Income Test

See NSA. For partners of people receiving Special Benefit, see Special Benefit above.

## 13.12 Parenting Payment

A recipient of the Parenting payment must have qualifying child under 16 (sole and partnered parents) or a child over 16 with a Child Disability Allowance (sole parents only). It is paid to one member of a couple.

### Basic Rates of Payment

For sole parents (see Age Pension) the basic rate is \$354.60. For partnered parents the basic rate is \$65.10 and the additional rate (including the basic rate) is \$290.10.

The additional rate is higher if there is illness, a separated or respite care couple, or a partner is in gaol. There is a Pharmaceutical Allowance of \$5.40 per fortnight for sole parents or eligible partnered parents. An Education Entry payment of \$200 may be payable and an Employment Entry payment of \$100 may be payable (sole parents only).

### Income Test

For sole parents, see Age Pension above. For partnered parents the test is as follows. The basic rate is, $PP_B = \$65.10$, and additional rate, $PP_A = \$225.00$ per fortnight. Let $Y_R$, $Y_S$ and $Y$ denote the taxable fortnightly incomes of the reference person, spouse and household respectively, with $Y = Y_R + Y_S$. The full allowance of $PP = \$290.10$ per fortnight is given if $\min(Y_R, Y_S) = Y_{Min} \leq \$60$ and $\max(Y_R, Y_S) = Y_{Max} \leq \$Y_c$ per fortnight, where $Y_c$ is the 'cut out' income defined above.

An income test is applied to the additional component of the parenting allowance, where $PP$ is reduced as follows. For $Y_{Min} \leq Y_c$, define:

$$
\begin{aligned}
PP_1 = 290.10 \quad &- \max\left[0, 0.5\left(Y_{Min} - 60\right)\right] \\
&- \max\left[0, 0.2\left(Y_{Min} - 140\right)\right] \\
&- \max\left[0, 0.7\left(Y_{Max} - y_c\right)\right] \\
&+ \max\left[0, 0.7\left(Y_{Max} - \left\{Y_c + \tfrac{PA_B}{0.7}\right\}\right)\right]
\end{aligned} \tag{13.24}
$$

The last line ensures that the maximum deduction to the Parenting Allowance associated with the spouse's income does not exceed the additional component of the allowance, $PP_A$. For $Y_{Min} > Y_c$, $PP_1 = 0$. Then:

$$PP = \max[0, PA_1] \tag{13.25}$$

The Parenting Allowance in excess of $PP_B$ is taxable and the payment is made to the spouse with $y_{Min}$.

### Assets Test for Pensions and Allowances

Unless otherwise stated, the following outlines the assets test for all pensions and allowances paid by Centrelink. Let $A$ denote value of assets.

### Home-owners

Singles:    Benefit  $= \max[0, Max\,Benefit - 0.003(A - 127,750)]$

Couples:  Benefit  $= \max[0, Max\,Benefit - 0.003(A - 181,500)]$

$$\tag{13.26}$$

### Non-home-owners

Singles:    $R_p$  $= \max[0, Max\,Benefit - 0.003(A - 219,250)]$

$$\tag{13.27}$$

Couples:  $R_p$  $= \max[0, Max\,Benefit - 0.003(A - 273,000)]$

The maximum benefit includes the basic pension or allowance, Rent Assistance and Pharmaceutical Allowance.

## 13.13  Family Allowance

### Conditions of Eligibility

Family Allowance, FA, is paid for a child or children aged under 16 in care, or full-time dependent secondary students who are ineligible to receive a

Table 13.9: Basic Rates of Family Allowance

| Number of Children | Amount |
|---|---|
| Child aged 0-12, each | 96.40 |
| Child aged 13-15, each | 125.40 |
| Child aged 16-17, each | 60.20 |
| Minimum rate per child | 23.50 |
| Large family supplement (for 4th and subs child) | 7.70 |

Prescribed Education Scheme (PES) payment (such as Austudy), and is paid until the end of the calendar year in which they turn 18 or at the end of secondary studies, whichever happens first.

FA is paid to a parent, guardian or approved care organisation. To receive more than the minimum Family Payment rate for children of a previous relationship, reasonable action for maintenance must be taken. Blind pensioners are exempt from maintenance action test.

## Basic Rates of Payment

Fortnightly rates of payment are shown in Table 13.9.

### Guardian Allowance

This allowance, of $36.70 per fortnight, is paid to sole parents who receive minimum Family Payment.

## Income Test

Let $n_j$ be the number of dependent children in age group $j$, where $j$ takes values 1, 2 and 3 respectively for children 0-12, 13-15 and 16 years. The standard rate per child is $b_j$ in group $j$, where the values of $b_j$ in turn are $96.40, $125.40 or $60.20 per fortnight (see above). There is a large-family supplement of $s$ per child for the fourth and subsequent child, where $s = $7.70$

per fortnight. The maximum amount paid, $R$, is given by:

$$
\begin{aligned}
R &= \sum_j b_j n_j & \text{if } \sum_j n_j < 4 \\
&= \sum_j b_j n_j + s \left( \sum_j n_j - 3 \right) & \text{if } \sum_j n_j \geq 4
\end{aligned} \tag{13.28}
$$

The payments are subject to an income test, where incomes are specified in terms of annual, rather than fortnightly incomes as above.[1] Hence, let $y_R$, $y_S$ and $y_h$ now denote the annual taxable incomes of the reference, spouse and household respectively. There are two relevant income thresholds. First, $y_1 = c_1 + c_2 \left( \sum_j n_j - 1 \right)$, and second $y_2 = c_3 + c_4 \left( \sum_j n_j - 1 \right)$, where the $c$'s are given respectively by \$23,400, \$624, \$65,941 and \$3,298. The benefit, paid per fortnight, is given by:

$$
\begin{aligned}
FP &= R + RA & \text{if } y_h \leq y_1 \\
&= \max[c_5 \textstyle\sum_j n_j, R + RA & (13.29) \\
&\quad -0.5 \left\{ y_h - c_1 - c_2 \left( \textstyle\sum_j n_j - 1 \right) \right\} \tfrac{2}{52}] & \text{if } y_1 < y_h \leq y_2
\end{aligned}
$$

where $c_5$ is \$23.50 per dependent child. Further, $FP = 0$ if $y_2 < y_h$ The adjustment of $\frac{2}{52}$ converts the annual income into a fortnightly value. The non-taxable payment is given to the spouse with $\min(y_R, y_S)$.

## Assets Test

The assets test is applied to family's assets, not including the family home. FP is payable if assets are less than \$407,250. The minimum rate is payable if assets are less than \$604,250. The assets test does not apply if the income test does not apply. Rent assistance is paid with Family Allowance if eligible.

---

[1] This income test is applied only if an income support payment such as a DSS pension benefit or allowance is not received. There are also income tests relating to the incomes of a student's (age 16-17) annual income, and that of children under 16 years.

# 13.14 Maternity Allowance

## Conditions of Eligibility

The Maternity Allowance, MAT, is paid for all babies (including stillborn babies and babies who die shortly after birth). Recipients must qualify for Family Payment within 13 weeks of a baby's birth (or they would have qualified if the baby had lived). Where the recipient is not a natural parent, the child must be entrusted to care within 13 weeks of birth and be likely to remain in care for not less than 13 weeks.

## Basic Rates of Payment

There is a lump sum payment $750.00. In a multiple birth, MAT is paid for each child.

## Income and Assests test

See Family Payment/Allowance

## 13.14.1 Maternity Immunisation Allowance

One lump sum payment is paid for an 18-month-old immunised child born on or after 1 January 1998. Recipients must qualify for Maternity Allowance of Family Payment. This is not modelled in MITTS.

# 13.15 Family Tax Payment

## Conditions of eligibility

Children age under 16 in care, or full time dependent secondary students aged under 18. Part B is only payable to families with a child aged under 5. Paid to parent/guardian.

## Basic Rates of Payment

Fortnightly rates of payment are as follows: for Part A: $7.70 per child; for Part B: $19.24 per family.

## Income Test

Part B is paid to sole parents or in cases where one member of a couple earns less than $175.70 per fortnight. It is payable to families who are eligible for more than minimum family payment. There is no assets test

### 13.15.1   Child Disability Allowance

This is a payment of $75.10 per fortnight (with no income or assets test) for dependent children under 16 or full-time students 16-21 with a disability who requires substantially more daily care and attention than a child of the same age who does not have a disability. Payment is not payable when the child is receiving a Social Security payment in its own right.

# 13.16   Department of Veterans Affairs Pensions

Family Tax Benefit (A) and (B) and Rent Assistance may also be available for recipients of DVA pensions.

## Service Pension

Service Pensions are available to Australian Veterans and their families. The Service Pension comprises the Age Service Pension which is available five years earlier than the Centrelink Age Pension, the Invalidity Service Pension and the Partner Service Pension. The pension rates are the same as the Centrelink Age Pension. Pharmaceutical Allowance is also payable to Service

Pensioners. The Income and Assets test are the same as for the Centrelink Age Pension.

## War Widow's Pension and Income Support Supplement

War Widows Pension is payable to a widow or widower of an eligible Australian veteran. The maximum pension comprises an indexed component of $361.40 per fortnight and a non-indexed component of $24.00 per fortnight. Thus the total maximum payment available is $385.40 per fortnight.

For eligible war widows, an Income Support Supplement of $120.10 is available in addition to the basic War Widow's Pension. For widows or widowers receiving the maximum supplement, this rate is 'frozen' (that is, non-indexed) while for those in receipt of less than the maximum rate, the payment is indexed twice yearly.

### Income Test

War Widow's Pension is not income or assets tested. The Income Support Supplement is income tested in the following manner. Let $Y_R$ denote the reference person's income, $Y_S$ the spouse's income, $Y = Y_R + Y_S$ the combined income (not including income from the pension). The reduction in the Age Pension per fortnight is given by:

$$
\begin{aligned}
\text{Singles:} \quad ISS_1 &= ISS_B + \$5.40 \quad -max[0, 0.5(Y - 190.40)] \\
ISS &= max[0, ISS_1)
\end{aligned}
$$

$$
\begin{aligned}
\text{Couples:} \quad ISS_1 &= ISS_B + \tfrac{\$5.40}{2} \quad -max[0, 0.25(Y - 500.20)] \\
\text{(per person)} \quad ISS &= max[0, ISS_1]
\end{aligned}
$$

$$(13.30)$$

For each additional child, add $24.00 per child to threshold. Half the married rate is payable to one of a couple if the partner is not receiving a pension, benefit or allowance. War widow pensioners are also eligible for the Pharmaceutical Allowance of \$5.40 per fortnight.

**Assets Test**

Let $A$ denote value of assets.

**Homeowners**   For singles:

$$
\begin{aligned}
Benefit \ &= 0 && \text{for } A \geq 251{,}750 \\
&= maxISS - 0.003(A - 211{,}750) && \text{for } 211{,}750 \leq A < 251{,}750 \\
&= maxISS && \text{for } A < 211{,}750
\end{aligned}
$$
(13.31)

For couples:

$$
\begin{aligned}
ISS \ &= 0 && \text{for } A \geq 388{,}500 \\
&= maxISS - 0.003(A - 308{,}500) && \text{for } 308{,}500 \leq A < 388{,}500 \\
&= maxISS && \text{for } A < 308{,}500
\end{aligned}
$$
(13.32)

**Non-homeowners**   For singles:

$$
\begin{aligned}
R_p \ &= 0 && \text{for } A \geq 343{,}250 \\
&= MaxISS - .003(A - 303{,}250) && \text{for } 303{,}250 \leq A < 343{,}250 \\
&= MaxISS && \text{for } A < 303{,}250
\end{aligned}
$$
(13.33)

For couples:

$$
\begin{aligned}
R_p \ &= 0 && \text{for } A \geq 480{,}000 \\
&= maxISS - 0.003(A - 400{,}000) && \text{for } 400{,}000 \leq A < 480{,}000 \\
&= maxISS && \text{for } A < 400{,}000
\end{aligned}
$$
(13.34)

## Disability Pension

The Disability Pension is available to veterans who have suffered injuries or diseases as a consequence of war or defence service on behalf of Australia. The payment depends on the degree of incapacity suffered. The payments are: Special rate $636.80; Intermediate rate $439.60; and a general rate that ranges from $241.60 for 100 per cent disability to $24.16 for 10 per cent disability. Extreme Disablement Adjustment (EDA) is paid in respect of extreme incapacity to veterans over 65. It is paid at 150 per cent of the General Rate.

Disability Pension is not subject to an income or assets test.

# Bibliography

[1] Allen, R.G.D. and Bowley, A.L. (1935) *Family Expenditure: A Study of its Variation.* London: P. S. King.

[2] Apps, P. and Savage, E. (1989) Labour supply, welfare rankings and the measurement of inequality. *Journal of Public Economics,* 47, pp. 336-364.

[3] Atkinson, A.B. and Sutherland, H. (1988) *Tax-Benefit Models.* London: STICERD.

[4] Atkinson, A. B. and Sutherland, H. (1998) Microsimulation and policy debate: a case study of the minimum pension guarantee in Britain. *University of Cambridge, DAE Working Paper,* no. 9815.

[5] Banks, J., Blundell, R. and Lewbel, A. (1996) Tax reform and welfare measurement: do we need demand system estimation? *Economic Journal,* 106, pp. 1227-1241.

[6] Blundell, R. and Meghir, C. (1987) Bivariate alternatives to the Tobit model. *Journal of Econometrics.* 34, pp. 179-200.

[7] Blundell, R., Ham, J. and Meghir, C. (1987) Unemployment and female labour supply. *Economic Journal,* 97, pp. 44-64.

[8] Blundell, R.W., Meghir, C., Symons, E. and Walker, I. (1986) A labour supply model for the simulation of tax and benefit reforms. In *Unemploy-*

*ment, Search and Labour Supply* (ed. by R.W. Blundell and I. Walker), pp. 267-293. Cambridge: Cambridge University Press.

[9] Callan, T. and Van Soest, A. (1996) Family labour supply and taxes in Ireland. (Tilburg University).

[10] Chesher, A. and Irish, M. (1987) Residual analysis in the grouped and censored normal linear model. *Journal of Econometrics*, 34, pp. 33-61.

[11] Cornwell, A. and Creedy, J. (1997) *Environmental Taxes and Economic Welfare: Reducing Carbon Dioxide Emissions.* Aldershot, Hants: Edward Elgar.

[12] Creedy, J. (1996) *Fiscal Policy and Social Welfare: An Analysis of Alternative Tax and Transfer Systems.* Aldershot, Hants: Edward Elgar

[13] Creedy, J. (1998) *Measuring welfare changes and Tax Burdens.* Cheltenham: Edward Elgar.

[14] Creedy, J. (2001a) Tax Modelling. *Economic Record*, 77, pp. 189-202.

[15] Creedy, J. (2001b) Labour supply, welfare and the earnings distribution. *Australian Journal of Labour Economics*, 4, pp. 134-151.

[16] Creedy, J. (2001c) Quadratic utility, labour supply and the welfare effects of tax changes. *Australian Journal of Labour Economics*, 4, pp. 272-280.

[17] Creedy, J. and Duncan, A.S. (2000) Behavioural microsimulation methods for policy analysis. In *Taxes, Transfers and Labour Market Responses: What Can Microsimulation Tell Us?* (ed. by T. Callan), pp. 23-58. Dublin: The Economic and Social Research Institute.

[18] Creedy, J. and Duncan, A. S. (2001a) The Melbourne Institute Tax and Transfer Simulator. *The University of Melbourne.*

[19] Creedy, J. and Duncan, A. S. (2001b) Aggregating labour supply and feedback effects in microsimulation. *Melbourne Institute Working Paper*, no. 15/01.

[20] Creedy, J. and Duncan, A.S. (2002) Behavioural microsimulation with labour supply responses. *Journal of Economic Surveys*, 16, pp. 1-39.

[21] Creedy, J. and Kalb, G. (2001) Measuring welfare changes with nonlinear budget constraints in continuous and discrete hours labour supply models. *Melbourne Institute Working Paper*, no. 9/01

[22] Creedy, J., Kalb, G. and Hsein, K. (2001) The effects of flattening the effective marginal rate structure in Australia: policy simulations using the Melbourne Institute Tax and Transfer Simulator. *Melbourne Institute Working Paper*, no. 10/01.

[23] Creedy, J., Duncan, A.S., Harris, M. and Scutella, R. (2001) Wage functions for demographic groups in Australia. *Australian Journal of Labour Economics*, 4, pp. 300-320.

[24] Deaton, A.S. and Muellbauer, J. (1980) *Economics and Consumer Behaviour*. Cambridge: Cambride University Press.

[25] Duncan, A.S. (1993) Labour supply decisions and non-convex budget sets. In *Empirical Approaches to Fiscal Policy* (ed. by A. Heimler and D. Meulders). London: Chapman Hall.

[26] Duncan, A.S. and Giles, C. (1996) Labour supply incentives and recent family credit reforms. *Economic Journal*, 106, pp. 142-155.

[27] Duncan, A.S. and Giles, C. (1998) The labour market inpact of the working families tax credit in the UK. (Paper presented to International Institute for Public Finance conference, Cordoba, Argentina).

[28] Duncan, A.S. and Weeks, M. (1997) Behavioural tax microsimulation with finite hours choices. *European Economic Review*, 41, pp. 619-626.

[29] Duncan, A.S. and Weeks, M. (1998) Simulating transitions using discrete choice models. *Proceedings of the American Statistical Association*, 106, pp. 151-156.

[30] Duncan, A.S., Giles, C. and Stark, G. (1995) An algorithm for calculating piecewise linear budget constraints. *Institute for Fiscal Studies.*

[31] Ermisch, J. F. and Wright, R. E. (1994) Interpretation of negative sample selection effects in wage offer equations. *Applied Economic Letters*, 1, pp. 187-189.

[32] Gallagher, P. (1990) Australian tax benefit and microsimulation models. In *Tax-Benefit Models and Microsimulation Methods* (ed. by B. Bradbury), pp. 29-79. Sydney: University of New South Wales.

[33] Gourieroux, C., Monfort, A., Renault, E. and Trognon, A. (1987a) Generalised residuals. *Journal of Econometrics*, 34, pp. 5-32.

[34] Gourieroux, C., Monfort, A., Renault, E. and Trognon, A. (1987b) Simulated residuals. *Journal of Econometrics*, 34, pp. 201-252.

[35] Greene, W. (1981) Sample selection bias as a specification error: comment. *Econometrica*, 49, pp. 795-798.

[36] Harding, A. (ed.) (1996) *Microsimulation and Public Policy.* New York: Elsevier.

[37] Heckman, J. (1979) Sample selection bias as a specification error. *Econometrica*, 47, pp. 153-161.

[38] Heimler, A. and Meulders, D. (eds.) (1993) *Empirical Approaches to Fiscal Policy Modelling.* Melbourne: Chapman and Hall.

[39] Hellwig, O. (1990) Overseas experience with microsimulation models. In *Tax-benefit Models and Microsimulation Methods* (ed. by B. Bradbury), pp. 5-29. Sydney: University of New South Wales.

[40] Immervoll, H., O'Donoghue, C. and Sutherland, H. (1999) An introduction to Euromod. *University of Cambridge Department of Applied Economics Euromod Working Paper*, no. EM0/99.

[41] Keane, M. (1995) A new idea for welfare reform. *Rederal Reserve Bandk of Minneapolis Quarterly Review*, spring, pp. 2-28.

[42] Keane, M, and Moffitt, R. (1998) A structural model of multiple welfare program participation and labour supply. *International Economic Review*, 39, pp. 553-590.

[43] Klevmarken, N.A.(1997) Modelling behavioual response in Euromod. *University of Cambridge, DAE Working Paper*, no. 9720.

[44] Lambert, P.J. (1993) *The Distribution and Redistribution of Income.* Manchester: Manchester University Press.

[45] Launhard, C.F.W. (1885) *Mathematische Begründung der Volkswiirtschaftslehre*: translated by H. Schmidt and edited and introduced by J. Creedy as *Mathematical Principles of Economics.* Aldershot: Edward Elgar (1993).

[46] Maddala, G.S. (1983) *Limited Dependent And Qualitative Variables in Econometrics.* Cambridge: Cambridge University Press.

[47] McFadden, D. (1987) Regression-based specification tests for the multinomial logit model. *Journal of Econometrics*, 34, pp. 63-82.

[48] Miller, P. and Rummery, S. (1991) Male-female wage differentials in Australia: a reassessment. *Australian Economic Papers,* 30, pp. 50-69.

[49] Moffitt, R. (1992) Incentive effects of the US welfare system: a review. *Journal of Economic Literature*, 30, pp. 1-61.

[50] Moffit, R. (2000) Simulating transfer programmes and labour supply. In *Taxes, Transfers and Labour Market Responses: What Can Microsimulation Tell Us?* (ed. by T. Callan), pp. 1-22. Dublin: The Economic and Social Research Institute.

[51] Olsen, R. (1982) Distributional tests for selectivity bias and a more robust estimator. *International Economic Review*, 23, pp. 223-240.

[52] Orcutt, G., Merz, J. and Quinke, J. (1986) *Micro Analytic Simulation Models to Support Social and Financial Policy*. New York: North-Holland.

[53] Pagan, A. and Vella, F. (1989) Diagnostic tests for models based on individual data: a survey. *Journal of Applied Econometrics*, 4, pp. s29-s59.

[54] Proops, J.L.R., Faber, M. and Wagenhals, G. (1993) *Reducing $CO_2$ Emissions: A Comparative Input-Output Study for Germany and the UK*. Heidelberg: Springer-Verlag.

[55] Redmond, G., Sutherland, H. and Wilson, M. (1998) *The Arithmetic of Tax and Social Security Reform*. Cambridge: Cambridge University Press.

[56] Stern, N.H. (1986) On the specification of labour supply functions. In *Unemployment, Search and Labour Supply* (ed. by R.W. Blundell and I. Walker), pp. 143-189. Cambridge: Cambridge University Press.

[57] Sutherland, H. (ed.) (1997) The Euromod preparatory study: a summary report. *University of Cambridge Department of Applied Economics Working Paper*, no. 9725.

[58] Sutherland, H. (ed.) (1998) *Microsimulation in the New Millenium: Challenges and Innovations.* (Conference Proceedings, University of Cambridge).

[59] Symons E., Proops J. and Gay, P. (1994) Carbon taxes, consumer demand and carbon dioxide emissions: a simulation analysis for the UK. *Fiscal Studies*, 15, pp. 19-43.

[60] Van Soest, A. (1995) Discrete choice models of family labour supply. *Journal of Human Resources*, 30, pp. 63-88.

[61] Van Soest, A. and Das, M. (2000) Family labour supply and proposed tax reforms in the Netherlands. In *Taxes, Transfers and Labour Market Responses: What Can Microsimulation Tell Us?* (ed. by T. Callan), pp. 59–80. Dublin: The Economic and Social Research Institute.

# Index

239